DATE DUE		
MAR 1 5 1991		
MAR 1 8 1991		

OCT 2 6 1990

Children's Ideas
in Science

Children's Ideas in Science

Edited by Rosalind Driver,
Edith Guesne and Andrée Tiberghien

Open University Press
Milton Keynes · *Philadelphia*

Open University Press
12 Cofferidge Close
Stony Stratford
Milton Keynes MK11 1BY, England

and
242 Cherry Street
Philadelphia, PA 19106, USA

First published 1985
Reprinted 1988, 1989

British Library Cataloguing in Publication Data
Children's ideas in science.
    1. Science—Study and teaching (Secondary)
    2. Concept learning
    I. Driver, Rosalind   II. Guesne, Edith
    III. Tiberghien, Andrée
    370.15'6   Q181

ISBN 0-335-15040-3

Library of Congress Cataloging in Publication Data
Children's ideas in science.
    includes index.
    1. Science—Study and teaching. 2. Students—
Attitudes—Evaluation. I. Driver, Rosalind.
II. Guesne, Edith. III. Tiberghien, Andrée.
LB1585.C42 1985   372,3'5044   85-7104

ISBN 0-335-15040-3 (pbk.)

Text design by Clarke Williams

Typeset by Mathematical Compostion Setters Ltd,
7 Ivy Street, Salisbury, UK.
Printed in Great Britain by M. A. Thomson Litho Limited,
East Kilbride, Glasgow, Scotland.

Contents

Preface

This book concerns secondary school children's ideas about a range of natural phenomena and how these ideas change and develop with teaching. It has been written in such a way as to give an overview of children's conceptions to teachers and others concerned with science education in the middle and secondary school years; it is not intended to be an academic review.

Our plan has been to present findings which will be helpful in enabling the teaching of science to be better adapted to children's understandings. The idea of writing the book was born in Paris in 1978 when the three of us first met to exchange ideas and information about the studies we had been undertaking over the previous few years on children's conceptions in science.

Since that first meeting there has been a rapid growth of research into students' conceptions worldwide. Articles documenting students' ideas and their development and modification during teaching have been appearing in science education journals in North America, Europe, Australasia and elsewhere. A number of international meetings have also been held which have resulted in the publication of useful collections of papers. With this rapid explosion of interest, the idea of a book which would make the findings, at present scattered in various informal reports and journal articles, accessible to science teachers, seemed even more important.

The research literature is growing to such an extent that it has become less feasible for such a book to be written by the three of us alone. We have therefore invited a number of people who have undertaken significant research in the field to contribute chapters.

Each chapter focuses on studies of children's ideas about a particular topic area or class of phenomena. The areas we have chosen are those relevant to the physical sciences where a significant amount of research has been undertaken. However, there are still a number of topics which, regretfully, the book does not address.

As well as being on different topics, the chapters differ from each other in a number of respects. Some, for example, give an overview of what is currently known about children's thinking in a particular topic area drawing together the findings of studies carried out in different places. Other chapters are written from the perspective of a case study of the ideas of children in classrooms and how they changed as a result of specific instruction.

It has not been a straightforward task preparing the book with contributions from different countries. Several of the chapters are based on studies with children whose first language is not English, and care has had to be taken to keep the translation as close as possible to the original meanings of the children's written and spoken comments.

Where examples of children's written work have been used in the text these have been reproduced exactly as they were written by the children (except where translation into English has been necessary). Similarly children's drawings have been faithfully reproduced.

We hope that the chapters with their various emphases give an insight into the conceptual world of children in our classrooms; an insight which we hope will be helpful in making science teaching and learning more rewarding to teachers and children alike.

Rosalind Driver, Edith Guesne, Andrée Tiberghien
June 1985

Acknowledgements

We are grateful to a number of people who have made helpful suggestions in the preparation of this book. We owe particular thanks to Jack Easley for his very helpful comments on drafts of a number of chapters.

The children's drawings in Figure 8.1 are reproduced from a Research Report by W. Dow, J. Auld and D. Wilson *Pupils Concepts of Solids, Liquids and Gases* with kind permission of Dundee College of Education.

The questions in Figures 6.7, 7.6, 8.4 and 8.5 were developed for use in the national science surveys conducted on behalf of the Assessment of Performance Unit and are reproduced from *Science in Schools, Age 15, Report No. 2* (1984) Assessment of Performance Unit, DES, by permission of the Controller of Her Majesty's Stationery Office. The pupil responses in Figures 8.2, 8.3, 8.4 and 8.5 are reproduced from the report *Aspects of Secondary Students' Understanding of the Particulate Nature of Matter* by A. Brook, H. Briggs and R. Driver, Centre for Studies in Science and Mathematics Education, University of Leeds, by permission of the Controller of Her Majesty's Stationery Office.

The examples of classroom activities illustrated in Figures 1.1 and 1.2 were first published in the *European Journal for Science Education* and are reproduced with permission of the publishers, Taylor and Francis Ltd.

It would have been very difficult indeed to complete this book without the financial assistance from UNESCO which has enabled us to meet to prepare the final manuscript. We are most grateful for their support.

Contributors

Rosalind DRIVER is a lecturer in Education at the Centre for Studies in Science and Mathematics Education at the University of Leeds where she is involved with the training of physics and science teachers. She has a longstanding research interest in children's conceptions about natural phenomena and is currently directing the 'Children's Learning in Science Project' which is exploring ways of promoting conceptual change in secondary school science classrooms.

Edith GUESNE is Maître de Conférences at University of Paris 6 where she has been involved in developing in-service training courses for secondary school physics teachers for the last eight years. She is a physicist; her earlier research was in solid state physics. Since working at LIRESPT*, her particular area of research has been investigating children's ideas about optics and their use in curriculum development.

Gaalen ERICKSON is an associate professor in the Department of Mathematics and Science Education at the University of British Columbia where he is involved with programmes for the preparation of both undergraduate and graduate students in science education. He has long been intrigued by children's intuitive ideas in a variety of science content areas and is currently directing a research project aimed at the development of teaching materials and strategies based upon students' intuitive thinking.

Richard GUNSTONE is a senior lecturer in Education at Monash University in Melbourne where he is involved with the training of science and physics teachers. His research has probed children's ideas in different areas of physics. He is currently concerned with exploring the implications of these ideas for teaching and curriculum.

---

*Laboratoire Interuniversitaire de Recherche sur l'Enseignement des Sciences Physiques et de la Technologie (LIRESPT) was set up by G. Delacôte at University of Paris 7. The research team is associated with CNRS (Centre National de la Recherche Scientifique).

Joseph NUSSBAUM is lecturer in the Department of Science at Michlalah, Jerusalem College for Women in Jerusalem, Israel, where he is involved in training future teachers of Science. He has long been engaged with research on pupils' understanding of science concepts and his work is currently concerned with the application of the findings to improving teaching strategies and materials.

Marie-Geneviève SÉRÉ is Maître de Conférences at Univeristy of Paris 6. She is a physicist who studied solid state optics before being involved in research about pupils' conceptions. She is in charge of in-service training courses for middle school teachers.

David SHIPSTONE is a lecturer in the School of Education at the University of Nottingham where his main concern is the training of physics and other science teachers, though with a strong interest in the psychology of education. His earlier work was in upper atmosphere physics but since becoming a teacher his research interest has shifted to the development of children's scientific reasoning.

Andrée TIBERGHIEN is Directeur de Recherche in CNRS and belongs to LIRESPT* (University of Paris 7). She is a physicist and has undertaken research on Physics Education for fifteen years specifically with elementary and middle school pupils.

Mike WATTS taught for eight years in comprehensive schools, both in this country and in Jamaica, before becoming a BP Schoolteacher Research Fellow at the Department of Educational Studies, University of Surrey. His research interests include developing techniques to study youngsters' understandings of physics, and to explore their perceptions of their experiences of school science in general. He is currently a Regional Project Leader with the Secondary Science Curriculum Review.

CHAPTER I

Children's Ideas and the Learning of Science

Rosalind Driver, Edith Guesne and Andrée Tiberghien

Two 11-year-old boys, Tim and Ricky, are studying the way a spring extends as they add ball-bearings to a polystyrene cup which is hanging from it. Ricky is intent on adding ball-bearings one at a time and measuring the new length of the spring after each addition. Tim is watching him, then interrupts: 'Wait. What happens if we lift it up?'

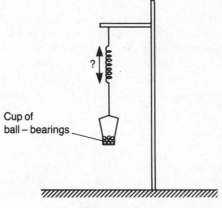

Cup of
ball – bearings

Figure I.1

He unclamps the spring, raises it higher up the stand, and measures its length again. Apparently satisfied that the length is the same as before he continues with the experiment. Later, when he is asked the reason for doing this, Tim picks up two marbles, holds one up higher than the other and explains:

> this is farther up and gravity is pulling it down harder the farther away. The higher it gets the more effect gravity will have on it because if you just stood over there and someone dropped a pebble on him, it would just sting him, it wouldn't hurt him. But if I dropped it from an

aeroplane it would be accelerating faster and faster and when it hit someone on the head it would kill him.

Tim's idea about weight increasing as objects are lifted higher from the Earth's surface is not an irrational one as his argument indicates (although from a scientist's point of view he seems to be referring here to gravitational potential energy).

Like Tim, many children come to science classes with ideas and interpretations concerning the phenomena that they are studying even when they have received no systematic instruction in these subjects whatsoever. Children form these ideas and interpretations as a result of everyday experiences in all aspects of their lives: through practical physical activities, talking with other people around them and through the media.

This book documents the conceptions that have been uncovered in children aged 10-16, in different physical domains, and indicates the importance of these for teachers and others concerned with science education.

What can be said about these ideas?

Do the ideas that children possess represent coherent models of the phenomena that are frequently presented in classroom settings? Experienced teachers realize that students do have their own ideas about phenomena, even if at times these 'ideas' may seem incoherent at least from the teacher's point of view. It is also recognized that such ideas often persist even when they are not consistent with the experimental results or the explanation of a teacher. In other words, they may be stable ideas. These characteristics of childrens' ideas— their personal nature, their coherence and their stability—will now be discussed in more detail.

These ideas are personal

When children in a class write about the same experiment they can give various diverse interpretations of it. Each one has 'seen' and interpreted the experiment in his or her own way. Our own behaviour is similar; when we read a text or discuss a topic with another person, we may or may not modify our own point of view. The extent to which we do modify our thinking depends at least as much on the ideas we have to start with as on what is written or said. A number of people attending the same lecture or reading the same book, even a scientific text, will not necessarily get from it and retain the same points.

Individuals internalize their experience in a way which is at least partially their own; they construct their own meanings. These personal 'ideas' influence the manner in which information is acquired. This personal manner of approaching phenomena is also found in the way in which scientific knowledge is generated. Most philosophers of science accept that hypotheses or theories do not represent so-called 'objective' data but that they are constructions or products of the human imagination. In this way of thinking, observations of events are influenced by the theoretical frameworks of the observer. The observations children make and their interpretations of them are also influenced by their ideas and expectations.[1]*

The fact that these ideas, whether of a child or a scientist, are personal does not necessarily mean that they may not be shared by many people (just as in the history of the sciences, it has happened that different scientists have independently developed and used the same theoretical framework). The following chapters will show that students, even those in different countries, may have the same ideas, or the same interpretations of similar events.

A child's individual ideas may seem incoherent

What teacher has not been struck by the different and at times contradictory interpretations of phenomena that have been proposed by individuals in a class. Even if students are confronted with what appear to be contradictions to the teacher, they will not necessarily recognize them. In addition, we will see that the same child may have different conceptions of a particular type of phenomenon, sometimes using different arguments leading to opposite predictions in situations which are equivalent from a scientist's point of view, and even switching from one sort of explanation to another for the same phenomenon. We will see many examples during the course of this book of such contradictions in students' thinking. Why these contradictions? The need for coherence, and the criteria for coherence, as perceived by a student are not the same as those of the scientist: the student does not possess any unique model unifying a range of phenomena that the scientist considers as equivalent. Nor does the student necessarily see the need for a coherent view, since *ad hoc* interpretations and predictions about natural events may appear to work quite well in practice.

These ideas are stable

It is often noticed that even after being taught, students have not modified their ideas in spite of attempts by a teacher to challenge them by offering counter-evidence. There are a number of examples in the chapters which follow which illustrate this issue: students may ignore counter-evidence, or interpret it in terms of their prior ideas. Although students' notions may be persistent, as we have already argued, this does not mean that the student has a completely coherent

---

*Superscript numerals refer to numbered references at the end of each chapter.

model of the phenomena presented, at least in the scientist's sense of the word coherent. The students' interpretations and conceptions are often contradictory, but none the less stable.

How do these ideas affect the learning process? A possible model

Students' minds are not blank slates able to receive instruction in a neutral way; on the contrary, students approach experiences presented in science classes with previously acquired notions and these influence what is learnt from new experiences in a number of ways. These include the observations made of events, the interpretations offered for such observations and the strategies students use to acquire new information, including reading from texts and experimentation.

The child, even when very young, has ideas about things, and these ideas play a role in the learning experience. Many different authors such as Ausubel, Piaget and Wallon, have incorporated this notion as an integral part of their theory. What children are capable of learning depends, at least in part, on 'what they have in their heads', as well as on the learning context in which they find themselves.

A model introduced by cognitive scientists fits well with what we now know of the interaction between the child's different ideas and the manner in which these ideas evolve with teaching. This model is based on the hypothesis that information is stored in memory in various forms and that everything we say and do depends on the elements or groups of elements of this stored information. Such elements or groups of elements have been called 'schemes'.* A scheme may concern an individual's knowledge about a specific phenomenon (for example, the sensation of cold elicited by a metallic object), or a more complex reasoning structure (for example, the association of one variable with another that leads some children to anticipate that 'the brighter the light bulb, the larger the shadow will be'). Thus, the term 'scheme' denotes the diverse things that are stored and interrelated in memory. These 'schemes' also influence the way a person may behave and interact with the environment, and in turn may be influenced by feedback from the environment.

We will illustrate the idea of 'scheme' using as an example a person's notion of a high school.[2] This scheme may incorporate relationships between events or situations that comprise it and which are themselves schemes. Some of these represent physical features, e.g. one or more buildings, stairways, corridors, rooms, a playing field; or people, including a large number of students, teachers, technicians, cleaners and a principal or head.

---

*Here the word 'scheme' does not have the meaning attributed to it by Piaget but rather the meaning derived from studies of memory and information processing.

Other aspects of the person's general scheme may include the types of relationships or attitudes between the people involved, such as friendship, submission and power, and the activities of these people including, going up or down the stairs, writing, talking, playing musical instruments and teaching.

Thus this relatively simple 'scheme' of the high school contains different elements organized among themselves to form a structure. This structure may be linked to schemes in other structures (for example, teachers, students, education, etc.).

In scientific theory there are some very elaborate 'schemes' representing knowledge in a particular domain such as mechanics, light, or chemical reactions. Such scientific 'schemes', integrated as they are into structures, are composed similarly of elements and relationships between them. However, they differ from the example just used of a high school in that some elements in the structure of a scientific theory do not correspond to direct perceptions.

This model of the organization of schemes integrated into structures can be used to describe learning or the acquisition of a new piece of knowledge. First we will consider an analogy with the grouping of students in a class. Students relate with one another and form groups for different activities such as sports, drama and science lessons. These groups are not static but change as friendships and interests change; some students may not relate to others at all but remain isolates. Consider what may happen when a new boy arrives in the class. When he arrives, there are various possibilities for what might happen: he might not relate with the other students at all and remain isolated; he might join a group that already exists; or his presence might provoke a reorganization of friendship groups of the class as a whole. The same student could also be integrated differently depending on the class that receives him.

The analogy with learning is clear; the way a new piece of information is assimilated depends both on the nature of the information and the structure of the learner's 'schemes'. Thus the same experience provided for students in their science lessons may be assimilated differently by each individual.

These images of the organization of schemes and the acquisition of new schemes may account for the existence of these personal, contradictory and stable ideas. Each one of us has a characteristic organization of schemes. Acquired information is linked to other information and even if this new information is the same for several people, the link established between this acquired information and already stored information has little chance of being the same from one person to the next.

When a student states several contradictory ideas, different schemes are brought into play; these ideas may all be stable in so far as the schemes leading to them are integrated into structures, and to change any one of them may require the modification of a structure, not merely of an element of that structure.

In learning science, a pupil may note an event that is contrary to his or her expectations, that does not fit in with his or her schemes. Simply noting such a discrepant event however is not necessarily followed by a restructuring of that student's ideas—such restructuring takes time and favourable circumstances. To help students to accomplish such reorganization in their thinking about natural phenomena, science teaching can play an important role in giving children a wide range of experiences relating to certain key ideas. This is illustrated in later chapters, particularly those relating to children's ideas about heat transfer (Chapter 4) and about gases (Chapter 6). In both cases examples are presented and discussed which illustrate the conceptual 'schemes' used by students in lessons indicating that changes in some of these ideas do not take place readily despite the practical activities the children have undertaken.

What purposes are served by understanding students' ideas?

Taking account of students' prior ideas is one of the strategies, though certainly not the only one, which enables teaching to be better adapted to students. This can occur in a number of ways:

(1) *The choice of concepts to teach.* In some teaching schemes used with secondary school pupils, some concepts have been considered to be obvious and have been taken for granted in planning a course. Yet, as the findings in Chapters 4 and 8 indicate, studies of children's ideas suggest that even some apparently simple notions such as the conservation of matter or the intensive nature of temperature may not be appreciated by many secondary school students. Failure to appreciate such basic ideas then leads to further and more serious learning problems.

(2) *The choice of learning experiences.* If students' prior ideas are known then these can be challenged directly by experiences which conflict with expectations, so provoking students to reconsider their ideas. However, challenging students' current ideas is not by itself enough to promote change; alternative ideas have to be offered and these need to be seen by students not only as necessary but also reasonable and plausible. Knowledge of students' ideas enables us to choose teaching activities which are more likely to be interpreted by students in the way intended. The case of the reflection of light by objects, described in Chapter 2, is an example of this. Most children aged 13-14 recognize that a mirror has the property of reflecting light, even though they think that the light remains on other objects. To support this idea, they refer to the fact that with a mirror one can

light up an object or flash a light at someone. One can introduce similar experiences to convince them that light is reflected by ordinary objects. At noon in midsummer, a piece of white paper will glare when struck by the light from the sun. In a dark room, one can easily perceive a light-coloured object being lit by light reflected by a sheet of white paper. We also see that, on the other hand, knowledge of children's conceptions allows us to reject certain classical teaching experiments, which are not interpreted by the child in the way we expect them to be.

(3) *The presentation of the purposes of proposed activities.* In formulating the purposes of learning tasks it is important to bear in mind that pupils may reinterpret the intentions of the teacher in terms of their own understandings. This is illustrated in the following example where secondary pupils were programmed through a series of activities on work-cards. One group of girls carried out an experiment in which an immersion heater was placed in blocks of equal weight but made of different metals (Figure 1.2). The function of the experiment was to demonstrate variation in heat capacity. The pupils had been instructed to draw a temperature–time graph as each block was heated. Towards the end of the lesson the girls were instructed to look at the graphs they had produced and compare them, suggesting an explanation. The teacher (T) enters their discussion:

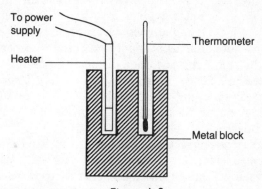

Figure 1.2

T: What has your experiment shown you?
P2: That different... um... that different materials and that... see how heat could travel through them.
T: What did you find out?
P1: Well... er... that heat went through the... the... iron more easier than it did through the er...
P2: Aluminium.

The pupils had had first-hand experience—they had collected their data, but these had been assimilated into a scheme concerned with conductivity, rather than in the way intended.

While it is necessary to bear students' ideas in mind while teaching, it certainly is not easy to put this into practice. The teacher has responsibility for the class as a whole and may consider it quite unrealistic to take the varied ideas of each student into account.

One of the recurring themes in the studies which are reviewed in the following chapters is that, although there is variety in the ideas children use to interpret phenomena, there are clearly some general patterns in the types of ideas that children of different ages tend to use. Studies of childrens' conceptions relating to a number of scientific topics have been undertaken in different parts of the world with children whose experience of formal science teaching has varied considerably. Despite this, quite independent research studies have reported similar patterns of ideas held by young people. For example, studies in the area of students' conceptions of dynamics (Chapter 5), their views of the Earth (Chapter 9), and their ideas about heat (Chapter 4) have been undertaken in a number of countries and the findings paint a consistent picture with students' early experiences of phenomena dominating their thinking. Studies reported on the particulate theory of matter in Chapters 7 and 8 indicate how difficult it is for many students to assimilate aspects of that model despite carefully designed teaching sequences. The report on children's ideas about electricity in Chapter 3 gives a rather disturbing finding; the proportion of students using an incorrect 'sequence' model for electric current remains dominant as students go through secondary school.

Studies of this kind suggest that despite the apparent variety of ideas suggested in science classrooms, there may be some value in attempting to take account of general trends in childrens' thinking, both in planning learning activities and in order to improve communication in the classroom itself.

In this chapter we have given an outline of a particular view of learning; a view in which learning is seen to take place through the interaction between, on the one hand, a learner's experiences and, on the other, the 'mental entities', the 'ideas' or 'schemes', used to interpret and give meaning to those experiences.

Throughout the following chapters various terms are used to describe these 'mental entities' and each has a slightly different connotation. Some terms, such as 'intuitive notion' or 'intuition' are suggestive of the origins of the ideas; some, such as 'conception', 'rule' or 'prototypic view', hint at the generality of use of the ideas. In some cases the organization of ideas and the relationship between them is emphasized in the use of such terms as 'cognitive structure', 'frameworks' or 'childrens' models'. In other cases the term used is qualified with the word 'alternative' (e.g. 'alternative conception', 'alternative framework'), thus emphasizing the difference between childrens' ideas and accepted scientific theory.

In our view, this plurality of terms reflects both the multifaceted nature and the variability which characterizes childrens' ideas; a variability which exists from one type of phenomenon to another, between contexts and between children themselves.

We have not, therefore, attempted to impose a common terminology throughout the following chapters. As in the story of the blind men describing an elephant, each of the various terms used reflects some aspects of the central concern of this book: the description of childrens' thinking about phenomena in the natural world.

References

[1]Driver, R. (1983). *The Pupil as Scientist?* Open University Press: Milton Keynes.
[2]Tiberghien, A. (1980). Quel rapport y a-t-il entre ce que les éleves "ont dans la tête" et ce qu'ils font ou disent? In *Sciences Physiques*, pp. 197–202. Livre du Professeur 3ème coll Libres Parcours, Hachette, Paris.

CHAPTER 2

Light

Edith Guesne

For the physicist, light is an entity that propagates in space from a source, that interacts with objects it encounters in its path and then produces various perceptible effects (warming, a contrast between zones differently illuminated or which reflect light differently). It possesses a certain number of properties: in homogeneous space, it propagates along straight lines; its speed of propagation is finite, i.e. light always takes a certain amount of time to travel from one place to another; it can disappear, partially or totally, when it crosses a material medium, and is conserved as long as it does not encounter any absorbing medium.

What is light to children? We propose here to assess this for 10 to 15-year-old children, by seeing what the word light evokes in them, which properties they attribute to it, and how they interpret phenomena which, for the physicist involve light, such as shadows, vision or the burning of a piece of paper placed behind a magnifying glass.

The results reported here were obtained by interviewing children individually, and in some cases by written questionnaires. The children had not received any systematic instruction about light;[*] nevertheless, they had ideas associated with the word 'light', and interpretations for the phenomena related to it.

'Where is there light?'

Children aged 10-11 and 13-14 were asked: 'Where is there light in this room?'[2,4,9] The interviews took place in daylight and, in a systematic fashion for the children aged 10-11, in a sunny room.

---

[*]In only one case, which is indicated later in the chapter, will we refer to an investigation conducted after teaching in optics.

Some children responded 'everywhere' or 'in space'; these are
responses that a physicist might have made. But others replied:

> On the ceiling... light is there, but it isn't on (Véronique, 12 years, point-
> ing to the electric light bulb).
>
> In the bulbs. It's the bulbs that light up (Marie, 14 years).
>
> Lionel, 11 years: There [pointing to the ground].
> Interviewer: Why do you say that?
> L: Because the sun beats down and you can see that it's lighter than in
> the shadow.

The first two children here identify light with its source, the third identifies it with its effect (the luminous patches produced on the ground
by the sunlight), instead of considering it (as the physicist does) as a
distinct entity, located in space between its source and the effects it
produces.

Light is also sometimes defined as a state: 'Light is a brightness...
which comes depending on the weather; it's lighter one day than
another' (Lionel, 14 years). This definition is similar to the 'light-effect'
one. It is interesting to note that the child just cited is the same one
who, three years earlier, defined light as one of its effects (the luminous
patches produced on the ground by the sun); we will come across this
child again.

We thus find two different conceptions of light: light equated with
its source, with its effects, or with a state; and light recognized as a
distinct entity, located in space between its source and the effect it
produces.

In the following sections, we find other situations that provide
evidence for the definition, by some children, of light as its source or
as its effects. We will also see that the same child may call on one or
the other of the two conceptions, according to the situation, or even
switch from one to the other within the explanation of the same
phenomenon. A child cannot be judged, then, on the basis of a single
response. In order to know where he or she stands in relation to the
concept of 'light-entity in space', it is necessary to assess the range of
utilization of this notion by the child, by suggesting various
situations.

When this assessment is made for children aged 10-11 years, it
appears that they rarely use the concept of 'light-entity in space', and
generally equate light with its source or with its effects instead. At
13-14 years, children on the whole have clearly progresses, instead
but one still finds some of them defining light as its source or as its
effects. However, by this age most children happen to speak of light
as an entity located in space, in one or two situations at least.

However, if this does constitute progress, the acquisition of the
notion of 'light-entity in space' does not necessarily imply a conception of light that would completely satisfy the physicist. We will see
the limits of this notion in 13 to 14-year-old children.

Light and shadows

Children 13-14 years old were asked to explain what a shadow is, and how a shadow is formed.[2,4] Here are some characteristic responses:

> (A shadow)... it's a reflection but... it's a darker light (Pascal, 15 years).
>
> Interviewer: Is there any light on the chairs in the room?
>
> Laurent, 14 years: On some of them, there isn't any, because they're in the shade. ... Under the tables... (there's shade)... because there are... tables which hide the light... (A shadow)... it's the reflection of a person or a thing. ... You can't really see the person. ... You just see the shadow... the light shines on the person... behind the person, reflects his shadow.
>
> The light, uh... sets off. And then it meets and object. ... It lights it up, but behind, it can't cross it. ... So it's black, then that makes the shadow (Hevré, 15 years).

These three responses are not at the same level. The first two merely note the similarity of shape between the object and its shadow ('it's the reflection...'). Only the last child is capable of suggesting a mechanism for the shadow's formation; he considers light as an entity moving in space (it 'sets off', 'meets', 'crosses'), and he can then interpret shadow in terms of an obstacle blocking the passage of light. The two other children do not manifest this conception. The first child, Pascal, confuses light with its effects when he says that the shadow (effect) is a 'darker light'. When the second child says 'the tables hide the light', his understanding of light can be connected to the 'light-source' category. These conceptions do not provide children any means of explanation for the formation of shadows.

If we compare the responses of children aged 10-11 and 13-14, it appears that most of the 13 to 14-year-old children are clearly more advanced than the younger children. Almost all the 10 to 11-year-olds respond like Pascal or Laurent; they perceive the 'light-source' as being responsible for the phenomenon, but they only notice the reproduction of the object's form.[2] On the other hand, the majority of the 13 to 14-year-olds use the notion of 'light-entity in space' in order to interpret shadows, even if, as we have seen, some children still give their responses in terms of 'reflection', as do the younger children.

Lionel was questioned after a three-year interval; his development is interesting to look at. He was first questioned at the end of primary school. During the course of the interview, the interviewer placed a piece of cardboard in the path of the light from a lamp and asked: 'What happened to the light that was there?' Lionel (11 years) then answered:

> It disappeared, because if you put the cardboard there, it keeps the lamp from shining any farther; it's like putting a wall between the two. It disappeared because of the cardboard, because the cardboard makes shade.

His reply established a correct relationship of cause and effect between the presence of the piece of cardboard and the disappearance of the light; but it made no reference at all to 'light-entity in space' and suggested no mechanism for the formation of the shadow. Three years later, Lionel (14 years) first explains the formation of the shadow on the table, using terms that suggest the idea of a movement of light in space:

> If you take away the piece of paper, the light comes back on the table; if you put it back, the light can't pass through the paper and the table is bound to be in shadow.

Then, immediately after this explanation, he adds an interpretation of the 'light-effect', 'light-state' type:

> (The light)... is hidden under the shadow. It becomes the shadow of the piece of paper.

During these three years, Lioned has advanced. But the acquisition of the 'light-entity in space' notion has not driven out the notions of 'light-effect' and 'light-state'. All these ideas are available to him; he can shift from one to the other.

The propagation of light

The propagation time

In the preceding sections, we have seen children saying that 'light sets off, meets, crosses'. These terms suggest an idea of movement of light in space. Almost all the 13 to 14-year-old children we interviewed used such terms as rebound, go through, cross, etc., at least once during the interview.[2,4] They used them in greater or lesser abundance and in a greater or lesser variety of situations, according to the individual. Children aged 10-11, on the other hand, used terms of this kind much less often. These terms locate light in space. They are indicators of the recognition of an entity, 'light', distinct from its source and its effects. Can more be said? For example, that these terms, evocative of movement, indicate that the child has an idea of the movement of light in space?

Children rarely make explicit the idea of light moving in space. When they do, it is almost always only in the case of very great distances.[2,4] For example:

> Well, I know, for instance, that if all at once the sun...went out, well, you know, if the sun's flames stopped burning, you could say... well that... you'd have some... some light for quite a time, because the sun would already have sent out some... some rays... and the rays, well, they, they wouldn't go out... only... only the sun's core would... so during this time... during the... perhaps four months, I don't know how long it takes a ray to get to earth... it... it goes fast, okay, but it takes... takes time even so. ... It can't come just like that (13-year-old).

It is quite exceptional when children call upon the notion of propagation time when speaking of their immediate environment, where this amount of time is imperceptible. The child who gave the preceding speech regarding the sun, continued in this manner:

> [For the lamp]... it's not the light which takes time there, it's the electricity which is coming to the lamp... so as soon as the electricity gets there... well, the light... anyway the lamp reacts and starts... shining.

The idea of moving light is thus rather foreign to children, even when they consider light as an entity located in space.

This question obviously makes no sense to children, particularly 10 to 11-year-olds, who equate light with its source or with its effects. When they are asked if light moves, they reply either in terms of the movement of the light source, or in terms of the variations of an effect:[9]

> But there's some that moves, and some that doesn't move! For example, the one on the ceiling, it doesn't move; and the light from batteries, that moves, and from cars too... because light is the sun and the sun doesn't move (Véronique, 12 years).
>
> François, 11 years: Ah, yes it moves.
> Interviewer: Ah... then how does it move?
> F: Well, it's dark at night, and then it's light during the day.
> I: Yes, then how does this light move?
> F: Uh, the darkness ... it is the darkness that comes, because the darkness is dark and after that you can't see anything.

The straight path

The notion of a straight path of light can be completely dissociated from the notion of propagation time. Children can actually place light on linear rays without having any idea of the movement of light along these rays. But they can locate light on rays only if they have the notion of 'light-entity in space'. The question of the path of light makes no sense to children aged 10-11.

To test this notion of the straight path among 13 to 14-year-olds, we placed the following two experimental devices before the children at different times during the interview:[4]

(1)   The first device consisted of a small lightbulb (disconnected) placed in front of a vertical stick and a screen, as indicated in Figure 2.1. We asked the children to guess, before lighting the bulb, what would be the exact size and position of the stick's shadow, and draw it on the screen.

(2)   The second device is represented in Figure 2.2; the child could not see the lighting of the second screen. We asked him if he thought that that screen would be lit. If he replied yes, we asked him, after disconnecting the bulb, to draw very precisely on the second screen the part that was lit when the light bulb was on.

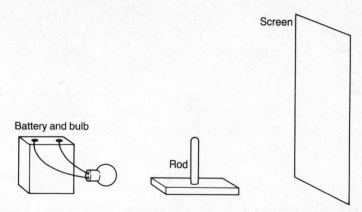

Figure 2.1: First device used to test the notion of a straight path of light with 13 to 14-years-olds.

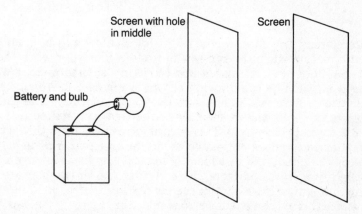

Figure 2.2: Second device used to test the notion of a straight path of light with 13 to 14-years-olds.

About a third of the children aged 13-14 correctly called upon the notion of the straight path of light to guess the size of the stick's shadow or the position of the luminous patch on the screen. This last result was confirmed by a written questionnaire given to 250 children.[5]

An additional number of children grasped the idea of a straight line, but in the horizontal direction only: the guessed, therefore, that the screen in Figure 2.2 would not receive light, because the hole was not 'across from' the lamp (in other words, they were not horizontally aligned). Altogether, the idea of a straight line was grasped by one-half of the children aged 13-14 that we questioned.

Among the children aged 10-11, it is only possible to test if they can place shadow, object, and source in the correct relationships. This was tested by three questions of a written questionnaire administered

Figure 2.3: Drawing designed to test whether children aged 10 to 11 were able to place a shadow, an object and a source in the correct relationship to one another.

to 94 children:[9] the child was asked if his shadow was in front of or behind him, first when the sun was in front of him, then when the sun was behind him; he was also asked to circle the shadow that was in the right position on the drawing shown in Figure 2.3. About 90% of the children answered the first two questions correctly. The children did not respond as well in the case of the tree represented in Figure 2.3 (66% correct responses). This may have resulted from the fact that this last situation does not evoke, as do the first two, a personal situation for the child, one in which he himself has been involved. This may also have resulted from the fact that the drawing presents a certain ambiguity: if we add up the percentages corresponding to the choice of either of the shadows to the left of the tree (the sun being on the right), 80% is obtained. One might say, then, that children aged 10-11 have a generally correct idea of the relative positions of the source, the object, and the object's shadow (at least in the case of everyday situations), even though they do not have the explanatory model given by the notion of the straight path of light.

Light and its interactions with matter (I): the role of a magnifying glass

Children know that a magnifying glass can be used to set something alight on a sunny day. At 13-14 years, many of them have already tried it. How do they interpret it?

> It makes it bigger. ... So it ought to make the light bigger. And as the light heats up anyway... because if you put it there, at the end of an hour, it's going to burn. ... But as the lens makes it bigger... there's going to be lots of light, I think (Jean-Marie, 13 years).

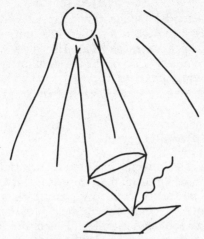

Figure 2.4: How a magnifying glass sets a sheet of paper alight (Oliver, 13 years).

Olivier, 13 years: It concentrates the light.
Interviewer: Yes, can you draw me a picture?
O: As the light is more or less hot. ...
I: Yes, here you are, draw it for me. Show me where the sun is, where you put the paper and the lens.
O: Well, here for instance is the sun. The paper is there. It spreads out all around. It goes like that and there it's concentrated [see Figure 2.4].
I: Is there more light behind the lens than in front?
O: No, but it's more concentrated in one spot.

These two types of response are equally given by 13 to 14-year-old children: 'the magnifying glass makes the light bigger' or 'the magnifying glass concentrates the light'. Among the children who think the magnifying glass 'makes the light bigger', some think, like Jean-Marie, that there is more light behind the magnifying glass; other think that there are 'just as many rays, but they're... they're stronger' (Roseline, 15 years). Children who believe that the magnifying glass concentrates light do not necessarily have a representation that is as

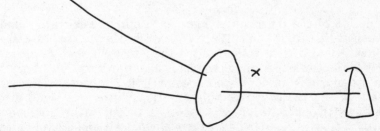

Figure 2.5: How Michel (14 years) imagines the concentration of light by a magnifying glass.

consistent with the model of the physicist as Olivier's one. Thus Michel (14 years) drew the picture shown in Figure 2.5 to show how the magnifying glass concentrates light. However, all these children have the idea of the conservation of the total quantity of light passing through the magnifying glass, as opposed to the children who think that the magnifying glass 'makes the light bigger'.

The conservation of light

We have just seen a case in which children do not take into consideration the conservation of light, in that they suggest that the magnifying glass has the power to multiply or intensify light. For the physicist, on the other hand, the quantity of light can only be diminished when it encounters a material medium; if it encounters a non-absorbant material (or a material only slightly absorbant, such as the glass of a lens), it is conserved.

We found another case in which children do not feel it is necessary for the light to be conserved, though there is no interaction with a material medium. For some, indeed, light alters with distance:

> At one point it stops because it's too far. ... At one point it can't go on... you can't see it any more. ... I think that it can't go through the air any more, or else it... it's because it can't go through the air any more, it's lost its... its density (Jean-Marie, 13 years).

We have seen that this same child thought that there was more light behind the magnifying glass because it 'makes the light bigger'; for him, light can be lost, can disappear or, on the contrary, be multiplied. Children's conceptions are linked to their perceptions: Jean-Marie associates the idea that light stops with the fact that it can no longer be seen. The presence of light is thus linked, for children, to a perceptible effect. For them, light is strong; when it loses its force, it ceases to exist.

Light and its interactions with matter (II): the reflection of light by objects

The notion of the reflection of light by a mirror was tested among children aged 10-11 and 13-14.[2,4,5] With the 13 to 14-year-old children, we also tried to find out if they thought that an ordinary object (a piece of paper, for example) is able to reflect light. Very few data are available on children's ideas relating to the various light-radiations and the colour of objects.[1] In addition, we found in our interviews that children rarely associate colour with light spontaneously. Colour is likely to be for them an intrinsic property of objects, quite independent of light and, therefore, we will not take into account the colour of the object here.

The 10 to 11-year-olds and mirrors

Most children 10-11 years old have no idea of the reflection of light by a mirror. This corresponds to the fact that they have no notion of 'light-entity in space', as was apparent in the previous examples. Let us return to Lionel, in his last year of primary school:

> Interviewer: Is there light on the mirror?
> Lionel, 11 years: Yes.
> I: What becomes of it?
> L: There really isn't any; it's the light of the lamp reflected inside... (Actually)... there's no light and when you put the mirror in front, the lamp reflects inside the mirror. You'd say there is another lamp behind.

The child evokes simply the image of the source (light-source) in the mirror.

The 13 to 14-year-olds and the reflection of light by objects

On the contrary, the majority of the 13 to 14-year-olds express the idea that the mirror reflects light, the light then being conceived of as an entity located in space.

The interview situation
In an interview, we tested the children for the notion of the reflection of light by mirrors and by ordinary objects by presenting them with a piece of white paper, then a mirror, placed in front of an electric torch (Figure 2.6). We then asked them: 'What does the light do, from the moment I switch on the torch?' We again found children who reason by assimilating light as its source or as its effect, and can only describe what they see in the mirror, as younger children do. Thus,

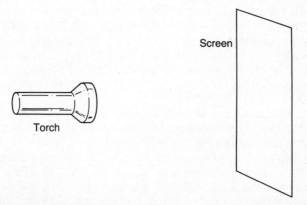

Figure 2.6: Device used to test the notion of the reflection of light.

Evelyne (15 years) tells us: 'You see the light... in the mirror... (you see) the lamp.'

In the case of the piece of paper, they limited themselves to observing the presence of the luminous spot on the paper:

Interviewer: What does the light do?
Evelyne: It makes a haze... it makes streaks [the spot was inhomogeneous].

But at 13-14 years, the dominant interpretation is the following: the light leaves the lamp and stays on the paper, but the mirror reflects it.

(The light)... it bounces off the glass [gesture of the child going from the torch to the mirror, then towards herself]. When the light falls on the paper, that makes a screen. ... It stays there... whereas the glass sends the light back (Christine, 14 years).

This conception follows directly from their perception: with the mirror you can light up something else or flash a light in someone's eyes, while with the paper, the most apparent effect takes place on the paper. This can be linked to the conception which we encountered above: for children of this age, light means intense light; when it is not intense enough to be perceptible, it does not exist any more.

The written test situation
But when the idea of the reflection of light by ordinary objects is tested in a situation where the child has no direct perception of the spot of light on the object, and where there is another possible receptor, the results are different. We tested that notion in a written questionnaire,[5] by presenting two diagrams (Figure 2.7).

The diagrams represent a shop window, first with a white wall, then with a black one. The children were asked whether the object placed in the shop window would be lit with the spotlight oriented in such a way. Just like the children who were interviewed, these children had never been taught physics either, but they answered quite differently: 30% of them answered, in the case of the white wall, that the object would be lit because the wall reflects light; the same answer was also given by 10% of the children for the black wall. The question was an open one, the children themselves introducing the word 'reflects' (or 'throws back', 'sends back', etc.). We can then say that the idea of the reflection of light is present among children of this age for objects other than mirrors, though that idea was exceptional in the interviews.

It appears again here, as with Lionel in the case of shadows, that a child can 'have' some given notion, but not use it systematically. We found that about one-third of the 13 to 14-year-olds were able to call upon the idea of the reflection of light by an ordinary surface, in a given instance (the questionnaire situation). But, in other instances (the interview situation), children can call upon other ideas (perception, light=intense light, etc.) and they can then be led to give answers contrary to the first notion.

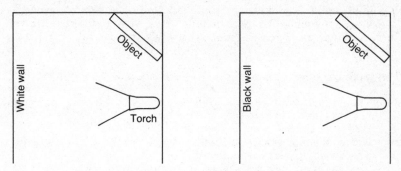

Figure 2.7: Written test about the notion of the reflection of light: the two sketches represent a shop-window seen from above; the first one has a white wall on the left, the second one a black one.

Pedagogical implications
Thus, children aged 13-14 will admit that light can be reflected by ordinary objects. But that idea can be driven back, for example when perception gives another clue to deal with the situation. Now this notion of reflection is fundamental to optics: one cannot understand the formation of images of ordinary objects (not in themselves luminous), as in photography for example, without this prior notion; it is likewise a prerequisite for understanding vision. Therefore, teaching has to encourage this idea to be held more firmly and more widely among children of that age. To do this, one can use as a basis the case of the mirror which is already fully recognized by most children as reflecting light. Children refer to the fact that with a mirror another object can be lit up or a light flashed at someone. With a light-coloured sheet of paper, similar experiences can be reproduced: at noon, in midsummer, a piece of white paper will glare in the light of the sun; in a darkened room, it is easy to perceive a light-coloured object being lit up by the light reflected from a piece of white paper. We see here how a knowledge of children's conceptions gives some indication both of pertinent objectives for the age group under consideration, and of some means of attaining these objectives.

Light and electric light

Children place electric light and sunlight in two quite distinct categories:

> There's sunlight that brings us daylight... and then there's the light which is made, electric light to illuminate us... (14-year-old).

Sometimes, only electric light is spontaneously associated by the child with the word 'light'. Thus, when asked, 'what is light to you?', Marie (14 years) tells us:

It's light bulbs that light up... and that... and the light is made by dams... or something like that... mainly dams. ... Well, the water turns in the turbines and it gives light. ... It's the (electric) current which gives the light.

When asked where is there light?', she continues by saying:

M: There's light everywhere. ... Well, yes, er... in the streets, in... there, in the houses... in cars too... everywhere.
I: And here, in this room, is there any light?
M: Not at the moment... you have to switch on, there...
I: There's no light at the moment?
M: Yes, daylight... not not the, er... electric light.
I: It's not the same?
M: No, because there's sunlight, and then there's lights like that.
I: And the sunlight, is it light?
M: Well, yes... because you can make light by... the sun... yes, with the sun. I don't know how really, but certainly... well, I don't know, the sun should... yes certainly.
     (There is light)... in houses, outside, in cars... well pretty well everywhere... everywhere where there are people, where you have to light up; not particularly for people, also in factories, well everywhere, for... so that... so that you can see.
     (Here)... there's light, but it's not turned on. ... Well... you'd have to switch on there, at the switch, and there'll be light.

Thus, when asked to speak freely about light, this child thinks only of electric light. To be sure, she speaks of daylight, in reply to a remark by the interviewer, but she returns immediately to the assimilation 'light = electric light'. For her, sunlight is light 'because you can make light with the sun', she does not know how, but is sure you can; perhaps someone has told her about solar cells, as well as about dams.

We have already quoted Marie in a preceding paragraph; she belongs to the group of children who identify light as its source. Like her, in general, children who identify light as source usually identify light as an electric light-bulb. Thus, the assimilation of light as its source is generally coupled with the assimilation 'light = electric light'.

Light and daylight

At 13-14 years, children see a cause and effect relationship between sun and daylight, but this relationship remains rather vague, as it does for the 14-year-old who told us earlier: 'there's sunlight that brings us daylight'.

They are capable of interpreting the alternation between day and night when considering the lighting of the side of the Earth facing the sun:

Twelve hours a day, the light is... it's on us... on France... and for twelve hours, it's no longer on France, I don't know what country it's on. ... It's because the Earth is round, it's spherical, so when there's one side of the Earth which is facing the sun, the rays go where they can, they won't go round the Earth to light up the other side, behind the Earth... so they light up the side which is... facing the sun... so... the other side is not lit up. it's night-time for the other part (F4, 13 years).

But this age group tend to be at a loss to interpret the 'sunbath' into which we are plunged when it is daytime. The terrestrial day actually takes place due to the diffusion of light by the atmosphere; when one knows that these children are not quite convinced of the reflection of light by solids, one can conceive that they do not understand the result of an interaction between air and light. In fact, their notions about daylight are rather muddled.

There's light everywhere [in the room]... well, it's not light, it's something to enable us to see, I'd say... it's not really light. ... When you look at a candle or a lamp, you say, well, that, that makes light; whereas there, that's not light, you can't say, well, there, that, that makes light, you're in a room, there's light there, but it's... it's... the room doesn't make the light (14-year-old).

[It's daytime] because there's sunshine. ... Well sometimes, there's not always sunshine, it rains, but... nevertheless it's daytime. ... I don't know why that is... [When there is sunshine, that is to say]... it's good weather... it lights up more... because when it rains or when it snows, well... it's dark... because there are clouds... grey clouds... so it covers the sun... not the sun, the sky... well it makes the sky dark (Marie, 14 years).

The first of these two children is hindered because she cannot manage to identify the source of the light. How can one understand the lighting of a room that does not receive direct sunlight, a room with north-facing windows in Europe or North America for example? The second child, for her part, does not understand how there can be daylight when there is no sun. In her case, she lacks the notion of 'light-entity in space', which would permit her to interpret daylight as light that reaches us from the sun, more or less attenuated by passing through clouds. This is a first stage, preliminary to the comprehension of situations in which the sunlight cannot reach us in a straight line, but reaches us only after having been diffused in all directions by the atmosphere.

Light and vision

There is a strong association between light and vision for most children. The questions, 'what is light to you?' and 'what does light do?', when asked at the beginning of an interview, bring out two dominant ideas: light lights things up; light allows vision.

With children 13-14 years old, we tried to find out what, for them, was the mechanism of vision and what role light played in it.[3,4] We asked them two questions: one concerned vision of a primary source, a glowing stick of incense; the other dealt with vision of an ordinary object, a multi-coloured cardboard box.

Is the eye conceived of as a receptor of light?

We first presented the stick of incense, asking the child if he saw its (glowing) tip so that he would be quite conscious of seeing it. Then we asked him, 'does it give off light?', in order to find out if, for him, vision was linked to the reception of light by the eye.

Most children think that it does not give off 'any' light, or that it sends it 'not very far', not as far, at any rate, as where they are, about one metre from the stick of incense.

> It doesn't send out any, it stays where it is (Christine, 14 years).
>
> Interviewer: Is this end sending out light?
> Jean-Marie, 13 years: Yes... but much less than that [he points to the torch which has just been used].
> I: Much less strong... how far does it go?
> J-M: I don't know. ... Well, much less far, only a little. You have to put it... very close... [he holds the incense stick close to a sheet of paper]... Oh, even like that, it's not sending out any light. ... You can see it, because it's red, otherwise...

Here again, Jean-Marie links the presence of light to the manifestation of an effect intense enough to be perceptible: the lighting up of a piece of paper. Now the fact of seeing an object is not accompanied by any violent physical sensation; one is rarely dazzled. By not recognizing light except when it provokes marked perceptible effects, children do not think that their eyes can be receptors of light. Light is necessary in order to see an object, but light does not necessarily reach the eye. This is what David (13 years) explicitly expresses.

> I: Is it sending out light?
> D: Yes.
> I: Yes. Why?
> D: Because you can see it in the dark. ... You can see it in the dark, so it gives out light otherwise you couldn't see it. ... Unless there's another light...
> I: Where does it send out light to?
> D: There [he indicates a point a few centimetres from the stick].
> I: When you see, does your eye receive light? Is there any light which goes in your eye?
> D: Not necessarily.
> I: Not necessarily, no...
> D: No, because with the incense stick, for instance, if I had binoculars, it could be one kilometre away, and I would see it just the same.

Only a few children respond to the question, 'Does its light reach you?': 'yes... otherwise I wouldn't see it' (Hervé, 15 years). These responses are still very vague. One or two are, however, more explicit:

My idea is that the moment you see something, if it's in the dark, it must be sending out light. ... If I see something in complete darkness, and I see that thing, like that [he points to the lighted incense stick] or a lamp, I think it must be sending out light. If I see it a hundred metres away, it must be sending out light to a hundred metres. If I see it at a hundred and fifty metres, it's sending out light to a hundred and fifty metres... at least provided that it's in complete darkness. Because if I see a cupboard or my coat because there's light, I see it. But if in complete darkness I see something... and I can't see anything else, well I think it must be sending out light. Because I can see it (Karim, 12 years).

Here, Karim clearly distinguishes between the case of incandescent objects and the case of ordinary objects. If the recognition of the reception of light by the eye is rare in the case of an object such as a stick of incense, it is even rarer in the case of ordinary objects. Only one child, who had given a response conforming to the physicist's model in the case of the glowing stick, extended this response to the case of the cardboard box.

... if I see the object... it must be because it gives me a bit of light. So... I can see it... (the light)... it gets to my eye... and then my eye it records. And it makes it possible, er... in my brain to form an image of the object (Michel, 14 years).

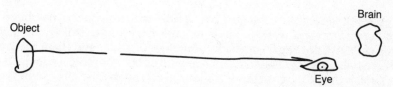

Figure 2.8:   A drawing by Michel (14 years): vision is correctly conceived as resulting from the reception of light by the eye.

Another conception:

Hervé considered the eye as a receptor of light in the case of the glowing stick, but in the case of the cardboard box he tells us:

Here my eyes can go right up to the box. ... It's my sight. ... If it [the box] was fifteen kilometres away, I couldn't see it, because... my sight isn't strong enough. ... Because a box doesn't move, it hasn't any energy. A lamp for example, it moves, the light gets there. ... The box, it's stuff that isn't alive.

Here, a model of vision appears in which the eye is not a receptor but is, on the contrary, an active agent. Jacques (14 years) similarly tells us:

It's pretty much like the light, because it comes out. ... The eye sees like this... it comes out like this... [he draws lines going forwards or upwards from the eye, according to the direction in which the eye is looking]. ... The eyes haven't got any light of their own, so they have to have a light that lights up what you want to see.

Everyday language, which may reflect and reinforce the common ways of thinking, conveys the same idea: it attributes an active role to the eye, while the object 'looked at' has only a passive role; an eye examines, probes, scrutinizes; in romantic literature, eyes flash fire, one looks daggers at someone. Indeed, when looking at an object, there is more a feeling of being an active subject than a passive receptor. A comprehensive theory of vision includes physical, physiological and psychological aspects. This feeling of the activity of the subject, which is linked to psychological aspects, is found also in the 'visual fire' notion of Plato and the Pythagorean school. For Plato.

... the Gods cause the pure fire within us, which is akin to that of day, to flow through the eyes in a smooth and dense stream. ... So whenever the stream of vision is surrounded by daylight, it flows out like unto like, and coalescing therewith it forms one kindred substance along the path of the eyes' vision. ... And this substance distributes the motions of every object it touches, or whereby it is touched, throughout all the body even unto the Soul, and brings about that sensation which we now term 'seeing' (*Plato's Dialogues: the Timaeus*).

The Pythagoreans believed that vision was solely the result of an invisible fire coming from the eye; this fire (or, according to Euclid, this collection of rays) touched upon objects and made them recognizable as shapes and colours. At the end of the fourth century, Theon of Alexandria thought that luminous rays emitted by the eye must be somewhat separated from each other, because

a thing cannot be seen completely with one glance: sometimes, when looking for a small object on the ground, a needle for example, one does not see it, even though it is not hidden by any obstacle; but one can see it without difficulty when one has directed one's look on where it is actually found; in the same way, one does not see simultaneously all the letters on a written page.[10]

For children, the movement starting from the eyes to the object remains abstract; it thus clearly differs from the 'visual fire' of the ancient theories, the 'emanations' from witches' eyes in fairy tales, or the red rays that shine from Superman's eyes. Only the idea that the subject is the origin of a process, instead of being its receptor, is common to these representations of vision. It is a qualitatively important conception. But we have encountered it only among very few children; it should not be given more importance than it has quantitatively, in spite of the attraction an historic model always exerts.

The dominant conception:

Most children do not bring in any mediator between the eye and the object, in either sense.

> Interviewer: How is it that you see this box at this particular moment?
> Patricia (14 years):   Because it's in front of my eyes, here, I see it... I can see it on account of daylight, because in the dark I wouldn't see it... because in the dark there's no light... there's no daylight. ... The eyes need daylight, need light, in order to see clearly.
>
> It's thanks to the light that we see the box... (its role is)... to light up objects so that we can see them (Daniel, 15 years).

Some of them reproduce a sketch, such as that in Figure 2.9, of the inverted image at the back of the eye. This is only a memory from school, recited without having attached to it any means of explanation.

What do the two crossing lines represent? The child who drew them (Jean-Marie, 13 years) does not know. All children recognize light as a factor necessary for vision; but, for most of them, it only serves to light up the object, or it constitutes a general bath (daylight) surrounding object and observer. The eye 'sees' without anything linking it to the object. This conception appears to be widely spread. We have quoted French children here, but studies conducted with Swedish[1] and German pupils[6,7] gave similar results, even after teaching in optics.

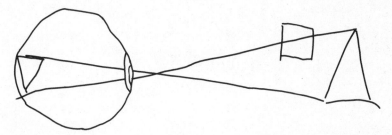

Figure 2.9:   A stereotyped drawing about vision by Jean-Marie (13 years).

Conclusion

Children's conceptions about seeing an ordinary object can be summarized by Figures 2.10 to 2.13. Figure 2.10 represents the 'bath of light': no mechanism is defined between the eye, the light and the object. In the case of Figure 2.11, the necessity of a mediator between the eye and the object is also not perceived by the child, but light plays a more precise role—it lights up the object. These two figures are equally representative of the ideas held by a very large majority of children. We have seen, indeed, that few children imagine 'seeing' as

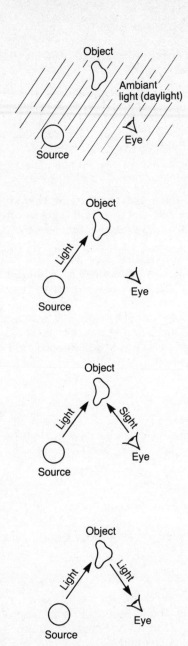

Figures 2.10 to 2.13: The progession in conceptions of vision encountered among 13 to 14-years-olds, towards that of a physicist.

a movement from the eye to the object (Figure 2.12). We have also seen that the physicist's model, presented in Figure 2.13, is very rare among children, especially when objects are not themselves luminous. This is in keeping with the fact that the idea of the reflection of light by objects is not firmly established among children.

These conceptions of vision are in themselves important: the physicist's model, which considers the eye as a receptor of light, is not acquired; it therefore becomes a teaching objective. These conceptions of vision are also important when we consider the validity of certain classic experiments in physics teaching, and when deciding the readiness of children for some topics, such as virtual images.

Indeed, many teaching courses on optics and light assume that children already appreciate the idea of light travelling from an object to the eye. Often a teaching course will start by establishing the propagation of light in a straight line. To accomplish this, it will show pupils that they cannot see a candle's flame through a series of holes punched in card unless the holes are aligned. Children cannot appreciate this demonstration; they cannot interpret the experiment in terms of the path of the light from the object to the eye, when they do not link the vision of the flame to a reception of light by the eye.

The lack of a correct model of vision is also probably one of the reasons for the difficulty, which pupils traditionally have, of grasping the notion of the virtual image. The physicist interprets the virtual image of an object (O) in a mirror (Figure 2.14) by saying that the light issuing from the object reaches the eye of the observer after having been deflected by the mirror, *exactly as if* it came in a straight line from an object (O'), which would be symmetrical to the real object in relation to the surface to the mirror. The observer then has an identical perception to that which he would have looking directly at an object situated at O'. This model thus rests on the idea that an object

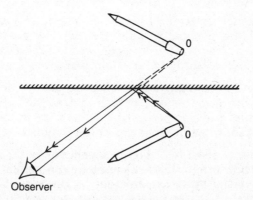

Figure 2.14: The physicist's interpretation of the virtual image of an object in a mirror.

is seen because of the light that comes from it and that penetrates our eye after having been propagated in a straight line in the intermediate space. It is not until 13–14 years of age, and possibly beyond, that children have this notion.

Teaching needs to produce a better model of vision; it cannot take this model as a basis, on the mistaken assumption that it is already acquired.

In conclusion: representations of light—teaching of optics

The representations of light

In the preceding paragraphs, we have seen two quite different conceptions of light: first, there is the more primitive notion of light assimilated as its source, as its effects, or as a state; secondly, there is the idea of light as a distinct entity, located in space. The first conception does not give children any means of interpreting phenomena: they can only notice the similarity of shape between an object and its shadow, or the presence of an image of a source in a mirror. The second conception constitutes clear-cut progress; children can now interpret shadows and wonder about the reflection of light by objects, a question that makes no sense as long as the notion of light in space has not been formed. But this is only a first step toward a notion consistent with the model of the physicist. We have seen the limitations of this among 13 to 14-year-old children who have this conception:

(1) the movement of light is not explicitly accepted; children often speak of light as if it were an entity in motion (it leaves, crosses, rebounds, etc.), but they refuse to make explicit the propagation time, except, sometimes, in the case of great distances;

(2) light does not exist for children unless it is intense, intense enough to produce perceptible effects; thus they are led to believe that, unlike the mirror, a piece of paper does not reflect light and that their eyes do not necessarily receive light when they look at an object;

(3) light is not necessarily conserved; for many children, it can disappear without any interaction with matter, when it is no longer intense enough to produce perceptible effects; or on the contrary, it can be intensified, when passing through a magnifying glass.

Children's ideas appear to be highly dependant on their perceptions. Instances of it are seen in children's answers concerning the reflection of light, vision or the 'variation' of light with distance. The quotations we gave to illustrate these points were drawn from our study with French children.[2,3,4] Other instances of the close relationship between children's interpretations and perception can be found in studies conducted in Sweden[1] and New Zealand.[8] A sketch where the beams from the headlamps of a car were drawn only along a certain distance led a majority of Swedish children to say that there was light only in that part; children from New Zealand stated that the light from a source goes further at night than during the day.

Some children also have an image of the entity 'light in space'. At 10-11 and at 13-14 years, this tends to be a material image. Frederic (11 years) uses an analogy with water to describe what happens when light is stopped by a piece of cardboard:

F: Just behind the cardboard there's no light, but on the side there's light because the light, I think maybe it strikes and goes over there.
I: It strikes, it strikes against the cardboard?
F: Yes and it scatters, going back here [he points to the sides of the cardboard].
I: What does that mean?
F: It's as if it's water; water would come here, and then it would go by the sides to get to the other side.

Jean-Marie (13 years) describes light as 'solid'. Speaking about light shining from a lamp on a mirror, he tells us: 'Light... it is solid... so it must go back...'. When a piece of white absorbant cotton is being lighted by the lamp, he points out that the light will not go back from it 'because it's not firm'.

Such a 'material' image can help children interpret certain phenomena, such as the interaction of light and a mirror; but in other cases, it is a stumbling block, as it is for Jacques (14 years) in the case of the magnifying glass:

J: My idea is that the rays don't go through. It's the light that goes through. What I mean is that it doesn't go through, but it... how can I put it, it...
I: The rays aren't the same as the light?
F: Yes they are, but... the rays and the light are the same thing. They don't go straight through, there are no little holes for them to go through.

The development of children and the teaching of optics

It appears that children pass successively from the assimilation 'light = source, effect or state' to the conception of light as an entity in space: at 10-11 years, in fact, the majority of children have the first conception, whereas at 13-14 years, most children tend to call upon the second conception. But children do not pass all at once from one conception to the other. When a child acquires a new idea, the old conception is not automatically driven away. We saw several instances where the child called upon one conception or another according to the situation. Thus, many 13 to 14-year-olds call upon the notion of light in space only in a limited number of situations. At this age, not all children have reached the same level of development, some of them even still assimilate light strictly as its source or as its effects.

The notion of light in space, dissociated from its source and from its effects, is a prerequisite necessary to touch upon problems in optics. In many countries, the 13-14 age group is taught optics. The teacher will have, then, to assess where his/her own students are in relation to the notion of light in space: this notion will constitute a primary objective of his/her instruction if the children do not have this idea, or do not use it systematically.

When this notion is acquired, the entity 'light in space' is often endowed with properties that do not entirely conform to the physicist's model. We have seen that before being in a position to grasp a phenomenon such as virtual images, adolescents have many stages to go through. We have also seen how a knowledge of childrens' ideas helps in the invention or the choice of experiments likely to help them to conform to the physicist's more universal and more powerful model.

References

[1]Andersson, B. and Kärrqvist, C. (1983). How Swedish pupils, aged 12-15 years, understand light and its properties. *European Journal of Science Education* 5(4), 387-402.

[2]Guesne, E., Tiberghien, A. and Delacôte, G. (1978). Méthodes et résultats concernant l'analyse des conceptions des élèves dans différents domaines de la physique. Deux examples: les notions de chaleur et de lumière. Revue *Française de Pédagogie* 45, 25–32.

[3]Guesne, E. (1978). Lumière et vision des objets: un example de représentation des phénomènes physiques préexistant à l'enseignement. In *Physics Teaching in Schools* (Ed. G. Delacote), pp. 265-273. Taylor and Francis: London.

[4]Guesne, E. (1984). Children's ideas about light. In *New Trends in Physics Teaching*, Vol. IV, (ed. E. J. Wenham) pp. 179-92. UNESCO: Paris.

[5]Guesne, E. (1985). Contribution à la définition d'un enseignement sur la lumière et l'optique pour des enfants de 13-14 ans. Thesis submitted to the University of Paris XI.

[6]Jung, W. (1981a). Ergebnisse einer Optik-Erhebung. *Physica Didactica* 9, 19-34.

[7]Jung, W. (1981b). Conceptual frameworks in elementary optics. In *Proceedings of the International Workshop on Problems Concerning Students' Representations of Physics and Chemistry Knowledge*, Ludwigsburg, West Germany.

[8]Stead, B. F. and Osborne, R. J. (1980). Exploring science students' concepts of light. *Australian Science Teachers Journal* 26 (3), 84-90.

[9]Tiberghien, A., Delacôte, G., Ghiglione, R. and Matalon, B. (1980). Conceptions de la lumière chez l'enfant de 10-12 ans. *Revue Fran*çaise de Pédagogie 50, 24-41.

[10]Ronchi, V. (1956). *Histoire de la lumière*. Armand Colin: Paris.

CHAPTER 3

Electricity in Simple Circuits

David Shipstone

Electricity is a difficult subject. Many adults will freely admit that they never understood it, which is not so often the case with some other areas of physics, mechanics for example, where they do at least *believe* that they understand. In their study of electrical phenomena children are asked to reason in terms of abstract notions such as current, voltage and energy and two particularly important consequences appear to stem from this. First, they experience great difficulty in differentiating between the concepts in this subject area. In consequence, though much of the terminology of basic electricity is acquired even before formal instruction, we frequently find the terms energy, current, power, electricity, charge and voltage used synonymously. Secondly, as a group, children form a variety of conceptual models through which they 'understand' the phenomena with which they are confronted. As in several other topic areas, recent research has revealed that some of these models, once formed, tend to be surprisingly resistant to change through instruction.

For reasons of space, this chapter will deal with only some of the most important aspects of electricity in D.C. circuits constructed from batteries, resistors, lamps, ammeters and voltmeters. Foremost amongst these aspects is that there must be a complete circuit if any continuous processes are to take place. The behaviour of any such circuit depends upon the interplay of voltage and resistance values within it as these determine the rate at which energy is supplied to each element. The voltages across any number of components connected in parallel must be identical and the sum of the voltages across any series of elements comprising the external circuit, that is excluding the battery itself, must equal the voltage between the terminals of the battery. There will be a current in any conductor which has a potential difference between its ends, a voltage across it, and no current otherwise, though it is usual to treat the voltages across connecting wires as negligibly small. The current transports energy from the battery to the various circuit components which make up the load. The current is a flow of charge around the circuit and, is conserved, which is to say that the current entering any element of the circuit must be equal to that leaving, and currents at junctions divide up or recombine so that none is lost or gained. The total resistance of a circuit determines the current through a given battery—the higher this resistance the lower the current. Except in special circumstances where the source has no internal resistance, it is not possible to change the current in one part of a circuit without changing it in all other parts.

In an attempt to help pupils come to terms with electrical circuit phenomena modern courses make extensive use of pupil experiments. Mounted 1.25 V MES lamps (torch bulbs) are employed in many countries now as indicators of intensity of current. Pupils use these to explore the properties of a wide range of circuits, often in conjunction with circuit boards such as those made popular in Britain through the introduction of the Nuffield science courses.

There is no universally accepted sequence of topics though instruction should commence with the requirement of a complete circuit: thereafter practices differ. In many countries it is the concept of electric current that is introduced next, probably in connection with the identification of conductors and insulators, or with the investigation of series and parallel circuits. In the United States, though, the Science Curriculum Improvement Study (SCIS) materials introduce the concept of electrical energy before that of current. This approach deserves more attention and we shall return to it later in the chapter. The concept of resistance is normally introduced in conjunction with current. Voltage, however, is recognized by teachers to be more difficult, more abstract concept so that this may not even be given a place in an introductory course. Instead its introduction may be delayed until the study of electricity is taken up again later in the secondary school years where more quantitative work, involving applications of Ohm's law and calculations on power and energy, is encountered.

A general alternative framework for current electricity

Several investigators[1,2] have examined children's beliefs about electricity before formal instruction through their attempts to make an unmounted lamp light when equipped with a battery and a number of connecting wires. Many of their subjects, aged about 8-12 years, failed in this task and typical examples of the arrangements that they tried are shown in Figure 3.1. It is not, of course, surprising to find that many young children fail at this task. Unfortunately, however,

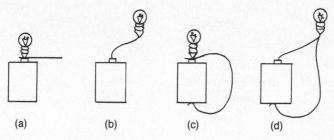

(a)   (b)   (c)   (d)

Figure 3.1: Examples of circuits which indicate a source-consumer model.

investigations have shown that many students at the end of secondary level courses[3,4] also try arrangements such as those shown, treating the lamp as a one-terminal 'sink'.

The underlying idea that children bring with them at the beginning of formal instruction and which many retain is one in which there is a source, such as a battery, and a consumer such as a lamp or a motor.[1-8] Electricity, current, power, volts, energy, 'juice', or whatever, is stored in the source and flows to the load where it is consumed. The battery is usually seen as the active agent or 'giver' in this process, with the load being the 'receiver', but it is also common to find the load regarded as the active agent, as a 'taker', drawing what it 'needs' from the battery.[5]

Prior to instruction the concept of what it is that is 'used up' is very nebulous and it is not always clear what children intend by the terms they use. However, during the early stages of formal instruction in this topic it is the electric current that usually receives most attention and it is to this quantity that the properties of storability and consumability are quickly ascribed. In one study in Germany[5] about 85 per cent of a very large sample of 13 to 15-year-olds, who had completed an introductory course, agreed with the statements:

> In every new battery is stored a certain amount of electric current...
> [and]... the current contained in a battery will be consumed by electric appliances in the course of time.

Forty per cent of a group of 36 university level students planning to become physics teachers also decided that these statements were correct.

The popular conceptual models for current in simple circuits

In explaining how what is 'used up' gets from the source to the consumer children will turn to one or more of a variety of detailed models depending upon the circumstances. The four outlined in Figure

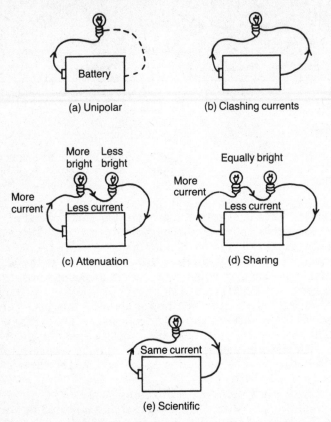

Figure 3.2:   Children's models for current in simple circuits.
(Adapted from Osborne[2,6].)

3.2(a-d) enjoy considerable support. In describing them the term 'current' has been used for convenience: it is not necessarily the term that a child would employ.

(1)   *The unipolar model (Figure 3.2(a)).*   There is no current in the return path. Essentially only one terminal of the battery is regarded as active. Some pupils think that only one wire will be sufficient, while there are others who regard the return wire as a necessary but passive link. In one study the second wire was explained away by one child as a 'safety wire', by another as 'just required to get the bulb alight' in the manner of a catalyst.[6]

(2)   *The clashing currents model (Figure 3.2(b)).*   Current flows to the bulb from both terminals of the battery. This model was so named[2] following one subject who explained that the lamp lit because

Two things clashing let out an electric current... just a force... an argument between forces.

It represents a clear attempt to assimilate the necessity for the second wire to a source-consumer model.

(3) *The attenuation model (Figure 3.2(c)).*   Current flows around the circuit in only one direction. It leaves the battery by one terminal and some current is 'used up' in the lamp so that less returns to the battery. Where the current passes through a number of identical components in series each successive one will receive less. This is a very prevalent view familiar to all physics teachers.

(4) *The sharing model (Figure 3.2(d)).*   Where a series circuit is made up of a number of identical components the current will be shared equally between them. Identical lamps in series are predicted to be all the same brightness, for example, but current is not regarded as conserved.

In addition to these source-consumer views we also find some children subscribing to the accepted scientific model, in so far as they regard the current as being in one direction in the circuit and as being conserved (Figure 3.2(e)).

Just how some of these models are used in practice is revealed by the following extracts from an interview I had with an 11-year-old girl. Ann had not been taught formally about electricity but had encountered a number of its uses through a circus of experiments on energy transformations. The apparatus used in the interview consisted of a cylindrical 1½ V battery which had been run down completely and a set of MES lamps to which wires had been soldered in various arrangments. I explained that the battery was flat but that I wanted to know whether the lamp would light if it was connected to a good battery in each of the ways demonstrated. The interview concluded with questions about some working circuits set out on a circuit board. Note particularly how Ann's responses are influenced by her beliefs about the functions of the various parts of the lamp and battery. Ann said the tip of the lamp 'passes the energy through... to the light' but wondered about the threaded stem: 'Does it help it to stop in?. ... Stop in your torch?' She believed that the metal stud on the end of the battery 'gives out the energy to the... whatever object it is', but didn't know what the metal plate on the other end does.

Shown the arrangement in Figure 3.1(b) Ann said that the lamp would light, but not when the single connection was moved up to the battery's negative terminal. When connected as in Figure 3.1(d) the lamp lights, she said, because 'the energy in the middle of the battery goes out both wires to the light bulb' where it 'comes to the top and then lets the light go on'. With both wires moved to the thread on the lamp, Ann's response to the bulb not lighting was:

Don't know. ...'Cos the energy can't get through there.

Next she was shown the arrangement in Figure 3.2(b) and the interview proceeded as follows:

> Interviewer: Would that light up?
> Ann: Yes, but not as bright as the other ones with both wires at the
> bottom.
> I: I see. Why is that?
> A: 'Cos the energy goes through the bottom [tip of the light bulb] 'cos
> it can't get through there [the threaded part].
> I: What's happening in this other wire? Anything or nothing?
> A: The good energy goes up here [from positive] and the one as what's
> been used goes back down there.
> I: I see. Now in that case you said you've got energy going up one wire
> and then back down the other. In this case [Figure 1(d)] remember,
> when we had the two wires soldered onto the bottom of the lamp, can
> you remember what you said about that one?
> A: Both of them go up to the top.
> I: Yes. Why is it different there?
> A: 'Cos in that one [from positive] the energy comes up and in that one
> the energy comes up 'cos they're both at the bottom, but when
> they're on there, onto the one where you fix it into [the screw
> thread], the energy goes out, what's been used.

Asked about a simple working circuit on a circuit board, where the
connections to the lamp were not clear because of the socket, she
assumed again that energy travelled to the lamp from both ends of the
battery. Among Ann's responses you will find evidence of her using
the unipolar, clashing currents and attenuation models according to
the circumstances, though all of her ideas fall within the source-
consumer framework. Her answers are not typical in that she has used
the term 'energy' where most children would refer to 'electricity' and
others might easily assign different roles to the various parts of a
battery and a lamp, but such switching between models as circumstances are altered is quite common.

The relative popularity of the various models changes with the
pupils' ages and experience. A few years ago I examined children's
beliefs about current, resistance and voltage in closed circuits. The
subjects came from three 11-18 British comprehensive schools and
one sixth form college.[9] All had studied electricity in the year in which
they were tested, the sixth form pupils having completed their
advanced level studies. Figure 3.3 gives one of the questions used.
From the responses to this, at times supported by evidence from
elsewhere in the ten-item test, it was usually possible to deduce the
current model employed.

Of the models previously described all except the unipolar one were
distinguished in the responses. Its incidence was expected to be very
low, however, since a survey of New Zealand children[10] revealed that
generally less than 5 per cent of pupils over this age range use this
view when presented with a complete, simple circuit. Consequently it
was absorbed into the attenuation model. The age distributions of the
models as revealed by that study are shown in Figure 3.4.

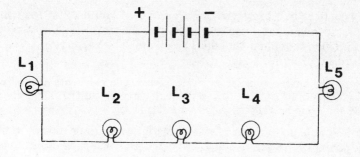

(i) Read each of the sentences below and put a tick in the box
   if you think the sentence is true.
   (a) L_4 is dimmer than L_5 ☐
   (b) L_3 will be lit up ☐
   (c) L_2 and L_4 are same brightness ☐
   (d) L_3 is brighter than L_1 ☐

(ii) Will the brightness of L_2 be MORE THAN ☐
                              LESS THAN ☐
              or THE SAME AS ☐
   the brightness of L_1? (Tick which)
   Why do you say this?

Figure 3.3: One of the questions used to investigate children's ideas about electricity.

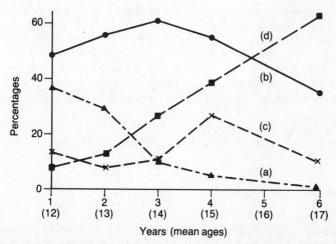

Figure 3.4: Variations in popularity of some conceptual models for current. (a) The clashing currents model, (b) all unidirectional non-conservation models, (c) the sharing model, (d) the scientific model.

Uncertainty in classification arose in a number of ways. For example, it was sometimes impossible to distinguish clearly between the scientific model and the sharing model. The response that L_1 and L_2 would be of equal brightness

> because the bulbs are in series which means they all obtain power from the same supply which is divided equally among all the bulbs giving them the same brightness (pupil, year 3)

might follow from the use of either model depending upon the meaning of 'power'. Uncertainty also arose where responses did not clearly fit any one of the models described and, in some cases, through children's use of different models in different questions. Figure 3.4 gives the best estimates for the incidence of the various models when the uncertainties are taken into account, though in some cases these were considerable.

The use of the 'clashing currents' model (Figure 3.4(a)) decreases sharply with increasing age and so seems to be readily challenged by teaching. The results presented here for the incidence of this model are very similar to those found in New Zealand.[10] Figure 3.4(b) gives the proportions using any of the other non-conservation models, including the sharing model. The initial rise here is brought about by a shift from the clashing currents model, in which current is not conserved, to one of the unidirectional models in which current is still not conserved. It is difficult to be certain what proportion of the decline in these models, coinciding with a switch to the scientific view, resulted from teaching rather than from self-selection of courses by those pupils who were more able at physics. There was a steady increase with age in the percentage of subjects who conserved current in these questions though at least 27 per cent of the sixth-year group definitely did not. The initial decline in the proportion of subjects who described current as being shared out (Figure 3.4(c)) was not statistically significant. In year four, however, there was a sharp rise in the number of clear statements of this model to a level which was significantly higher than in the other year groups. This may indicate some confusion between current on the one hand and energy, power and voltage on the other, all of which would be shared out equally between the lamps in Figure 3.3. Apart from one small second-year group these were the first pupils to have experienced any serious treatment of voltage.

A model for more complex circuits

If the total resistance of a series circuit is increased then the current will decrease. This is the case whatever the positions of the resistors in the circuit. The question shown in Figure 3.5 was used to investigate children's understanding of these two rules. They were asked to indicate the effects upon the brightness of the lamp of increasing or decreasing the variable resistors, R_1 and R_2, separately.

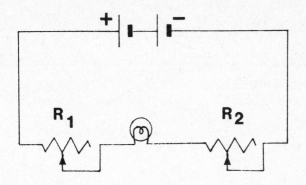

R₁ and R₂ are resistors which can be either increased or decreased.

a) If R₁ is *decreased*, will the brightness of the lamp

   INCREASE ☐ DECREASE ☐ or STAY THE SAME? ☐
   (Please tick which)
   Why do you say that?

b) If R₂ is *increased*, will the brightness of the lamp

   INCREASE ☐ DECREASE ☐ or STAY THE SAME? ☐
   Why do you say that?

c) If R₁ is *increased*, will the brightness of the lamp

   INCREASE ☐ DECREASE ☐ or STAY THE SAME? ☐
   Why do you say that?

d) If R₂ is *decreased*, will the brightness of the lamp

   INCREASE ☐ DECREASE ☐ or STAY THE SAME? ☐
   Why do you say that?

Figure 3.5: Question for revealing use of the sequence model.

The most important response types from the point of view of the current model used were those in which only a variable resistor situated 'before' the lamp is regarded as having any effect upon it; a variable resistor located 'after' the lamp is thought to have no effect. For example, one sixth-form pupil said that the brightness of the lamp will stay the same if R_1 is decreased because:

> R_1 is after the lamp (considering electron flow), hence it will not hinder the voltage

but if R_2 is increased the brightness of the lamp will decrease because:

> R_2 is before the lamp, therefore it will hinder the energy reaching the lamp (lower voltage) since electron flow is − to +.

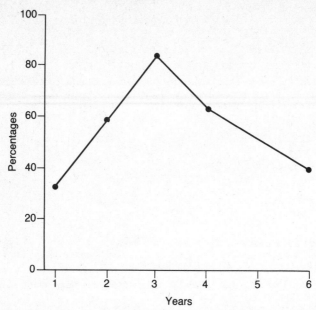

Figure 3.6:   Variation in popularity of the sequence model across the secondary school years.

The variation in the incidence of responses of this 'before and after' type across the year groups, as revealed mainly by this question but also elsewhere in the test, is shown in Figure 3.6. Pupils who had shown any indication whatever of reasoning in terms of a clashing currents model were omitted from the sample. These would have given apparently correct responses because R_1 would always control the current in one direction around the circuit while R_2 controlled the current in the opposite direction.

The 'before and after' responses imply a model in which current is influenced by each circuit element in turn. If a change is made at some point then the current is influenced when it reaches that point but not before. Information about a change having occurred is carried only downstream in the direction of the current. Actually, a change made at any point will result in electromagnetic wave pulses travelling away from that point in both directions around the circuit. As a result the voltages and currents in all parts of the circuit are altered and a new steady state is quickly established. The children's model is readily visualized and therefore very appealing. It has been referred to elsewhere as a 'time-dependent model'[11] and as a 'sequence model'.[9] The latter will be used here since spatial factors are at least as important as temporal factors in this view. The importance of this misconception is due both to its high incidence in the middle years of the secondary school and to its persistence amongst able students who have specialized in physics: it was found, for example, in seven out of a group of 18 graduate physicists and engineers who were training to be physics teachers.[9]

According to the sequence model, if a resistor is to have any effect at all that effect must be to alter the intensity of the current passing through it, so that the current leaving the resistor differs from that entering. An association would therefore be expected between use of the sequence model and failure to conserve current. There was no evidence of such a relationship in the first two years where relatively few held the sequence model and yet nearly all failed to conserve. At this stage it seems that non-conservation arises from intuitive source-consumer beliefs. With advanced students, in year six and at the postgraduate level, there was evidence of a close association.[9] The sequence model is not needed for reasoning about the very simple circuits encountered in the early stages of instruction and, in the main, appears to be developed by pupils as a response to the need to reason about more complex circuits. There is some evidence that it is the more able pupils who develop the model most rapidly. It may be that our failure to teach the principle that current is conserved is linked to our pupils' development of the sequence model. The scientific model that we are teaching cannot be assimilated into this view to which so many subscribe.

Currents in branching circuits

Research into experienced students' responses to electrical circuit problems has revealed instances in which they treat the current flowing from the battery as constant, unaffected by changes in the external circuit[11,12] and, in more general terms, a strong tendency for them to adopt local reasoning about circuits, ignoring the effects of a variation at one point upon the whole circuit.

Consider the circuit shown in Figure 3.7. If the variable resistor R is increased, what effect will this have, qualitatively, on the brightness of the lamps L_1 and L_2? To give a really satisfactory solution to this problem we should work in terms of the whole circuit and that entails

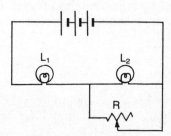

Figure 3.7: Diagram used to investigate children's beliefs about current in a branching circuit.

reasoning in terms of voltages as follows. If R is increased then the total resistance of the parallel combination will increase. The proportion of the applied voltage that is dropped across L_1 therefore decreases while that across the combination of L_2 and R increases. So L_1 will become dimmer and L_2 brighter. (The effects of internal resistance will have been ignored: few secondary school pupils would introduce it into a problem voluntarily.) Pupils making correct predictions of the changes in brightnesses usually arrived at these by a different route involving local reasoning, however, and argued as follows: if R is increased then more current will take the easier path through L_2 (ignoring, for the moment, the fact that the total current would change). L_2, therefore, becomes brighter. But increasing R will also increase the total resistance of the circuit so that L_1 carries less current and becomes dimmer.

When the sequence model is applied to this problem the conclusion is that L_2 does not change since the current through L_2 has already divided from that to R before the change takes place. Information about the change in R is only carried forward in the direction of the current, not backwards. Actually it has been found, even with physics undergraduates, that in qualitative questions a disturbing number reason that the current, having no 'knowledge' of what lies ahead, will divide into two equal parts at a junction.[13] Predictions about L_1 depend upon the current direction used. For conventional current the sequence model leads to the conclusion that L_1 will not change. In this instance, then, its use results in both local reasoning and the expectation that the current from the battery will remain constant.

'Most current takes the easier path' is a popular algorithm which enables many pupils to predict the increase in brightness of L_2. But I found that some fourth-year pupils reinterpreted this rule of thumb and concluded that L_2 would remain unchanged, e.g. 'Because the current will take the easier route via L_2', implying that *all* of the current would go by that (assumed) easier path. Some others in year four concluded that L_2 would become dimmer by assuming that any increase in resistance would decrease the current through it irrespective of the circuit geometry. Where sixth-year pupils reached the same conclusion it tended to be by a much more sophisticated route: if a variable resistor forming part of a parallel combination is increased the current through it will increase because in parallel circuits it is I/R that determines the current!

Voltages in circuits

Much evidence has now been accumulated to the effect that children experience great difficulty in discriminating between current and voltage. In one German study[5] children were presented with a succession of true–false questions about voltage and current including:

(a)   voltage can occur independently of the occurrence of current; and
(b)   Voltage is part of the current.

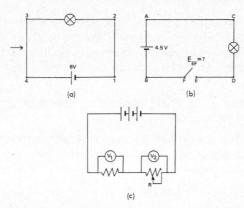

Figure 8: Diagram used to probe students' understanding of voltage.
(a) After Maichle[5] and (b) von Rhöneck.[8]

Approximately two-thirds of a sample of about 400 13 to 15-year-olds
judged (a) to be false and (b) as true. In another task these same
children were asked to give the voltages between neighbouring points
(1 and 2, 2 and 3, 3 and 4) in the circuit shown in Figure 3.8(a), first
with the circuit in the simple form shown and then with a second lamp
added in the position indicated by the arrow. The majority of those
secondary level pupils who answered the question stated that the
voltage would have the same value, namely 6 V, in every case. These
results follow naturally if children represent voltage as part or property of the current. In fact the mistake was made by 84 per cent of
all who disagreed with statement (a) and more than 80 per cent of
those who agreed with (b).

The resistance of this belief to instruction was demonstrated in
another German study[8] where pupils were asked to give the voltmeter
readings across the switch in Figure 3.8(b), first with the switch open
and then when it was closed. Fourteen out of 16 pupils, before instruction about voltage, stated that the readings would be 0 V and 4.5 V
respectively, whereas the reverse is actually the case. When tested
four months after instruction 22 out of 26 pupils gave the same
responses.

Several studies have indicated that current is the primary concept
used by students even at quite an advanced level, while potential difference is regarded as a consequence of current and not as its cause.
This approach largely determined British fourth-year pupils' reasoning about the circuit shown in Figure 3.8(c) when asked to describe the
changes which occur to the readings on the voltmeters, V_1 and V_2, as
R is increased. The question may be answered simply by stating that
the proportion of the applied voltage which is dropped across R will
increase so that the reading on V_2 increases and that on V_1 decreases.
There is no need to consider the currents through the voltmeters,
since these are usually chosen to have very high resistances compared
with the components across which they are connected and consequently draw negligible current. In year four, however, 75 per cent of

pupils made no reference whatever to voltage despite having studied this as part of the electricity course in that year. They explained their reasoning in terms of current, electricity or power. One pupil, for example, concluded that the reading on V_2 would increase because:

> The current flowing through the circuit will try to take the easiest possible path through it, therefore instead of going through the resistor it will take the easiest path.

In 31 per cent of those explanations in which there were references to voltage it was treated as something which flows. For example, the reading on V_2 increases

> Because more voltage is passing through the current in V_2.

For those holding the sequence model and reasoning in terms of current this question proved to be very similar to the parallel circuit question of Figure 3.7. According to this view the current entering V_2 has already divided from that entering R, so V_2 cannot be affected by changes taking place in the other branch of the circuit. And where the conventional current direction was assumed there could be no change in the reading on V_1, which the current had already passed when it encountered the variable resistor. It is interesting to note that none of the sixth-year pupils who held the sequence model had successfully assimilated the rules for the distribution of voltages in circuits.

Analogies and pupils' learning

In introductory courses, at least, many discussions must be in terms of analogies. The use of these, and in some instances of analogue models, is widespread in the teaching of current electricity, the water circuit analogy being the most popular among teachers. But there is evidence that pupils in early adolescence do not find the analogies particularly useful. Piaget's work suggests that this should be so, since concrete operational children cannot be expected to transfer logical deductions readily from one physical system to another.

An inquiry with 33 second-year comprehensive school pupils in Britain[14] demonstrated that one problem in the use of the water analogy is children's poor understanding of water flow. The pupils studied were taken from the top stream and one of the middle streams in the school and all had been introduced to the water flow analogy as part of their second-year course in electricity. Although about 50 per cent could explain how the rate of flow of water might be measured, only two out of the entire sample appeared to have a satisfactory conception of rate of flow in a water circuit in which there were constrictions. Approximately 60 per cent of the group thought that the rate of flow through a constriction in a pipe would be less than the flow in the wider pipes to either side of it even though the majority accepted that the speed of flow in the narrow section would be greater.

It was possible to classify these pupils into four groups according to the extent to which they used the water analogy in reasoning about electrical circuits. The results, set out below, speak for themselves.

Pupil response	Percentage of pupils
The pupil sees and notes the similarity between the flow of water and of electricity	54
The pupil claims that these similarities aid his understanding of the electrical case	33
The pupil actually appears to use the analogy when faced with a problem situation	27
The pupil uses the analogy correctly	6

It is important that we recognize the limitations of the analogies we use, together with those of their aspects which pupils find difficult. For a few children in this study, for example, one problem was that electrical conductors are not hollow whereas water pipes are. A further danger is that some pupils will assimilate an analogy to an existing misconception, which thereby receives support. In a separate inquiry[2] one 11-year-old child explained the lighting of a lamp as follows:

> I think it is to do with positive and negative... the positive would make it [the current] go in [to the bulb]... the light bulb would make it go negative and the negative would go back.

Following the introduction of an analogy which related to blood flow and heat transfer in the body this child said:

> I think [the analogy] is right because also blood changes also... when it gets oxygen it turns red... so it is different kinds... different currents.

The use of analogies in teaching will be discussed briefly in the next section.

Teaching elementary electricity

A lot of evidence has been presented about the widespread confusion existing among school pupils and older students concerning the phenomena occurring within even quite simple circuits. It is now time to use this evidence as a guide in suggesting some possible remedies.

The first task confronting us is to establish the requirement of a complete circuit if any continuous processes are to take place. As has been explained, some of our problems may arise from the use of MES lamps, the design of which is not immediately clear. In fact, to a pupil, the design is decidedly misleading as it suggests a one terminal device. We would be unwise to use these lamps to establish the requirements for a complete circuit without first making their nature very clear. It might be better still to begin by demonstrating these requirements using the linear 'festoon' bulbs which have two very conspicuous contacts (6 V bulbs of this type are available as motorcycle spares). The problem of lighting an unmounted MES lamp using a battery and some wires could then be set. This would serve to reinforce and generalize the newly acquired principles through their application to this more complex device, the design of which could then be explored.

Our next problem, and probably the most intractable, is to assist pupils to discriminate between the concepts of electric current and electrical energy. Without this discrimination common sense tells them that 'it' gets used up. One possible approach starts from the fact that the children's source-consumer model, in its various guises, comes much closer to the scientists' idea of electrical energy than it does to the concept of current. If in our teaching we adopt the time-honoured principle of 'starting from the point the children are at and leading them from there to where we want them to go' the concept of electrical energy should be introduced before the idea of current is encountered, as is the case in the American SCIS materials. There is no need to throw away the school's supply of circuit board lamps. These blatantly consuming devices are far better as indicators of the amount of energy used up (to do something) than they are of current which is conserved. We might start by instructing our pupils to set up a range of simple circuits and encourage them to describe their observations in terms of the supply of electrical energy to the lamps which form their principal elements. In this way we might begin to form a bond between the acceptable term 'electrical energy' and the idea children already have of what it is that is 'used up' in a circuit to light lamps, run motors, etc.

Of course the concept of energy is itself difficult if we take it as a whole. But the aspect that children find problematic is conservation of energy and we are only concerned with its use, at the very most with its transformation from one form to another, and these are aspects which children comprehend much more readily.

Current could be introduced later, and as a quite separate entity, through its magnetic effect, for example. This leads naturally to the introduction of the ammeter and its use to indicate both the intensity and the direction of a current. Probably the best approach to the issue of current conservation is to exploit cognitive conflict by letting children outline their own models initially. Most, if not all, of those described earlier in this chapter would emerge and the pupils could then be asked to predict the readings on a demonstration centre-zero ammeter according to the various models they hold. Finally, these predictions would be checked experimentally, giving support to the accepted model.[2]

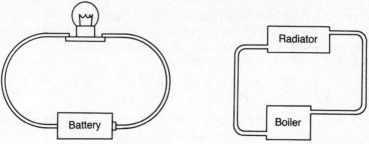

Figure 3.9: Simple circuit and heating system analogue.

Children will naturally wish to know what the electric current does since it doesn't get used up. Several analogue models have been described,[15] one of which is shown in Figure 3.9, for explaining the role of the current as a circulating, conserved carrier of electrical energy. The use of analogies in teaching electricity seems to be unavoidable but the evidence presented in the previous section suggests that we must not expect too much from them. Pupils seem to make little use of analogies in reasoning about circuits so their main value appears to be as aids to us in establishing the behaviour of circuits to them. All analogies have their weaknesses, however, the one shown in Figure 3.9 being no exception, and we must guard against pupils taking them too literally. If we make use of a wide range of analogies in teaching then pupils will be more likely to divorce the essential features that we are aiming to convey from the often irrelevant, and sometimes troublesome ancillary attributes of any single concrete model.

The consequences of introducing the current–energy distinction in the early stages of courses are being investigated in several countries. Work with all-ability 12 and 13-year-olds in Britain and Australia[16] has shown that the more able half of the population can at least learn the relationship between these concepts. Few would make use of this new learning when faced with a novel situation, however, so further effort needs to be directed towards building their confidence in applying these ideas. A German study with 15-year-olds has reported some promising improvements in learning with this approach.[17]

The concept of electrical resistance needs to be introduced early in a course. In doing this it is not sufficient simply to consider the effects of adding more lamps to a series circuit. To many pupils lamps are lamps and not resistors so that these should be introduced as quite distinct elements. With pupils who pursue their studies of electricity beyond the elementary level, at least, we must discuss what happens when we make changes in circuits. Many children are curious about, and some will ask, such questions as how the battery 'knows' that a switch has been opened or closed, or how the magnitude of the current from a battery becomes determined. We must try to explain these processes and how information about any changes is transmitted 'backwards' as well as 'forwards' in the direction of the current. Such an emphasis upon the fact that changes affect all parts of a circuit may help to counteract the impression so often given that a current experiences a series of events as it travels round a circuit. Have you said anything like this to your pupils:

> Current leaves the battery at this terminal and travels round through this ammeter to this junction where it splits up...?

Intuitively, we should expect that an approach to circuits in terms of energy will facilitate the introduction of the voltmeter. If we set up a series circuit containing dissimilar lamps then, of course, these will be at different brightnesses, indicating that they are receiving energy at different rates. Voltmeters connected across the lamps will give readings related to their brightnesses, the brighter the lamp the higher the reading. In fact the reading on a voltmeter tells us, for each unit of current, how fast energy will be supplied to that section of a circuit across which it is connected. Linking voltage to energy seems preferable to the common approach of describing it as the 'push' which produces the current, the main problem there being that a push can act at a point, and the energy approach may help us to emphasize that a voltmeter must be connected to both ends of the section of the circuit in which we are interested.

Throughout this section it has been assumed that our courses and objectives are to remain as they are at present. It is not, however, self-evident that all children need to understand the mechanism of the simple circuit. For most it would be sufficient to know about electrical safety, what electricity can do for us and what one needs to do to bring these desirable results about. With these pupils it is much more important to talk about electrical energy than it is to introduce electric current.

References

[1]A. Tiberghien, A. and Delacôte, G. (1976). Manipulations et représentations de circuits électriques simples chez les enfants de 7 à 12 ans. *Revue Francaise de Pédagogie* **34**, 32-44.

[2]Osborne, R. J. (1983). Towards modifying children's ideas about electric current. *Journal of Research in Science and Technological Education* **1**, 73-82.

[3]Andersson, B. and Karrqvist, C. (1979). *Elektriska Kretsar [Electric Circuits]*. EKNA Report No. 2, University of Gothenburg, Mölndal, Sweden.

[4]Fredette, N. and Lochhead, J. (1980). Student conceptions of simple circuits. *The Physics Teacher* **18**, 194-8.

[5]Maichle, U. (1981). Representation of knowledge in basic electricity and its use in problem solving. In *Proceedings of the International Workshop on Problems Concerning Students' Representations of Physics and Chemistry Knowledge*, Ludwigsburg, West Germany.

[6]Osborne, R. J. (1981). Children's ideas about electric current. *New Zealand Science Teacher* **29**, 12-9.

[7]Osborne, R. J. (1982). Investigating children's ideas about electric current using an interview-about-instances procedure. Science Education Research Unit, University of Waikato, Hamilton, New Zealand.

[8]von. Rhöneck, C. (1981). Student conceptions of the electric circuit before physics instruction. In *Proceedings of the International Workshop on Problems Concerning Students' Representations of Physics and Chemistry Knowledge*. Ludwigsburg, West Germany.

[9]Shipstone, D. M. (1984). A study of children's understanding of electricity in simple D.C. circuits. *European Journal of Science Education* 6, 185-98.

[10]Osborne, R. J. (1982). Bridging the gap between teaching and learning. Paper presented at the New Zealand Science Teachers' Association Conference, Hamilton, New Zealand.

[11]Riley, M. S., Bee, N. V. and Mokwa, J. J. (1981). Representations in early learning: the acquisition of problem-solving strategies in basic electricity/electronics. In *Proceedings of the International Workshop on Problems Concerning Students' Representations of Physics and Chemistry Knowledge*, Ludwigsburg, West Germany.

[12]Cohen, R., Eylon, B. and Ganiel, U. (1982). Potential difference and current in simple electric circuits: A study of students' concepts. *American Journal of Physics* 51, 407-12.

[13]Closset, J.-L. (1983). Sequential reasoning in electricity. In *Proceedings of the International Workshop on Research in Physics Education*, La Londe des Maures, France.

[14]Wilkinson, D. J. (1973). A study of the development of the concept of flow with reference to the introduction of current in the early years of the secondary school. Unpublished M.A. Dissertation, University of Leeds.

[15]Härtel, H. (1982). The electric circuit as a system: A new approach. *European Journal of Science Education* 4, 45-55.

[16]Shipstone, D. M. and Gunstone, R. G. (1984). Teaching children to discriminate between current and energy. *Paper presented at the International Workshop on The Representation of Students' Knowledge in Electricity and its Uses for the Improvement of Teaching*, Ludwigsburg, West Germany.

[17]von. Rhöneck, C. (1983). Semantic structures describing the electric circuit before and after instruction. In *Proceedings of the International Workshop on Research in Physics Education*, La Londe des Maures, France.

CHAPTER 4

Heat and Temperature

Gaalen Erickson and Andrée Tiberghien

Introduction: The scientific point of view

Why is it that pupils seem to have so much difficulty in grasping some aspects of the scientific conception of heat and temperature? That this topic area has attracted attention from researchers recently is not surprising. The ideas are given prominence in science courses in many countries and are encountered, in some way, at virtually all age levels, yet there are many aspects of heat and temperature phenomena which are counter-intuitive, or at least troublesome, for many pupils. For example, school children are often puzzled that a thermometer will record a similar reading for all objects in a room even though a metal saucepan feels much colder than a plastic mixing bowl. Or they are surprised that an ice cube wrapped in wool or shredded newspaper will 'last longer' than one placed in metal foil.

Many children appear to have constructed various simple explanations to account for everyday situations they encounter involving heat and temperature. These explanations may subsequently become an integral part of the child's explanatory framework when she or he is faced with similar sorts of problems in a school setting.

Before discussing the findings of the research on pupils' beliefs, it is important to recognize some of the confusion which seems to surround their use of the term 'heat', confusion which probably stems in part from everyday usage of the term. The word 'heat' and its literal and metaphorical derivatives are commonly used as nouns, verbs, adjectives and adverbs. It is the use as a noun, which creates most of the conceptual confusion from a scientific and more specifically from an energy point of view. For example, we frequently hear expressions such as 'close the window and keep the heat in' (or conversely 'keep the cold out'). In classrooms we may hear pupils saying that 'heat is gained or lost' by an object when it comes into thermal equilibrium with some other substance, or that heat 'travels along a metal rod' when the metal rod is heated by a flame at one end.

These expressions illustrate a tendency to imply that 'heat' is substantive in nature. In the examples above 'heat' is described in terms of its ability to make objects hotter; to be stored in objects and transferred from one object to another; and to travel from one location in an object to another.

Why does it seem so natural to describe heat as a type of material substance which can cause predictable changes in other objects? (e.g. increase in temperature or an increase in volume). Some people think it may be a linguistic remnant from the Caloric theory of heat from the eighteenth and nineteenth centuries (when heat was conceptualized as a subtle, weightless fluid capable of penetrating all material bodies*). We know, however, that the notion of heat was more closely defined in the Caloric theory than in its present everyday meaning.[1] Others argue that there is a natural tendency to describe our common sense world in metaphorical terms wherein cause and effect relationships are seen in terms of interactions between types of matter.†[2] Regardless of the origin of this usage, it seems apparent that the predisposition to think of heat as in some sense substantial may be one of the important conceptual barriers that students must overcome if they are to be initiated into the current scientific way of thinking.

At this point, it is useful to review briefly the concepts of temperature, energy and heat from a scientific point of view, before describing studies of children's thinking about these ideas.

Temperature is one of the parameters that describes the state of a system. Knowledge of temperatures (along with other parameters) is essential information for predicting the changes which will occur in one system when it interacts with another system. Consider a saucepan full of water as an example. The question can be asked: 'if the saucepan is heated on a stove what will happen to the water?'. It is impossible to answer the question if the temperature of the water is not known. If the water is at $100°$ C, then the water will pass from the liquid state to the gaseous state. If the water is between $0°$ and $100°$ C, then the temperature of the water will begin to increase.

Temperature is a macroscopic property which expresses the state of agitation or disordered motion of particles; it is therefore related to the kinetic energy of these particles.

The *energy* of a system corresponding to a state of particle agitation is referred to as a form of *internal energy* of that system—sometimes called *thermal energy*.

---

*For a good description of the caloric theory see Conant[3] and Fox.[4]

[2]Lakoff and Johnson[5] have argued that one of the most powerful linguistic tools that we use to structure and interpret physical phenomena is a set of 'substance and entity' metaphors.

Heat is a parameter that describes the interactions between systems; more precisely, it is one process of energy transfer. It is the *difference of temperatures* between two systems which determines whether heat transfer will occur. For example, when a mass of water is heated by a gas flame, there is a difference of temperature between the flame (temperature of combustion) and the water. So, heat is transferred from one system (gas + air) to the other system (water).

It is important to realize that heat transfer is only one way of altering the internal energy of a system. For example a mass of water at temperature T_1 and internal energy E_1 could reach temperature T_2 and internal energy E_2 either by being heated (i.e. where heat transfer occurs, or by being agitated by a paddle wheel (i.e. Joule's experiment where work is involved). Since there are several pathways for passing from a state with an internal energy E_1 to another state with an internal energy E_2, it implies that the internal energy state of any system is independent of the type of energy transfer used to achieve that state.[2]

A system can thus change its *internal energy* without energy being transferred in the form of heat. In everyday usage however the word 'heat' has a less specialized meaning and this leads to a confusion between the energy which is *in* a system (i.e. internal energy) and a form of transfer of energy between systems (i.e. heat).

In addition there is also confusion over the use of the term *thermal energy* in teaching: sometimes it is used to refer to the quantity of energy transferred between systems (i.e. in the form of heat), rather than as we have done, to the energy of particle agitation.

Since much of our everyday experience entails some form of transfer of energy between objects at different temperatures, the physicists' concept of heat plays an important role in interpreting these experiences. For example, as body temperature is higher than normal room temperature, any time we touch an object which is at room temperature or lower, energy is transferred from our hand to that object. Likewise, any time we cook food or turn on a heater to increase the temperature of a room there is a transfer of energy. But it is important to reiterate that in these contexts our conventional language tends to suggest that objects contain heat, while from the physicists' perspective they have the potential (because of the difference in temperatures) to transfer energy to another object at a lower temperature.

In the next part of the chapter we review studies, based on interviews and written surveys, which have documented pupils' use and understanding of these ideas.

Part A:

An Overview of Pupils' Ideas

Gaalen Erickson

Introduction

The studies discussed below have used a variety of different methods for identifying pupils' ideas about temperature or heat. These methods vary from interviews with individual children, to paper-and-pencil questionnaires, to observational studies in classrooms. Each of these methods provides different types of data and address different sorts of questions about pupil thinking in this topic area and so are interesting in themselves. However, since this chapter is organized around different topic areas, in many instances the data presented on any one topic are likely to have been generated by two or more different researchers who may have employed quite different techniques of data collection and analysis. The following descriptions, then, represent a summary of my interpretation of results from a number of different studies. Much of the work reported in the first section is based upon interviews with children ranging in age from 4 to 13. Later sections will refer to work done with older students, many of whom have received some formal instruction in the kinetic molecular theory.

Pupils' understanding of the concept of heat

Use of the term 'heat'

The terms 'heat' and 'hot' are usually a part of children's vocabulary from the age of 2-3 onwards. While these terms are used to describe some aspects of their many encounters with hot objects, it is not until they are 8 or 9 years old that they begin to talk about 'heat' in terms of a 'state of hotness' of a body along a continuum from cold to warm to hot.[6] Typically, when children aged 8-12 are asked: 'What does heat mean to you?', they tend to associate it with living objects, sources of heat, the degree of hotness of an object, and the effects of heat on objects such as phase changes, expansion, etc.[6,7,8] For example, when an 8-year-old was asked to give an example of heat he replied:

> Heat rises up, the sun has it. It has I think, the sun has, ... heat rises off the gas and it is hot and the sun burns it and it shines and comes down and makes the Earth hot.

Also, a 12-year-old girl volunteered the following response when asked what heat meant to her:

> Heat, it makes everything melt; lead, gold, iron, aluminium, zinc too I think.

In one study a large group of 12-16-year-olds were asked 'to say in a couple of sentences what heat is'.[7] Although some of the 16-year-old pupils described heat in terms of energy, most of the younger ones and about one-third of the older pupils equated the idea of heat with a hot body or substance or described it as being given off from a heat source. Examples of these types of response follow:

> Heat is energy; when it heats something up it will transfer the heat energy to what it is heating up.
> Heat is warm air.
> Heat is a warming fluid or solid.
> ... when you touch it it feels hot—if anything has got the heat in it.

Thus, even though many of the 14 and 16-year-old pupils have been exposed to formal instruction in this topic area, most pupils still seem to associate the term 'heat' with the meanings they have constructed for it during their everyday encounters with hot and cold objects rather than from those encountered in the classroom.

Pupils' intuitive understanding of the notion of heat as a transfer of energy

Research on the developmental acquisition of the notion of heat reveals that even at the age of two, children have developed a notion of a 'hot body' which is capable of producing feelings of warmth in oneself.[6] But it is not until the age of 5 or 6, that they actually disassociate these hot objects from feelings in themselves and differentiate between a heating source and the object which is affected by the source. They become aware of a movement from the source to an object. For example, to the question: 'Who makes the outside hot?', a child (6 years) answered:

I don't know, the sun shines [she raises her hands] you see, like this [moves her hands] it gets from the sun to the air.[6]

These are, however, the primitive beginnings of the notion of heat transfer and the recognition of 'hotness' as a property of objects which can be altered. By 8 or 9 years of age many children appear to have constructed, from a variety of interactions with their physical and linguistic environments, a set of relatively coherent beliefs about the nature and behaviour of hot and cold objects in their immediate world. They have become aware of the process of heating and cooling and tend to discuss 'heat' in terms of the representation of the 'state of hotness' of a body along a continuum from cold to warm to hot. Many children also invent the entity of 'cold' as a counterpart to 'hot'.

In interpreting common situations, very often children use the verb 'to heat' and not the noun; they describe the situation in terms of action.[9] For example, in discussing a situation where an empty flask is supported just above an alcohol lamp with a thermometer suspended in it, a child of 9 years said:

Well, I think the flask would be heated and that would heat the air and the air is surrounding the thermometer, and I think the thermometer would get hot. It's open at the top, and heat rises, so, ... it's just a guess.[9]

When we examine how pupils tend to describe the movement or transfer of heat from one object to another (or even movement within a single object) we find different ideas being used. In some instances pupils seem to use a substantive description of 'heat' which implies an inherent motive force. Hence, as the above example suggests, 'heat rises' of its own accord. Other expressions where heat tends to be treated like a substance include the use of more metaphorical terms such as 'fumes', 'rays' or 'waves'. It may be that the use of these terms emerge from direct observations of some phenomena (e.g. the appearance of 'heat waves', or 'fumes' rising from an electric toaster and from a pavement on a hot day) or from common linguistic expressions.

An example which suggests a physical mechanism for the movement of heat is provided by Ron (12 years old). He described a situation where a metal rod was being heated at one end by a candle.

The whole rod gets hot because 'the heat builds up in one part until it can't hold anymore and then moves along the rod.[10]

In other instances, however, many pupils seem unwilling to imbue heat with its own internal motive force and instead invoke some intermediate agent or medium (most frequently air) to convey the heat from one subject to another or even from one location to another in the same object.

Those researchers who have engaged children in discussions about various phenomena involving heat transfer have documented many properties which tend to be associated with heat. A very common property which is used extensively to make predictions and explain observations is the relative strengh/weakness of the 'heat' in that given situation. Hence the observation that some objects (e.g. wooden or plastic blocks) do not seem to get very hot when placed on a hot plate is explained in terms of the heat not being very strong and unable to penetrate those substances. For example, explaining how a metal block is heated, Ricky said:

> The heat, the heat isn't very strong. And it won't go through the metal very easily.

And comparing the rate of heating of wood and metal he said:

> Cause wood isn't as strong as metal. ... The heat will go through this wood faster than it will through the metal.[9]

Here, the strength is not only a property of heat but also of metal. Often, the property (such as strength or weakness) which is attributed to 'heat', is related to a property of the substance in which heat is moving.

As we will see in subsequent sections, this way of thinking about heat influences the sorts of judgement and predictions which pupils make in more school-related tasks: such as pencil-and-paper tests or questionnaires.

Pupils' understanding of the mechanisms of heat transfer

Two common mechanisms of transfer are normally discussed under this general heading—conduction and convection. I shall deal with each of these separately.

Conduction
Virtually all pupils are aware that one hot object is capable of 'heating up' another cooler object when they come into direct contact. The earliest experiences of this sort are personal such as when a child touches a hot stove, a light bulb or other hot object and discovers heat transfer in a memorable fashion. This perceptual experience is transferred to other contexts and thus researchers report that pupils of all ages rapidly refer to the 'movement of heat' from one object to another. The substance notion of heat is used extensively by children to account for this transfer phenomena. Typically, the mechanism hypothesized for transfer (for example, a flame heating a metal rod) is a transitive one, and is illustrated by one pupil who during an interview explained that the whole metal rod gets hot (even though it is only being heated at one end by a candle)

> because the heat keeps moving from one point of the rod to the next until the whole rod is hot.[11]

When pupils are asked to explain the results of typical conduction experiments—placing several objects made of different materials in contact with the same heating source—several common response patterns seem to emerge. The observation that metals become hot much more quickly than wooden or plastic objects is explained by pupils in terms of a metal's inherent attraction for and tendency to hold heat. For example, several pupils discussed these conduction phenomena as follows:[11]

> A metal just pulls in heat... I can't remember the word... and it sucks it in and keeps the heat.

> Well heat... it will be attracted to it... like pulls the heat towards it... as if it was like a magnet.

> ... metal holds heat... heat easily gives into it... wood doesn't hold heat.

Another common explanatory mechanism employed by younger pupils (up to age 13) to account for conduction phenomena is the strength criterion mentioned earlier. For example, some subjects predicted, without actually testing these predictions, that air would heat up the fastest and metal the slowest because of their respective 'strengths'.[7] Similar claims were found in the context of classroom discussions about the effectiveness of various insulating materials.[10] This belief that air readily transmits heat because it is weak, obviously becomes a serious source of confusion when the data from insulation experiments are actually obtained and discussed.

A related conduction situation, that of touching different objects at room temperature, is usually not seen by pupils in terms of a heat transfer from their hands to the object. Rather, their explanation of their sensation that metals feel colder than wood or plastic is, as in the other instances of conduction, attributed to an *ad hoc*, inherent property of metals. Some pupils explain that metals feel colder because, in this context at least, they attract cold or they lose their heat to the surrounding air. Less inventive subjects simply assert that metals are by nature a cold substance; that metals feel colder because they have smooth, shiny surfaces. If pupils were able to 'see' this phenomenon in terms of a transfer of energy from their body to the object, this sort of situation would likely be less of a problem than it seems to be at present.

Convection

Pupils also appear to possess an intuitive notion of convection which is most often anchored in terms of previous perceptual experiences. For example, most subjects are able to respond to a question such as: 'How does a radiator heat up a room?', with explanations like: 'heat gets out of the radiator; that's just like smoke which gets away and gets into the whole room, and the radiator is the same, it's the smoke that you can't see that gets into the whole room'.[8]

Another example of these sorts of intuitions is provided from a two-month case study of a 13-year-old boy.[12] When asked to explain 'how heat travelled from one place to another' the boy responded by writing the following:

> Most heat travels through some kind of rays. There are other kinds of heat like fire which gives off heat (I do not think these have anything to do with rays). Gas heats water. ... The heated water flows through pipes into a container. ... The rays from the hot water are very strong because they are new. The rays from the sun are old by the time they reach the Earth, though they were much stronger when they left the sun than the hot water which the boiler warmed by the gas.

This short excerpt illustrates a number of interesting intuitions about mechanisms for heat transfer other than conduction. While some subjects to appear to require some intervening medium (usually air) 'to carry the heat', others, as the above description of heat rays indicates, seem quite content to accord heat with an inherent propensity for movement.

In summary, the research in this area suggests most pupils are very aware of the transfer of heat from objects at a higher temperature to those at a lower temperature and they also possess a number of intuitions about plausible mechanisms for this process. Most of these mechanisms draw heavily upon the 'heat as a substance' metaphor in order to explain a variety of phenomena involving heat transfer. Furthermore, many of these explanations rely heavily upon simply ascribing plausible properties to heat (e.g. 'heat is strong', 'heat rises') or to the interacting objects (e.g. 'metals get hot quickly because they attract heat').

Pupils' understanding of the concept of temperature

Introduction

As with the term heat, temperature is a word that even very young children recognize, as they encounter it frequently in discussion about the weather and at later ages (e.g. 5-7 years) in the kitchen while observing or engaging in cooking activities. But unlike 'heat', they do not tend to use the term spontaneously in conversation. Rather, they tend to make observations about the relative 'hotness' of objects in qualitative rather than quantitative terms.

It has been observed that by 8-9 years of age, pupils seem to have developed a notion that temperature is related to levels or degrees of heat as expressed by a scale such as that used for reporting the air temperature or the dial setting for a heating device.[6] Others have noted that while pupils in the age range 8-12 are able to use and read a thermometer to take temperature readings, they tend to make judgements about the temperature of an object based more on the nature of the material than on the temperature of the surrounding medium.[13] Some pupils thought that objects of different materials in the same room were at different temperatures. For many pupils, metal objects were colder than wood objects. For example, a child who was asked if a casserole, full of water, left for a long time in a room would be colder, hotter or the same as the water inside it, said: 'The casserole will be colder than the water...it depends on what the casserole is made of'.[8]

It seems then, that up to the age of 12 or 13 pupils are familiar with the term temperature and are able to use a thermometer to assess the temperature of objects, but they actually have a fairly limited concept of the term and rarely use it spontaneously to describe the condition of an object. When asked to make specific judgements about the temperatures of different objects or systems of interacting objects most pupils are able to do so, but as we will see in the next section they frequently use a very different framework from that of physicists for making these judgements.

Pupils' understanding of the notion of temperature changes

This section will be subdivided into two parts: the first will focus on the pupils' understanding of temperature as an intensive rather than an extensive property of objects. The second is concerned with pupils' understanding of temperature during phase changes.

Temperature as an intensive property

In certain experimental situations, many pupils appear to believe the temperature of an object is related to its size. For example, more than 50 per cent of the 12-year-old children who were interviewed in one study thought that 'a larger ice cube would have a colder temperature than a small ice cube' and hence the larger ice cube would take longer to melt.[11] In another study[16], groups of 8 to 14-year-olds (totalling 324 pupils) were asked the following question: 'What can you say about the temperature of the ice blocks?' (Preceding this question was a diagram of a large and small block of ice.) Fifty per cent of the younger group (8 to 9-year-olds) used size as the criterion for temperature, whereas only 15 per cent of the 13 to 14-year-old group did.

These predictions follow quite logically from another apparent belief among pupils that temperature is simply a measure of the amount of heat (or in some instances cold) possessed by an object. It is reasonable to conclude, then, that larger objects contain more heat (cold) and hence are likely to have a hotter (colder) temperature.

Items that have been used extensively on many large-scale achievement tests ask pupils to predict the final temperature of a mixture of two quantities of water given the initial temperatures of the components from which the mixture is made. Detailed research studies on this question have found that the extent of the difficulties experienced by children depend upon the form in which the temperature problems are presented.[14,15] Two basic types of situation were used:

(1) similar amounts of water at the same temperature are mixed; and
(2) both similar and different amounts of water at different temperatures are mixed.

For the two types of situation, both qualitative and quantitative questions were asked. Figure 4.1 shows one example of these questions for each case, and Figure 4.2 gives the types of results obtained. In each case, qualitative tasks are easier than quantitative ones. And, the mixing of water at different temperatures is more difficult than the mixing of water at the same temperature. For example, it is not before the age of 12 or 13 that a task like that shown in Figure 4.1d is solved. Another study which used the same type of questions found an even smaller percentage (from 10 to 25 per cent) of their 13 to 14-year-old age group responding correctly to this type of quantitative problem.[16] The pupils' responses were categorized according to 'strategies' used to solve this problem and it was found that while the younger group (8 to 9-year-olds) preferred an 'addition strategy', the older group tended to opt for a 'subtraction strategy'—a strategy which at least acknowledges that the final temperature should lie somewhere in between the initial temperatures. Similar results were also obtained with

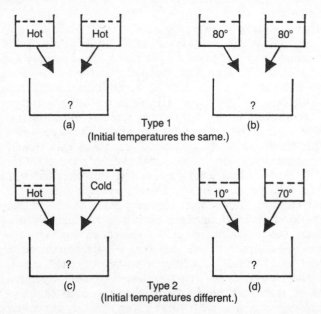

Figure 4.1:   Four water-mixing questions requiring qualitative and quantitative responses.
(After Stavy and Berkovitz[14].)

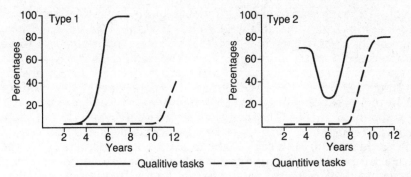

Figure 4.2: The success rates of pupils at different ages on the two types of water-mixing questions (after Strauss[15]).

another group of pupils aged 12 to 16 years, where even the 16-year-olds used the additive or subtractive strategies with about the same frequency as an averaging strategy.[7]

These results are somewhat perplexing since it would appear that most pupils, even at a very young age, possess a good intuitive grasp of this notion of intensivity when discussing phenomena in qualitative terms. It has been suggested that the main difficulty in problem contexts of this sort is the conflict which exists between two representational systems for temperature (qualitative and quantitative) and hence when the problem supplies quantitative data, most pupils employ those strategies normally used with quantitative data—that is, addition and subtraction.[15] Another complementary explanation for the popularity of an 'additive strategy' is the linking of the frequently expressed belief that temperature is simply a measure of the amount of heat possessed by an object with the operation of mixing together two quantities of water which then leads to a prediction of an overall increase in temperature. Whether one or both of these explanations adequately accounts for pupils' conceptual difficulties on this sort of problem, the fact remains that considerable confusion is still in evidence even among 16-year-olds.

In order to overcome this problem one study[14] undertaken with 10-year-old pupils as part of a larger curriculum project, used a conflict-inducing strategy which was quite successful in encouraging pupils to distinguish between the ideas of temperature and heat. The conflict was introduced by means of deliberately juxtaposing two different representational systems, a system in which predictions of various water mixing experiments were requested in qualitative terms, such as hotter or colder, and a system in which predictions were requested in numerical terms.

Temperature and phase changes
A 'standard' laboratory exercise is to plot a time-temperature graph of water (or some other liquid) from room temperature to its boiling

point. Although pupils can readily observe that the temperature of the boiling liquid remains relatively constant regardless of how vigorously or how long it is heated, this observation appears to be counter-intuitive to many pupils and exclamations such as 'this thermometer is not working properly' are frequently encountered.

A survey of over 400 Swedish pupils has shown that the majority of 12 to 15-year-olds predicted that the temperature of boiling water would remain at $100°$ C so long as the switch setting on the hot plate remained constant.[17] If this setting was increased, then 80 per cent of the grade 6 and 54 per cent of the grade 9 pupils predicted that the temperature of the boiling water would increase. In another study a similar type of response was noted, although it was not nearly as pronounced for one of their 14-year-old groups.[16] It would seem that pupils can easily learn the 'fact' that water has a boiling point of $100°$ C and that it may remain invariant in certain conditions (e.g. over time); however, most do not appear to have any clear understanding of why the temperature remains invariant during a phase change. This understanding would seem to require some explanation of what is happening to the liquid, at the molecular level, in order for temperature invariance to make sense. While the phenomenon of boiling is explained in most text books in terms of a kinetic molecular theory of matter, many pupils appear to have difficulty understanding this explanation.

The following brief excerpt from an interview which was conducted with a 12-year-old illustrates this need to relate phase change to some theory of matter (he subscribed to a 'cell' theory of matter), so that the invariant temperature of boiling water, which he had read about in a book, would make sense to him.[10]

I: Can we heat this ice cube up?
S: Yes.
I: How hot do you think we can get an ice cube?
S: Until it melts do you mean?
I: Well how high a temperature do you think we can get the ice cube?
S: Well it would melt at 32 degrees. But uh, you can boil it. Water will get uh, when water starts to boil it can't get any hotter. So when that ice cube starts to boil the cells won't expand anymore. That's what a uh, man told me. No, it's in this science lab book, my brother's lab book. It says once water starts to boil it might be boiling just slowly but it won't get any hotter. It might boil more rapidly, but it's not getting any hotter.
I: Why do you suppose that is?
S: The cells cannot expand anymore. The cells have reached their, you know, like after a while you can't blow a balloon up any farther or it will burst. You can call a balloon a cell. When, it's like we had a balloon over at Simon Fraser [University] and when we stuck it in liquid oxygen it would contract, it would go ssshh crumple. Take them out in the air and they would go, you know, back to the same point. You can heat them, you know, and they will expand until they burst. But water, it just stops at a certain point.

Others have examined the conditions which bring about these phase changes for a variety of different substances.[13] When pupils were questioned about whether these solids could become a liquid given a sufficiently high temperature, a majority of 12-year-old pupils indicated that some solids (e.g. iron, gold and lead) could indeed become a liquid; while other solids (e.g. aluminium, diamond and salt) could not. The reasons offered for these predictions were usually based upon either some type of previous direct or vicarious experience (e.g. 'because it is necessary to melt gold to make gold bricks') or an appeal to some observable property of the substance (e.g. 'because it is hard').

Pupils' understanding of the differentiation between heat, energy and temperature

As we discussed at the beginning of this chapter, heat describes the transfer of energy between two interacting systems at different temperatures. Temperature and energy describe the state of a system; but, temperature is an intensive parameter whereas energy is an extensive parameter and hence it is directly related to the amount of substance. This extensive property of energy seems to be more accessible to pupils in an everyday context. In one study which used two questions drawing upon familiar contexts—the melting of two ice cubes of different sizes and the boiling of different amounts of water using a similar heating source,[16] over three quarters of 11 to 14-year-olds responded correctly that the larger quantities of ice or water would require 'more heat' to melt or boil respectively.

It seems that many pupils have an intuitive notion of the extensive property of energy particularly when the problem setting and language is familiar to them. But as far as having a clear notion of energy or being able to distinguish it from the notion of temperature, much confusion is evident. Pupils of all ages (12-16) also experienced difficulty in differentiating between 'heat' and 'temperature'.[7] When asked to describe the difference between heat and temperature, the most common type of response (accounting for more than 25 per cent of pupils at all age levels) was that there is no difference between them. Other typical responses were that temperature is either 'a measurement of heat' or it is 'the effect of heat'. Some examples from pupils' responses to this question are:

Temperature you measure heat with, but heat is hot... you can feel heat.

Temperature is the amount of heat in that space... it tells you the hotness of the water.

Temperature is the amount of heat, and heat raises the temperature.

I don't think there is one, is there [referring to the question of a difference].

Well temperature, it's just like a thing—like the sun—when you get the sun shining you get a temperature then. But heat, you've got to get something to make heat. But for temperature, it just comes, it's just natural temperature.

There are, clearly, many types of responses here that are similar to those discussed in earlier sections.

In this part of the chapter we have reviewed studies which have given some insight into the kinds of ideas children have about heat and temperature. In the next part we draw on studies of particular classrooms to describe the way pupils' ideas change with teaching.

PART B:

The Development of
Ideas with Teaching

Andrée Tiberghien

Introduction

I describe here the way pupils' interpretations of phenomena concerned with heat and temperature change as a result of teaching. The
situations which will be considered are those commonly included in introductory science schemes involving ideas of heating, cooling and
thermal insulation. Our observations and comments are mainly based
on studies which have been undertaken for a number of years with
French children aged between 10 and 14, learning about aspects of
heat and temperature as part of an introductory physics course.[18]

Temperature

Very often the idea of temperature is not taught as such, except
for the temperature of change of state. Therefore, I will begin by
considering the evolution of pupils' conceptions concerning this
notion.

Temperature of change of state

Many pupils start learning about the stability of the temperature of
change of state by melting ice or boiling water. Here I consider what
they think about these phenomena and what they learn about them.

Results before and during teaching
Most pupils, aged between 10 and 13, do not know about the stability
of the temperature of change of state of water or ice unless they have
already been taught about it (in this study 20 per cent or less knew

about it or could give the temperatures at which water boils or ice melts).

The case of boiling water
For pupils the term 'boiling' is very often associated with the appearance of bubbles in heated water; the verb 'to boil' does not seem to have a specific link with the temperature of water. However, this is not a great problem for pupils as long as the teacher is aware of the issue and explains the meaning of boiling from the physicist's point of view.

When pupils boil water as an experiment, it has been noticed that those pupils who watch the thermometer are surprised by the rapid increase in temperature. Sometimes they are afraid that the thermometer will break. They are very surprised at the speed with which the reading on the thermometer goes up; often more than with the stability of the temperature when the water is boiling. The following comment made by a pupil after seeing that the temperature remained constant is typical:

> The water will be hot enough, very, very hot, the hottest that it can be...
> and then it is going to stop (11-year-old).

This pupil attributed a property to the water, i.e. he considered the temperature of change of state as a property of substance.

The case of melting ice
The results of several studies[13,16,17,18] in different countries are similar. The pupils are no more familiar with the temperature of melting ice than they are with the temperature of boiling water. Indeed, the analysis of different results show that pupils do not interpret the properties of ice and water in the same way. For example, let us consider the comments written by pupils during the following activities:

(1)   the water is in a vessel which is heated on a bunsen burner; and
(2)   the ice is in a vessel which is immersed in warm water

For pupils it is clear that *before* boiling, the purpose of the bunsen burner was *to heat* the water, whereas before melting the purpose of the warm water was *to melt* the ice (instead of warming or heating the ice). Therefore, ice has the property of melting or of cooling something; very seldom do they consider that the ice itself can warm, heat or cool, i.e. it can change temperature.

Results after teaching
When we consider the results after teaching on the stability of temperature of change of state, there is an improvement, particularly for boiling water and melting metals. For example, the following question regarding the apparatus in Figure 4.3 was given to pupils before and after teaching:

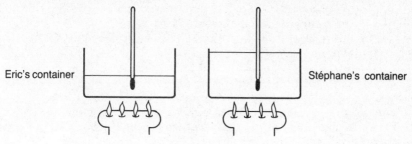

Eric's container

Stéphane's container

Figure 4.3.

In Eric's container there is a little water, and in Stéphane's container there is a lot of water. The two camping stoves are set at the same level. The two thermometers are the same.

(1) When the water is boiling in each of the containers, is the temperature read by Eric:
   (a) higher than the temperature read by Stéphane;
   (b) equal to the temperature read by Stéphane;
   (c) lower than the temperature read by Stéphane; or
   (d) I don't know.

(2) (a) What temperature does Eric read?
   (b) What temperature does Stéphane read?
   (c) I don't know.

At the beginning of the year 20 per cent of the pupils gave a correct answer to the first question, and at the end of the year 70 per cent of 300 pupils gave a correct answer. To the second question, less than 10 per cent gave a correct answer at the beginning of the year, but this increased to almost 60 per cent at the end of the year.

For a similar question about the melting of ice, there was less improvement over the year, though the progress made was still significant.

It is necessary to note that these results were obtained after a period of teaching in which the pupils carried out several experiments by themselves with ice, water and, in some classes, naphthalene. They also discussed the melting of metals and they were given exercises on both these points. However, despite these experiences, it was noted that these pupils still had difficulty in applying ideas about the temperature of change of state.

Responses to the following questions asked after teaching illustrate these difficulties.

Adele puts a piece of zinc in an oven at 1000° C. She reads the temperature of the zinc every minute. She got 30°, 70°, 200°, 420°, 420°, 420°, ...

(1) Why does the thermometer have several readings of 420° C?
Adele goes on to read the temperatures.

(2) Can you tell if:
(a) the temperature always stays at 420° C;
(b) the temperature is going to rise again to 1000° C; or
(c) I don't know.

The responses to the first question were:

'zinc is melting' (about 40 per cent of the pupils) and
'it is the highest possible temperature for zinc' (about 20 per cent of the pupils).

The responses to the second question were:

'the temperature always stays at 420° C' (70 per cent of the pupils); or
'the temperature is going to rise again to 1000° C' (17 per cent of the pupils).

These results suggest that, if the pupils accept the stability of the temperature, they may not ascribe it to the phenomenon of change of state, but rather to the maximum temperature that a substance can have when it is heated. In a certain way, they do not take into account that the liquid metal is an 'object' which is heated and, therefore, its temperature should increase until thermal equilibrium is reached. As we shall see in the next section, these points cause difficulties for pupils.

Remarks on the acquisition of the notion of temperature
This last difficulty shows that the notion of the temperature of an object is only partially acquired by many of the pupils. Here, I would like to emphasize two points concerning the notion of temperature.

First, scientists recognise that when an object is heated, its temperature increases of necessity except if there is physical or chemical transformation. However, the causal relation 'when a substance (or an object) is heated, its temperature increases' is not recognized systematically by all pupils. For some of the pupils this relation *depends on the substance*. Often, they establish a link between the heating and visible modifications (change of state, bubbles, change of colour, etc). For example, before teaching, only about a third of the pupils think that the temperature of sand, sugar and water increases when they are heated. Many of them predict that sand will not be hot 'because sand cannot heat', whereas water can heat up. For them the ability to be heated is a 'natural' property of particular substances.

After teaching more than 50 per cent of the pupils recognized that the temperature of these three substances increases when they are heated, but it remains a difficult concept for them. For example, it was noted that more pupils recognized the stability of the temperature of boiling water than recognized the increasing temperature of the three substances (sand, water, sugar) when they were heated. Very often in teaching, we consider that pupils are already familiar with such notions as the increase in temperature with heating, but it appears that this is not the case for them with every substance.

The second issue concerns thermal equilibrium. When several objects are in prolonged contact in the same room (or any other place which can be considered as a thermostat) they are at the same temperature. Pupils, however, have difficulties in recognizing the equality of temperatures at thermal equilibrium. For example, two plates (one made of metal, the other of plastic) in the same room are not considered by the majority of pupils to be at the same temperature, even after teaching.[19] Likewise, different materials (flour, nails, water) placed for several hours in an oven at 60° C are at different temperatures for the majority of the pupils. Typically, flour is at less than 60° C because flour does not heat up very much, nails are at more than 60° C because the iron heats faster, and water is at 60° C because it takes the temperature of the surroundings. Even if in this case there is some progress (from about 10 per cent before teaching to over 30 per cent after teaching) it remains a problem. Before, and sometimes after, teaching we find the same kind of interpretation as in the preceding case: that some substances cannot heat up. It appears that even after teaching, some pupils have difficulty in assimilating this notion.

Let us consider two examples which illustrate the difficulties of using the notion of thermal equilibrium in different situations. The first example illustrates pupils' use of different and even contradictory explanations for two experimental situations. To a question asking if the temperatures of different objects next to each other in the same room are the same or not, a pupil responds:

> They are in the room, therefore all of them have taken the temperature of the room. ... If one puts any object... in the room, this object is going to take the temperature of the room... irrespective of the material of which it is made (Nathalie, 13 years).

However, in response to a question about the choice of the best material in which to wrap a cold ball-bearing in order for it to remain cold for as long as possible, the same pupil chose aluminium foil and explained:

> ... because the material, like wool, has a tendency to heat something... because it is the material, it is like that... when it is aluminium, it is metal, therefore it remains at the room temperature.

The second example illustrates an incorrect use of thermal equilibrium. To a question about the handles of different spoons in hot water, a pupil responds:

> the iron seems hotter (when you touch it), the end of the wood is almost

not (hot). ... I think that they are at the temperature of water... because they have been in the same water, at the same temperature, for the same time (Cécile, 12 years).

This pupil knows that different materials in a room are at the same temperature although they feel different. She applies this knowledge to another situation, though here ambient air intervened and she did not take it into account.

To summarize, it was noted after teaching that pupils had made more progress in their understanding of the stability of the temperature of change of state, particularly in the case of boiling water or melting metals, than they had with the following ideas:

(1)   the increase in temperature of an object (or substance) when it is heated (without physical or chemical transformations); and

(2)   the equality of the temperature of several objects in prolonged contact, i.e. at thermal equilibrium.

Knowledge of these difficulties leads naturally to a consideration of the *content* of the teaching and we will return to this matter at the end of this chapter.

Heat

In this section, we deal mainly with the notion of conduction, in so far as conduction is the process of the transfer of energy. Moreover, nowadays, the words conductor and insulator are much used, particularly in the media. Many of the pupils, even before teaching, know these words even if they do not use them very often. What do they mean by them? Does the use of these words imply a notion of the conduction of heat, and if so what are their ideas?

First, let us consider the meaning for the physicist. Being a conductor or insulator is a property of substances. This notion is connected with one of the processes by which energy is transferred: that of heating, which corresponds to the transfer of increased thermal agitation. This process can exist only if there is matter. The notions of conductor and insulator *cannot be separated* from the notion of heat and consequently *from the notion of energy*. Indeed, it seems very difficult to consider a transfer without specifying what is transferred (i.e. to deal with heat without considering energy). As we noted previously, heat is a characteristic parameter of interaction and, therefore, when we use the notions of conductor and insulator, we are dealing with systems in interaction.

Types of interpretations given by pupils of several experimental situations

A number of studies undertaken by researchers have involved asking pupils about situations, which to a physicist involve the notion of the conduction of heat.[18,19,20]

The situations presented to pupils included the following:

(S1)   which materials are good for the thermal insulation of a house?

(S2)   Which materials are good for the thermal insulation of a heated (or cooled) steel ball-bearing?

(S3)   Which materials are good for the thermal insulation of a hot drink or of ice?

(S4)   Why do metal and plastic plates feel different to the touch?

(S5)   Why do the metal and plastic parts of bicycle handlebars feel different on a frosty day?

(S6)   Why is the handle of a metal spoon hotter than the handle of a wooden or plastic spoon when they are placed in hot water?

Explanations given by pupils before and after teaching fall into several main categories *which are not exclusive*:

(1)   the material retains warmth or cold, better or less well;

(2)   the material has the property to be cold or warm because of its nature;

(3)   the material is hot (or cold), so consequently it heats (or cools);

(4)   the material becomes hot or cold, more or less quickly;

(5)   the material retains, lets in or lets out hot or cold air, better or less well;

(6)   the material absorbs, retains, lets out, stores, ... attracts, repels heat, better or less well;

(7)   the material transmits heat, more or less quickly; heat propagates, moves in the material, more or less quickly; the material transmits thermal agitation, more or less quickly;

(8)   the material takes the temperature of its surroundings; and

(9)   the material is a conductor or an insulator.

Pupils' interpretations before teaching

Interpretations before teaching

Before teaching, pupils tended to give the first five categories of the above explanations depending on the experimental situations.

The explanation 'the material retains heat or cold, better or less well' predominates in situations in which there is a container whose function it is to keep the inside at a given temperature for as long as possible (situations S2 and S3). For example, a pupil chose aluminium to wrap the ball-bearing with (S2) and said:

the aluminium keeps cold or better (Cécile, 11 years).

Another pupil chose an aluminium container for a hot drink because:

the iron preserves better (11-year-old).

In that case, the container has the property to preserve the hot or cold state of the object which is inside it; it could be said that it is similar to the case of canned foods where the can could have the function of preserving the food in it.

The explanation that 'the material has the property to be cold or warm' is also quite common in this same type of situation (S2 and S3), and in the situation in which touch is involved. For example, in the case of the thermal insulation of a hot drink or ice (S3) a pupil chose a metal container with ice in it because:

> the iron container is colder than an ordinary glass (11-year-old).

Another pupil chose a glass wrapped in cloth for his hot drink because:

> the glass wrapped in cloth will be hotter than the others since it is wrapped in cloth (11-year-old).

In these cases, pupils relate two properties which they ascribe to the material: the property to be cold (or warm) (i.e. the explanation type 2) and the property of keeping something cold (or hot) (explanation of type 1).

The second type of explanation is also found very often in situations where touch is involved (S4):

> it's metal and metal is cold (11-year-old).

The third type of explanation, 'the material is hot (or cold), so consequently it heats (or cools)', is also mainly found in situations in which there is a container (S2 and S3). Pupils establish a casual relation of this type, because the material is cold (or hot), it cools (or it heats). For example:

> metal cools things, metal is cold (Marie-Noëlle, 12 years).

The fourth type of explanation, 'becomes hot (or cold), more or less quickly', is mainly found in situations where metal is heated and when the question concerns the material itself (S6). For example:

> I've been told that metal heats up faster than any of the other three.

In that case, the material doesn't have the property to remain in a given state of hot or cold.

The fifth type of explanation, 'material retains, lets in or lets out hot or cold air, better or less well', is found in the case of the insulation of a house, where the house is similar to a container whose function is to keep the inside at a given temperature as long as possible (S1). In that case, the majority of pupils do not use the previous categories of explanation; they tend to take into account the transfer of air between the outside and the inside and because of this, they consider an action from the outside on the inside. For example (in situation S1):

> it (the material) lets the cold air into (the house) (Cécile, 11 years).

These first five types of explanation *are only in terms of properties of objects or events* (it is hot (cold), it retains the warmth (cold), it heats, it becomes hot (cold), etc.). The pupils do not use parameters, as the physicist does, to describe experiments (temperature, heat, energy, etc.). In addition, except for the last example, in which the air intervenes as an intermediary between the outside and the inside, there is neither the idea of transfer nor the idea of interaction or even action between objects or systems. The thinking of the pupils is very much divorced from the interpretation of the physicist.

The other explanations listed earlier are given mainly after teaching. It is important to note that the explanation 'the heat goes through, moves...' is found mainly in situations where there is a material substance between the source of heating and the place where the temperature is considered, such as in the situation where spoons are left in hot water. The situation very frequently used during teaching, in which a bar of metal is heated on one side and temperature is examined on the other side, produces this kind of interpretation.

Comments on differences between the physicist'
and pupils' interpretations
As we have already noted, most of the pupils give interpretations which are very different from those of the physicist. In considering the choice of a container to keep a drink hot or ice cold for as long as possible, if responding in an analytical way rather than by recall, a physicist would:

(1) *Identify* the interacting systems: the hot drink (or ice) the container, ambient air;
(2) *redescribe* the state of the systems with the parameter temperature;
(3) *compare* the temperatures of the different systems;
(4) *recall* a piece of knowledge which comes from the *principles* of thermodynamics: heat propagates from a region at higher temperature to a region at lower temperature;
(5) *deduce* that heat will propagate from the hot drink to ambient air (or from ambient air to ice) and from the hot drink to ambient air through the container;
(6) *recall* the piece of knowledge that, in a conductor, the heat transfers faster than in an insulator; and
(7) *choose* the most insulating material for the container.

In what way does this differ from the explanations given by the majority of the pupils?

The first difference which is very often found is that pupils do not take into account all the systems which interact (including in this case the ambient air); secondly, they do not redescribe the systems by using parameters of state (or by interaction parameters)—in this case temperature. Most often they describe or interpret situations in terms of:

(1)   events: it is heating, it cools, etc.;
(2)   properties that they have ascribed to the object: the substance of the object, or the fact that it is cold, hot, solid, hard, thick, etc.; and
(3)   function of the object: it has been made to perform a specific function, e.g. for drinking coffee or keeping food, etc.

Pupils tend to associate:

(1)   a property of the object with an event (it is cold so it cools);
(2)   one property of the object with another (it is made of metal so it will retain heat);
(3)   the recognized event with another one (it becomes hot so it will heat); and
(4)   the object with another analogous situation (there is aluminium in the vacuum flask, so the container made of aluminium will work the same way).

It appears that the physicist who interprets these experiments reasons in a different way from the majority of 12 to 15-year-old pupils.

The physicist identifies *systems*, then, in order to analyse the interaction, *describes* the systems using *parameters* such as temperature. Pupils, on the other hand, take into account only *objects* (not a real difficulty when systems and objects are the same), and in order to interpret the situations, very seldom do they describe them in terms of parameters, instead they use *properties*, *functions* or *events*. These two fundamental differences are evident at the beginning of a teaching sequence when pupils start reasoning about experimental situations.

Learning of the notion of heat

Before considering our results concerning what 12–13-year-old pupils learn about heat as a result of teaching, it may be helpful to outline the main features of what is taught on this topic. It is very difficult to say what is actually taught in any class but here we outline the objectives of the teaching given by teachers who participated in this research:

(1)   there is transfer (propagation of heat) between two points which are at different temperatures; there is (spontaneous) transfer from the place which is at the higher temperature to the place which is at the lower temperature;
(2)   different materials conduct more or less heat; there are conductors and insulators;
(3)   in the case of conduction, the transfer occurs without movement of matter;
(4)   in the case of convection, there is transportation of matter;
(5)   several objects in prolonged contact have the same temperature (when there is only one thermostat).

Here we will not examine the case of convection because conduction is the process of energy transfer which corresponds to heat and also because there are few results on pupils' understanding of convection.

After teaching, it is striking to find out that pupils tend to use the words heat, cold, conductor and insulator in almost all types of explanations and in almost all the situations. However, these words can have *very different meanings*, which vary not only from one pupil to another, but even for the same pupil according to the situation.

Cases where there is little or no significant change in pupils' explanation

Let us examine the case where pupils' explanations are of the same type before and after teaching, only words are added. In the following examples, these explanations were given for the same question concerning the choice of a container which has to keep a drink hot or ice cold for as long as possible. A pupil (12-years-old) chose an iron container with ice in it and said:

> the iron keeps the cold better than the others. It is an *insulator*.

He made the same choice for the hot drink and explained:

> because the iron container keeps the cold, it can keep the heat.

Another pupil (also 12-years-old) chose an iron container and said:

> the iron will keep the ice. ... It is a good *conductor*.

and for the hot drink:

> for the same reasons.

At the beginning of the year, this last pupil made the same choice for these questions, and gave a similar explanation for the hot drink:

> the iron keeps things better.

So, before and after teaching, we found the same type of explanation; material retains warmth or cold well or not as well, the only difference is the addition of a word, 'conductor' or 'insulator'.

These examples illustrate one type of learning which is found in a substantial number of pupils after teaching on heat. These pupils *do not change their minds*, their type of interpretation is the same, *they just accumulate a piece of knowledge*, in this case the words 'conductor' and 'insulator'.[21]

Cases where there has been noticeable development but still with significant difficulties

Example of conceptual change
Let us take a typical example where there has been some development even though after teaching the type of interpretation is not very close

to the physicist's one.[8,20] For example, in considering the choice of container before teaching, Marie-Noëlle (12-years-old) said:

> Surely not this one (in cardboard and plastic)... beause in my fridge it is not cardboard, it is not this material, it is iron or plastic.

And, after touching a metal container, she said: 'metal cools'. Of the cardboard-plastic container, she said:

> the cardboard container, it is warm enough.

Concerning a casserole full of hot water, left for a long time in a room, she said:

> the casserole will be colder than the water... it depends on what the casserole is made of.

The analysis shows that she used:

(1) Events and properties: coffee pots are metal; in the fridge, there is no cardboard but metal or plastic; metal is cold;
(2) Causal reasoning: because a material seems cold when you touch it, its temperature is above the ambient temperature; because a material is cold, it cools; because an object has a specific function, it has some properties.

Sometimes, she used the heat as an existing intermediary in an interaction but not often and only in very favourable circumstances.

We should note that almost all of these statements are correct, but the statements that link them are not.

During the teaching, this pupil made several experiments, the results of which were in contradiction to her predictions. However, even after several sessions, we observed that in the same session, she stated that cotton and aluminium are at the same temperature and she stated that cotton is warm so ice wrapped in it will melt more easily than in metal.

> I think that, that [metal] will keep it [the ice] frozen most easily, because that [cotton] is hotter and keeps the heat better.

Then, she carried out the experiment, and after she stated:

> The cold of the ice goes into the material [metal] and goes away, and there [the cotton] it keeps it. That one [cotton] keeps the heat more than that one [metal]. Here [metal] it's all right, it goes away, the heat or the cold.

After teaching, she compared materials using the criterion that heat transfers more or less quickly according to the material (insulator, conductor); for example: 'it is a conductor... heat of hot water will go in the sides, it will go through'.

She also distinguished between heat and a hot object and she ascribed to heat the property to move in a material. So she used a new idea; heat, as an entity which implies an action of one object (hot water, for example) on another one (container).

After teaching, she still reasoned in terms of the properties of an object but she did not use the same properties. She had modified her ways of explaining. She had, as least partially, restructured her ideas.

However, she can draw on several types of interpretation. So, during the same final test, in order to answer a question about the different sensations she felt when she touched metal and cotton, she used the fact that the movement of heat is more rapid in some materials than in others:

> The metal spreads out the heat quickly, while the cotton's heat stays in the same place.

But, for a question based on an everyday experience (pick a material for a container to keep soup hot the longest), she referred to a different situation:

> Coffee pots keep in the heat well. Aluminium keeps in the heat well.

Comments
Pupils use the words 'heat' and 'cold' with several meanings. Let us examine some of them. For example, mainly in situations in which touch is involved (S4 and S5), the explanations are of the type:

> Metal *absorbs* more cold than plastic does.

In situations concerning the insulation of a house, typical explanations are of the type:

> We try to insulate houses... in order that heat does not escape and cold does not go in (Nathalie, 12 years).

In situations in which spoons are placed in hot water, many explanations are of the type:

> ... metal is a conductor, *it conducts the heat* up into the metal... it transfers heat... transfers heat along it.

or,

> Water has heated the whole... it has heated the end, then it has gone up... heat has gone in the whole spoon (Béatrice, 12 years).

All these types of explanation take into account an entity, the heat. In all these cases, *this entity has the property to make the material (or object) hot*, and in its absence, the material is cold. Very often, cold is also an entity which has the property to make something cold (heat heats and cold cools). But there are important differences between the types of explanations. In the case where the material absorbs, retains, loses, or prevents heat from escaping, the heat has the property of being stored in an object (or material), and it should be noticed that most of the pupils who 'store' heat (or cold) do not consider that heat has a mass. In the case where the material transmits heat or heat goes through, or propagates in the material, the heat has the property of movement and *it is not necessarily stored*. Moreover, in that case, recognition of transfer from one object to another presupposes that one of the objects has an influence on the other; in other words there is an action of one object on the others.

Therefore, when heat transfer is taken into account, the pupil's interpretations are nearer to those of the physicist than before teaching. For example, these pupils recognized, at least partially, the interaction between the objects, and also used the rapidity of the movement of heat in order to compare materials. But, significant difficulties still remain. The use of the idea of heat transfer *does not necessarily imply a correct explanation*, because, in particular, it also requires: first, a correct choice of the systems (or objects) which interact, and secondly to take into account the difference between the temperatures as a condition of transfer.

Therefore, even if after teaching the word 'heat' is frequently used, we have to be careful not to infer that for pupils this idea of heat as an interaction parameter predominates in their explanations of all the situations in which a physicist would use it. The interpretations given by a substantial number of pupils of the different experimental situations show that the *idea of heat as a characteristic of interaction* is not as essential in explaining the phenomena as are the properties of materials.

Some difficulties in the reorganization of pieces of knowledge
Let us examine the different explanations given, after teaching, by the same pupil in different situations. First, in the situation with several spoons in hot water, this pupil said:

> the iron is a conductor... the iron one will be the hottest because it will conduct more quickly (Jean-Claude, 12 years).

In the situation where he has to choose a material in which to wrap a cold ball-bearing, which is supposed to have been taken out from a freezer, he chose aluminium foil and said:

> because metals keep the cold... the aluminium is a conductor.

The interviewer asked, 'the fact that it (aluminium) conducts, does that make it possible for it to keep the ball-bearing cold for the longest time?', and the pupil answered:

> Yes, because it will take the temperature of the marble... and it will keep it for a long time.

This example illustrates an interpretation which is given quite often. It is based on the following reasoning:

— a conductor heats (or cools) quickly;
— something hot (or cold) heats (or cools);

With only this reasoning, the pupil is right to choose aluminium foil, since aluminium becomes cold (or hot) faster and will cool (or heat) what is inside. These statements work in the majority of real life situations. However, they may lead to incorrect conclusions. They ignore two essential points:

(1) it fails to take into account all the systems which interact, in this case the ambient air;
(2) it does not fulfil the condition that heat goes from the hotter place to the less hot place.

To learn that a conductor heats (or cools) quickly is seen as progress, but it is not sufficient.

The case where pupils' interpretations after teaching
are close to the physicist's interpretations
This section will show that the idea that an object takes the temperature of the other objects with which it is in contact, can be very helpful in using correctly the notion of transfer of heat in a material. For example, after teaching, a pupil gave as an explanation for his choice of thermal insulation for a house:

the polystyrene... is a good thermal insulator... they [polystyrene, wood] prevent cold for coming in... the lead will take the temperature... of the cold [outside] and therefore will put it in the house, ... it [heat] goes through the piece of lead (Sébastien, 12 years).

In the situation in which he had to predict the temperature of different objects on a table, he stated:

[same temperature]... because there is the same temperature on the two sides of the material, nothing has an effect upon the other.

In the situation with spoons in hot water:

[an insulator]... means that it does not take the temperature of the surroundings, but, on the contrary, iron will take the temperature of the surroundings at once.

These types of explanations are close to these of the physicist in so far as there is use of the parameter temperature in order to redescribe situations and to predict what will happen.

It should be noted that these kinds of explanations are not frequently found. In this case, even before teaching, the pupil concerned already used in most of his explanations an entity (which he called energy) moving at various rates according to the material. Perhaps this kind of interpretation could be a step forward in the learning of this concept.

Implications for teaching

The results show the very significant difficulties that pupils have in acquiring the notion of temperature. Very often, pupils think that temperature depends primarily on the substance (or material) and possibly on the surroundings. This has a number of implications:

(1) In some cases pupils do not recognize that the same object can have different temperatures.
(2) They reason in terms of substance and case by case, i.e. according to the experimental situation; they do not establish a systematic causal link between the heating of a substance and the fact that its temperature increases.
(3) They do not recognize that several objects in contact (with only one thermostat) move towards the same temperature.

However, typical teaching programmes do not take these difficulties into account; they often assume that pupils have already acquired the notions in question. More appropriate teaching which might help pupils to acquire these notions and to overcome the difficulties identified would involve the following components:

(1) Various experiments in heating and cooling of very different substances. These would give pupils the opportunity to see what is happening to these substances *and* to take their temperature, the temperature of the surroundings and, if possible, of the source of heat (or cold).
(2) Several activities with boiling water, melting ice and other changes of state including, of course, taking temperature readings.
(3) Discussions, tests, etc. in order to help pupils to generalize the notions which have been taught to appreciate their range of application.

Such teaching could help pupils to learn, at least partly:

(1) to use the parameter temperature in order to redescribe an experimental situation (when it is pertinent);
(2) to use the principle (sometimes called the zeroth law of thermodynamics) that two bodies which are in contact for a long time, are evolving towards thermal equilibrium; when there are two bodies in thermal equilibrium with a third then there is thermal equibrium between all three;
(3) to know that temperature is one of the parameters which determines the physical state of a substance;
(4) to learn the range of application of the temperature of change of state and consequently the range of application of the increase of temperature of a substance when it is heated (without change of state or chemical reaction).

The introduction of the notion of heat appears to give students significant problems for several reasons. Very often this notion is introduced before that of energy and, therefore, a transfer is being considered without being explicit about what is being transferred. The use of the notion of heat also implies the use of the notion of temperature and this notion has not yet been acquired by a majority of the pupils. The pupils' attainments *after* the teaching of conduction of heat and insulation show that a substantial number of them used these notions incorrectly in different experimental situations. So, more generally it would seem that an *intermediary* step could be used in teaching the notion of heat. The pupils could be introduced to a notion of interaction between objects in so far as they learn that the temperature of an object depends *necessarily* on its surroundings.

References

[1]Zemansky, M. W. (1971). The use of the word 'heat' in elementary and in intermediate instruction in physics. In *Seminar on the Teaching of Physics in Schools* (Ed. S. Sikjoer). Gyldendal: Copenhagen.

[2]Dode, M. (1965). *Le deuxieme principe de la thermodynamique*. Sedes: Paris.

[3]Conant, J. (1957). *Harvard Case Histories in Experimental Science*. [See article by D. Roller in Vol. 1: The Early Development of the Concepts of Temperature and Heat: The rise and decline of the caloric theory.] Harvard University Press: Cambridge, Mass.

[4]Fox, R. (1971). *The Caloric Theory of Gases*. Oxford University Press: Oxford.

[5]Lakoff, G. and Johnson, M. (1980). *Metaphors We Live By*. University of Chicago Press: Chicago.

[6]Albert, E. (1978). Development of the concept of heat in children. *Science Education* 62 (3), 389-99.

[7]Engel, E. (1982). The development of understanding of selected aspects of pressure, heat and evolution in pupils aged between 12-16 years. Unpublished PhD thesis, University of Leeds, Leeds.

[8]Tiberghien, A. (1980). Un exemple de restructuration de l'organisation conceptuelle à l'occasion d'un enseignement concernant la notion de chaleur. In *Compte-rendus des Deuxièmes Journées sur l'Education Scientifique*. Chamonix; France.

[9]Triplett, G. (1973). Research on heat and temperature in cognitive development. *Journal of Children's Mathematic Behavior* 2, 27-43.

[10]Erickson, G. (1979). Children's conceptions of heat and temperature. *Science Education* 63 (2), 221-30.

[11]Erickson, G. (1980). Children's viewpoints of heat: A second look. *Science Education* 64 (3), 323-36.

[12]Crookes, J. (1982). The nature of personal commitment in changes in explanations. Paper presented at a Seminar on Investigating Children's Existing Ideas about Science, School of Education, University of Leicester, Leicester.

[13]Tiberghien, A. and Barboux, M. (1980). Difficulté de l'acquisition de le notion de température par les élèves de 6ème. In *Compte-rendus des Cinquièmes Journées Internationales sur l'Education Scientifique*. Chamonix: France.

[14]Stavy, R. and Berkovitz, B. (1980). Cognitive conflict as a basis for teaching quantitative aspects of the concept of temperature. *Science Education* 64 (5), 679-92.

[15]Strauss, S. (1981). *U-Shaped Behavioural Growth*. Academic Press: Orlando and London.

[16]Driver, R. and Russell, T. (1981). An investigation of the ideas of heat, temperature and change of state of children aged between 8 and 14 years. Unpublished manuscript, University of Leeds, Leeds.

[17]Andersson, B. (1979). Some aspects of children's understanding of boiling point. *Proceedings of an International Seminar on Cognitive Development Research in Science and Mathematics*, University of Leeds, Leeds.

[18]Tiberghien, A., Séré, M. G., Barboux, M. and Chomat, A. (1983). Etude des représentations préalables de quelques notions de physique et leur évolution. Rapport de recherche, LIRESPT, University of Paris VII.

[19]Engel Clough, E. and Driver, R. (1985). Secondary students' conceptions of the conduction of heat: bringing together personal and scientific views. *Physics Education* **20**. 176–182.

[20]Tiberghien, A. (1979). Modes and conditions of learning. An example: the learning of some aspects of the concept of heat. In *Proceedings of an International Seminar on Cognitive Development Research in Science and Mathematics*, University of Leeds, Leeds.

[21]Rumelhart, D. E. and Norman, D. A. (1978). Accretion, tuning and restructuring: three modes of learning. In *Semantic Factors in Cognition* (Eds J. W. Cotton and R. Klatzky). Lawrence Erlbaum Associates: Hillsdale, NJ.

CHAPTER 5

Force and Motion

Richard Gunstone and Michael Watts

Introduction

In the large numbers of studies of children's conceptions of natural phenomena which have been undertaken in recent years, no content area has received more attention than that described by 'force and motion'. The interpretations of students from primary school to university graduates have been explored in a variety of real world kinematic and dynamic situations. In this chapter we concern ourselves largely with the broad middle section of the 9-19 age range.

We have set out the chapter in five parts. First, we raise what we see to be some of the major issues, as a means of introducing this whole area of research. Secondly, we consider some of the aspects of both force and motion as they appear in school science. Thirdly, we attempt to draw out some of the implications from the wealth of research reports for all of this—what sort of consensus can be gleaned from the work that has been done. Fourthly, we discuss one or two of the differing approaches that have grown up around this work—differences that reflect upon the question of 'so what?'—the implications for classroom practice. Finally, we summarized what we have been saying throughout.

You will notice as you are reading that we tend to emphasize a number of points and it is as well for us to note some of these here. The work we consider in the third part of the chapter has a strong international flavour and represents research that has been conducted in a number of countries—not all of them English-speaking. The temptation is to suggest that youngsters develop the same kinds of conceptions in exactly the same way everywhere, despite great variations in school experience, language, culture, etc. We would not want to say that at all—we know too little about the context in which the responses were generated in each case. Nor do we know nearly enough about how to 'translate' between contexts, languages and cultures to try to be able to base assumptions on this work.

It remains a point of interest, however, that we find we *can* make comments about the similarities in what youngsters say, do and write even though they *do* come from differing cultures and different educational systems. We have done this by mainly suggesting some five 'intuitive rules' that youngsters seem to use when they are considering forces. This is our name for the interpretations we make of responses in our own and other people's research work. Elsewhere these kinds of 'rules' are termed 'alternative frameworks', 'alternative conceptions' and the like. It is important to remember that probably no one youngster would subscribe to any one of these rules as we have written them here, nor do the rules describe the wide variety of responses that students make. They are our attempts to make some tentative generalizations from all the research that has been done on the concepts of force and motion.

A point we do emphasize is how seemingly self-contained youngsters' responses are. We think that it is important to realize that their answers make sense to them, the answers work in the sense that they explain and cater for the problem at hand. To a physicist the answers may not only seem totally unacceptable but also quite off the point. However, for youngsters it is almost always *not* the case; to them the answers are acceptable and relevant. It is worth remembering that most people have a self-reference system that not only helps them to sort out the answer to a problem but helps them sort out what the problem was in the first place.

Some issues

By way of introduction to the considerable number of issues which arise from this work, consider the following four examples. Although examples 1 and 3 are anecdotal both represent relatively common situations.

Example 1

Abe, a physics graduate, was undertaking a one-year course in secondary teacher training. He, along with the rest of the students studying 'Methods of Teaching Physics', was shown a bell jar with a partially inflated balloon inside. He was asked to predict what would happen when air was evacuated from the bell jar:

A: The balloon will float.
I: Why?
A: Because gravity will be reduced.

Even apparently successful students of physics have interpretations of the world which are not in accord with orthodox physics and which clearly do not come from classroom teaching.

Example 2

A large group of 17-year-olds who were just about to complete a specialist two-year physics course were asked the following question about Figure 5.1:

> A pendulum is swinging from left to right. When it is at the point shown, which of the diagrams below best represents the forces acting on the pendulum? Friction is negligible.

Exactly 50 per cent of the students gave either answer C or D, both of which incorporate a view of motion as implying the existence of a force. This is a common intuitive rule used by students. It will be discussed later in this chapter.

Some interpretations of natural phenomena which are at odds with the ideas of physics (and other areas of science) are very common.

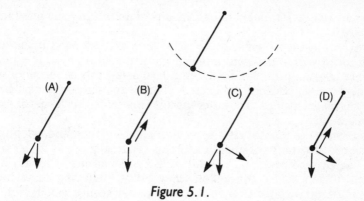

Figure 5.1.

Example 3

Lou, a 13-year-old, identified by his school as academically gifted, was one of 12 students participating in a special class. The students were asked to predict and compare the times taken for one-inch cubes of plastic and aluminium to fall about two metres. Lou answered:

> The heavier [aluminium] one will get there first.

He supported his prediction by claiming to have dropped objects of different weights from a bridge and to have seen the heavier one reach the ground first. When the two cubes were dropped there and then, Lou claimed to see the aluminium cube hit the ground first. Most people present saw the two cubes hit the ground together. Lou's belief that the aluminium would fall faster was apparently so strong that it influenced his observation. Half an hour later the students were asked to indicate 'true' or 'false', and to give reasons, for a number of statements. One of these was: 'Two objects of different mass will take the same time to fall the same distance.' Lou's response was: 'True— Newton's Law.'

It is not uncommon for students to learn the physicists' perspective and apply it to identifiably 'physics-type' situations, while still interpreting the real world in other ways.

Example 4

Tessa, a 14-year-old, was thought of in school as being a high achiever in science. She was being interviewed about certain situations where forces are involved and in particular about what she thought a force was. She was faced with describing why a balloon filled with hydrogen will rise upwards if released. She said:

> Well, I can't see it having any external propulsion. It's just in the nature of it, or in the nature of the gas inside. I suppose it is a force inherent in the object.

Here nature itself is called in as a means of describing the phenomena involved.

There are several issues in these examples that need untangling. When faced with a problem in science (in this case physics) students may not see the problem, or make a response to it, in terms of what we might call 'School Science'. There are some similarities in responses from students of different ages and different levels of school achievement.

Even when students give correct responses to standard physics questions, they may still hold onto quite contrary world views which they use to interpret real phenomena. Observations students make can be influenced by the beliefs they hold—'believing is seeing' is sometimes more apposite than the more usual 'seeing is believing'. An interesting addendum to the example of Lou above concerns the five students who predicted that the two cubes would take the same time to fall the two metres. All five independently justified their predictions by arguing that the force of gravity was the same on each cube.

Some of us who are exploring these issues have described students' conceptions of force and motion as Aristotelian, others have described the conceptions as similar to the medieval impetus theory. In one sense it could be argued that these labels are irrelevant, as no youngster has conceptions of these issues with the breadth and internal consistency of, say, Aristotle or the fourteenth-century French scholar Buridan. However, these labels do serve to remind us that Aristotelian and impetus views of force and motion were seen as logical and reasonable for fine minds for long periods of time. One major reason for this is, of course, that it is quite possible to make daily observations of phenomena which support either view. In general, it is very reasonable to suggest that large numbers of our students have themselves used such daily observations to build up models to allow them to make sense of their world. These models, albeit in some cases poorly articulated and inappropriate in terms of the current views of physics, are brought into the classroom.

There in the classroom, of course, they are brought into conflict with the usual school science of teachers and textbooks. In the next section we take a look at that part of school science involved with force and motion, to see where the conflicts might occur.

Force and motion in school science

The concept of force itself has quite a curious history. Even comparatively recently the concept was vague and not clearly isolated in science.

We have already mentioned some of the theories of early natural philosophers. Aristotle distinguished between 'forced' and 'natural' motion. It is useful (if not quite accurate) to think of this as an early version of the current distinction that is made between contact and gravitational (or other inertial) forces. For Aristotle, forced motion was maintained by forces. The source of this force was the air around a projected object (like a stone thrown in the air) which pushed it along on its way. Buridan's impetus theory was a development of this. Here, the maintaining force was the 'impetus', an internal source of force which the stone was given when thrown. In that case the force pushed the stone until it was used up. The 'natural' vertical motion then took over and the stone returned to earth.

All of this, of course, contrasts with Newton's synthesis—characterized by his three laws. In essence his first law delineates a system of mechanics: it says that unless a resultant force is acting on a body then it will move with constant velocity. That is, unlike Aristotle's theory, it is uniform constant velocity that is natural and needs no explanation. Change in motion, or acceleration, does need to be explained and this is provided in terms of resultant forces. The second law makes the relationship specific. Whereas previously it was force and velocity that were seen to be proportional to each other, in Newton's laws it is force and acceleration.

It is worth noting in passing that Newton's own concept of inertia was a mixture of the older conceptions of force with the one we have now. For him, inertia was very much an internal kind of force quite distinct from the externally applied one which resulted in a change of velocity.

Newton's formulation and his laws raises the need for two further broad conceptual areas. The first is for a notion of vectors and their combination, the second is for reference frames. Neither aspect is straightforward. Two short points, however, can be made. That force is a vector distinguishes it off from many other entities with which it is often associated—pressure and energy for example. And the 'small' matter of frames of reference, which even Newton realized was problematic, led eventually to Einstein's own reformulation of Newton's system. It is Newton's laws that form the basis of school physics. The formula $F = ma$ is the one that pupils are most frequently asked to work with. Seldom, however, are the subtleties that lie behind it made clear. The laws require a recognition of forces exerted on one body by another. Only by clearly distinguishing the individual forces acting on a body can one hope to make sense of the laws at all. An understanding of $F = ma$ is made all the more difficult because it often contrasts with pupils' intuitive conceptions of motion.

In the everyday world, where friction is present, a person must push on an object in order to keep it moving. Where friction itself is not recognized as a force, then a youngster might develop the intuitive implication that a constant motion requires a constant force. Moreover, in some cases youngsters regard force itself as synonymous with other physical entities like pressure, energy and/or power, and then this simply serves to compound matters.

In the next section, where we look at the outcomes of the research work concerning students' ideas on these sorts of issues, the importance of the ideas advanced above become ever more obvious.

A review of research work

It is never a straightforward matter to survey a wide selection of literature, not least because writers seldom work from the same starting points or with the same underlying assumptions. In this case we have made a few assumptions of our own. First, we have looked for the similarities we can see between various pieces of work rather than dwell too long on differences. We need to say this in case we generate a false sense of consensus. There certainly are considerable differences in the work being done, differences of opinion in psychology, philosophy and methodology (to name but a few). In looking for similarities, however, we hope to be able to discuss some fairly general and stable points in what we survey.

Secondly, although we consider some forces and motions (for example, weight, gravity, uniform velocity and circular motion) we do not consider others (like nuclear forces or random motion) as such. Our selection is constrained in part by the work that has been done, and in part by our focus on the kind of topics that commonly occur in school science.

On the whole in this section we have ignored the various 'camps' into which research workers tend to congregate. What we do concentrate on are the sorts of outcomes that are reported, particularly the most common kinds of outcomes. There are different facets to the work that has been done, and we discuss only some of those here. We have tried to establish what we think are some of the intuitive rules that students seem to operate by.

Some early work was conducted in the 1920s by Jean Piaget.[1] He tended at that time to have worked with children younger than the broad age range we wish to consider. However, his writings are worth noting for a number of reasons. He was concerned about children's conceptions of force and motion[2] (amongst numerous other ideas) which he describes in some cases as being animistic. That is, youngsters often talk about inanimate objects in terms of having a 'life force' or a 'vital force'. For instance, one way in which youngsters describe why a freely moving object should eventually stop is to say that it 'wanted to' or that it 'forced itself to stop'. These studies were some of Piaget's earliest work, hence they form one of the bases upon which he organized his theory of developmental stages. Animistic responses, he suggests, disappear at more advanced stages of conceptual development. This, then, gives us our first 'intuitive rule'.

(1) Forces are to do with living things

This kind of response has been reported by a number of researchers[3,4] and not only in young children. It is sometimes a mode of response that even advanced level physics students will adopt.[5] They talk, for example, of an object 'trying to fight its way upwards against the will of gravity'.

Our second rule is probably a more commonly reported one—also across a very wide age group.

(2) Constant motion requires a constant force

We will mention only a few of the reports which conclude that this 'intuitive rule' is very widespread. The first of these[3] involved over 100 London students, using an interview approach. They were in one of three age bands: 13, 14 and 17 years old, in their third, fourth and sixth years of secondary schooling. They were asked to discuss different situations in terms of their idea of force, such as a person sledging down a hill as shown in Figure 5.2.
Responses which showed this intuitive rule included:

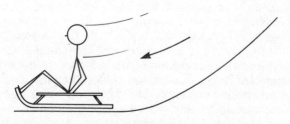

Figure 5.2.

If he wanted to keep moving along here [the horizontal] he would have to keep pushing, otherwise he'll run out of force and just stop (13-year-old).

To keep going steadily you need a steady push. If you don't force something to move its not going to go along is it? (14-year-old).

A second study,[6] this time just with 13-year-old London school-children, used written multiple-choice questionnaires. The questions have now been used many times over, in a number of different parts of the world (Leeds in England, Kenya, Portugal) with very similar results.

Paper-and-pencil tests were given to school and university students in Norway,[7] between 16 and 19 years of age, using some original questions and some adapted from other studies. The results highlight the strongly Aristotelian—or more appropriately Impetus Theory—responses of the Norwegian students. The authors conclude that a reasonable explanation of their data is that no learning of Newtonian physics takes place at all as students progress in their 'physics career'. Rather, they argue, more advanced students are simply better equipped to verbalize their impetus theories than less advanced students. We see this as a rather extreme and pessimistic view. Needless to say, some attempts to change students' views have been successful.[8] We will mention some of these attempts later in this chapter.

Another report[9] concerns higher education. Much of what has been said above is said again in this report, this time about select American honours physics students, not average-ability 13-year-olds. One of the earlier investigations of this nature was conducted by Viennot.[10] She used paper-and-pencil tests with a considerable number of senior secondary and university physics students in France, Belgium and Britain. Again the same intuitive rule was found. In addition, Viennot's investigation showed quite widespread use of intuitive rules 4 and 5 which will be discussed below.

The main point that clearly emerges from such written questions is that students often argue that constant motion requires a constant force. Langford and Zollman,[11] for instance, comment on the strength and persistence of the idea that a force must continue to act on an object if it is to continue in motion even under (simulated) friction-free conditions. If an object does not receive a constant force, then the force that causes it to move in the first place is said to be 'used up' during movement. In some cases when one force is used up then other forces (like gravity) 'take over' and move the object off in other directions. The students in Langford and Zollman's study were first allowed to explore the usual kind of carbon dioxide puck that moves almost friction-free on a glass-topped table. The puck could be blown by air from a hose connected to the 'blow' end of a vacuum pump. They were later asked to play with a computer simulation game that simulated the puck–table–hose arrangement. Both the amount and direction of the air could be controlled on the keyboard console.

The students were asked to 'make the puck move in a straight line across the table at a constant speed—not speeding up or slowing down after it gets started'. The authors report:

> It must be remembered that the population from which the sample was drawn includes only students with above average intelligence and who have a wider spectrum of experiences than would be found in most [American] school settings. Most of the students will enrol in the most prestigious universities. Over 50% of all the older students held the notion that a force must act on an object if it is to continue in motion.

These kinds of ideas are reported by many other researchers.

These same reports endorse our third intuitive rule, which might almost be a corollary of the second.

(3) The amount of motion is proportional to the amount of force

In lay terms it means the harder you push something, the faster (and further) it goes. This in itself is quite consistent with the effects of a single impulsive force, all else being equal. However, in this kind of intuitive rule, motion seldom has the same meaning as acceleration—which in any event requires a continuously acting force.

In the study with London school children already mentioned,[6] for example, youngsters were asked to tick and explain their choice in the question shown in Figure 5.3 (p. 94). A large number of students advanced very explicitly the association between force and movement—the force at the beginning being 'strong' (as it left the hand) and diminishing as the ball rises. As the motion stops (for a split second) so does the force, and then gravity is seen as pulling the ball down. For example:

> I think that the force is upwards as the person is throwing the ball up and putting all the force underneath the ball to move it up. Where the ball stops at point B, the force from the person throwing it up stops, and so the force of gravity pulls the ball back down. When the ball passes through point A the force of gravity is bringing it down, so the force would be here (13-year-old).

Moreover, the rule carried the (often stated) implication that if there is no movement, then there are no forces acting. 'Nothing is happening' it is said, 'and so there can't be any forces there.' This is our fourth rule.

(4) If a body is not moving there is no force acting on it

It has been said[12] that part of the problem lies not just with the word 'force' itself, but also with the other terms that are used to describe it. In physics a force is said to 'act' or to be 'exerted', in which case it seems reasonable to look for the source of the action or exertion.

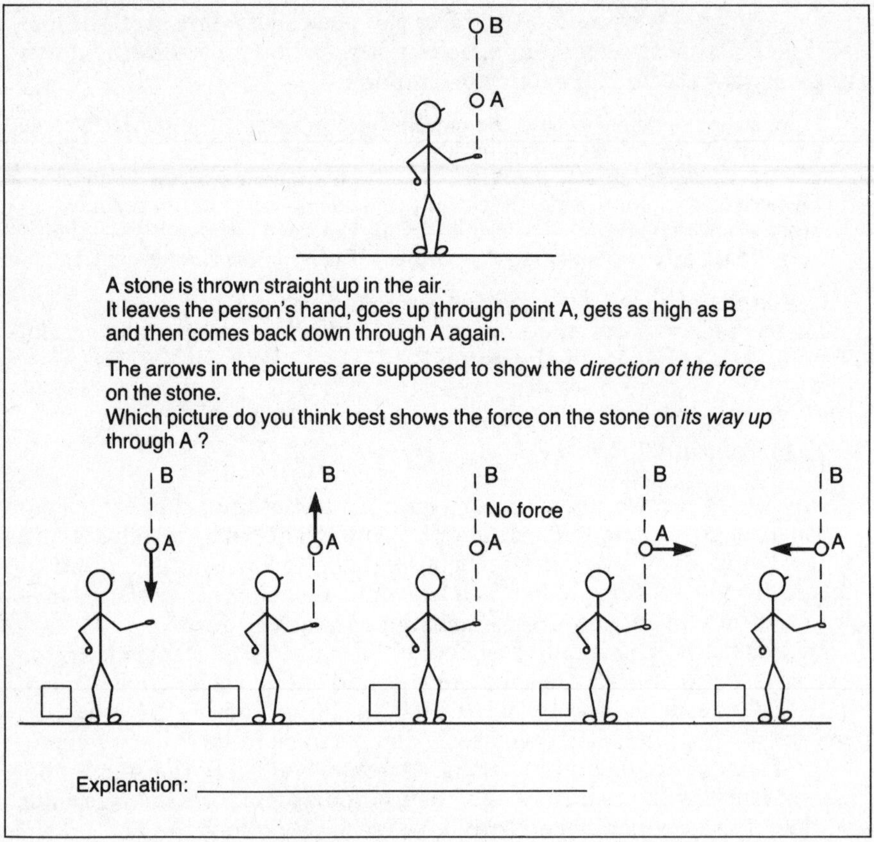

A stone is thrown straight up in the air.
It leaves the person's hand, goes up through point A, gets as high as B
and then comes back down through A again.

The arrows in the pictures are supposed to show the *direction of the force*
on the stone.
Which picture do you think best shows the force on the stone on *its way up*
through A ?

Explanation: _____

Figure 5.3.

Rule 4 seems to support the notion that it is pointless to look for a
force if there is no obvious action. Minstrell[13] asked a physics class at
an American high school to use arrows on a drawing to represent the
forces acting on a book stationary on a table. There were two
dominant views, indicated in Figure 5.4.

Approximately 50 per cent of the class believed that gravity and the
table were exerting opposite forces. The other 50 per cent believed
that only gravity was exerting a vertical force: 'the table was merely
in the way'. This 'no movement means no force' rule is often part of
the explanation given by children as to why something has stopped
moving. For example, Driver[14] asked an 11-year-old what made a ball-
bearing stop as it rolled along the floor. She was told:

I don't know. Why do they stop? It's just they always stop. After you
push it they go as far as the push... how hard it was, and after that wears
off it just goes back like it used to be.

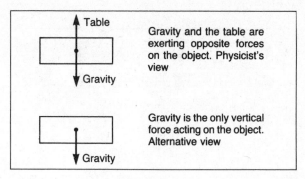

Figure 5.4.

Viennot,[10] in her work with more senior students mentioned above, found this sort of logic being expressed in the language of physics. In considering the forces acting on masses oscillating on springs, she found about 20 per cent of the students used statements such as '$V_3=0$; therefore $F_3=0$', 'M_3 is at rest, so $F_3=0$' to argue no motion means no force at the extreme position. This study also revealed that students use similar logic to support our fifth intuitive rule—one which has been widely reported.

(5) If a body is moving there is a force acting on it in the direction of motion

As we indicated in Example 2 (on p. 87) students commonly see the direction of the force as being necessarily in the same direction as the motion of an object.[6,7,10,15] It is a set of responses that has been widely reported. The first[6] has already been mentioned, where the work was with 13-year-old London school children, sometimes in terms of a ball being thrown upwards and sometimes in terms of pushing cards up a hill, etc. The Norwegian work already mentioned used a version of one of Viennot's questions, modified for use with school students rather than undergraduates, and presented as in Figure 5.5. (p. 96).

The main point about this question is that, from the information given, the *direction* of the force from the spring in B, C and D is not known. Whatever the case, the forces are identical in these positions. The authors acknowledge that this is a difficult question even in its modified form. The interesting category of response is where students argue that the force of the spring is greater than the weight in B, less in C and equal in D. That is, the net force acts in the direction of the movement. In a further study,[16] the author's note that the direction need not necessarily be in a straight line. That is, if an object is seen to be set in motion in a curved path (inside a curved hollow tube, for instance) it will be predicted as continuing to travel in a curved path afterwards (when it emerges from the tube).

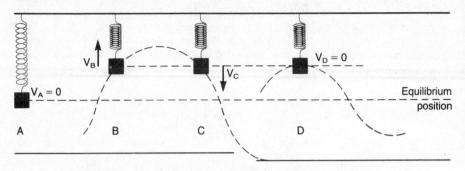

We then let the weight oscillate up and down around this
equilibrium position. Figure B shows the weight on the way upwards.
Figure C shows the weight on the way downwards shortly afterwards
in the same oscillation. (The dotted line indicates how the
position varies with time.)
Make a drawing of the forces acting on the weight in B.
Explain.
. . . . .
Make a drawing of the forces on the weight in C. Explain.
. . . . .
In Figure D the weight oscillates with a smaller amplitude. It
just reaches the same position as shown in B and C before it
returns downwards. (The dotted line indicates the movement.)
Make a drawing of the forces acting on the weight in D.
Explain.

Figure 5.5.

Similar views about the consequences of 'releasing' an object from
the constraints holding it in a circular path have been found by
Gardner[17] and Gunstone.[18] Their studies used the same paper-and-
pencil test with two groups of Australian school students—17-year-
old physics students who had completed a study of circular motion,
and 15-year-old general science students. Among the questions on the
test were a number which gave drawings of an object in circular
motion; questions which asked for labelled arrows to indicate the
forces acting on the object; questions which asked if the total force
was zero, or not zero and in the direction of motion, or not zero and
in some other direction; and finally questions which asked for an
explanation of their previous answers. The circular motion situations
were a tin attached by string to a peg in the centre of a smooth table,
a car travelling at constant speed around a circular curve, a passenger
in the car, and a moon of Jupiter. A force in the direction of motion
was often shown on the basis of 'force is needed because it is moving
in that direction', although this form of response was more common
with the 15-year-olds. The total force was frequently zero. This was

sometimes achieved by the use of centrifugal force by the 17-year-olds. However, centrifugal force was rarely mentioned by the younger students, their forces were often only tangential. One possible interpretation of these results is that the 15-year-olds tended to use our fifth intuitive rule (a force acts in the direction of motion) to explain the motions, while one of the consequences of the instruction which the 17-year-olds had received was to formalize previously vague notions about centrifugal force.

Warren[19] has asked a large number of English university entrants to draw an arrow showing the resultant force acting on a car travelling at constant speed around an arc of a circle. About 40 per cent of students indicated this resultant to be tangential and forwards, i.e. in the direction of motion. Equal numbers (about 28 per cent) showed the resultant to be radially inwards or radially outwards. Viennot[10] has argued that many university students treat circular motion as an example of an equilibrium situation, and this leads them to invent an outward (centrifugal) force to counterbalance the inward (centripetal) force.

The perceived relationship between direction of motion and direction of force which lies at the heart of our fifth intuitive rule can be seen in the results of studies which use computer simulations of motion.[20,21] In these simulations, for example, students have been asked to decide in what direction a force should be extended to change the direction of motion of an object by $90°$. The very common response is to apply a force in the direction in which the object should move, i.e. at $90°$ to the original motion. However, the use of these simulations has resulted in significant improvement in performance on questions exploring student understanding of force-motion relationships.

As a result of his studies, primarily with American physics undergraduate students, Clement[22] says:

> In conclusion, the data support the hypothesis that for the majority of these students, the 'motion implies a force' preconception was highly resistant to change. This conclusion applies to the extent that students could not solve basic problems of this kind where the direction of motion does not coincide with the direction of net force.

In contrast to what we have said here some students *do* include forces that are involved with non-movement. There are students who make a distinction between 'pulling forces' which seem to imply movement, and 'holding forces' which do not. Watts[3] has reported a similar distinction between what he called 'motive' forces and 'configurative' ones. Motive forces characterize those responses that students give where they see forces causing motion; configurative forces where they are seen as retaining objects in a particular set-up.

The five intuitive rules we have described above are not the only ones we could have extracted from the research reports. We could, for example, have explored what youngsters say about particular forces like friction or gravity in greater detail. Part of what they have said we have subsumed under the general term force, leaving a more specific analysis to other writers. Readers may be interested in another review of this area which McDermott[23] has produced.

In the next section we look at some of the classroom implications for what we have been saying.

Classroom implications

At the beginning of this chapter we suggested that much has been written about the nature of students' conceptions of force and motion. This comment could also be made about discussions of the classroom implications of these conceptions—a number of people have given ideas in this area.

(a) *Learners' heads are not empty vessels*
There appears to be uniform agreement about three issues among those who have written about the implications of this work. The first of these is central: the 'hydraulic model' of learning, which sees the transmission of knowledge from teacher to empty-headed student rather like water being poured from a jug into an empty glass, is clearly unreasonable. Students do have ideas about forces and motions before they enter science classrooms. It is arguable that this is true even in contexts where students may not be able to articulate a model. For example, consider a child who can ride a bike. It is clear the child does not have to learn from first principles when to peddle and when to brake on each occasion that the bicycle is ridden. The child has some view of the relationships between pushing peddles, applying brakes, and moving in various ways.

The second issue about which there is agreement in the literature concerns one important aspect of youngsters' views. While science places great emphasis on the need for theories and explanatory systems to apply to a wide variety of situations, young people do not. Youngsters do not seem to be too concerned if they have views we see as incompatible for different situations involving force and motion. It appears that parsimony of explanation is not an issue to them. Given this, it is not surprising that the third area of agreement is that it is very important to have learners articulate the views they hold about particular situations.

Arguments given to support the need for students to discuss and consider their own views vary in detail. However, in broad terms, there is consensus. Both pupils and teachers need to understand these views before any progress can be made towards changing views at odds with the tenets of physics.

Starting from these three broad areas—young people are not empty vessels, the views they hold may not be consistent across situations, articulating the views is an important first step—a number of other issues have been suggested in the literature. These are considered in points (b)-(h) below.

(b) *What seems to be conflict might not be conflict*

A careful analysis of the nature of students' views and the nature of the science to be taught may suggest that apparent conflict is only apparent. That is, the students' views and the scientists' views may not be in opposition to each other.

For example, consider normal reaction forces. It is common for students to begin formal physics learning with a view to force as being the result of dynamic, moving things (humans, or moving balls, and so on). Given this, it is not surprising that in an *apparently* static situation, such as a book lying on a table, many students do not really believe in the existence of a reaction force. Rather, the book does not fall because 'the table is rigid' or some similar logic. In this example, the reconciliation of the students' existing views of force with the physicists' logic of normal reaction must in part involve helping the students understand that the situation is not in fact a static one. In this way the origin of the reaction force can be shown in a way not inconsistent with the existing dynamic view of force. Minstrell has described a teaching sequence for the concept of normal reaction which is consistent without argument here.[13]

There may be some other areas of mechanics where a careful analysis of childrens' views and the science to be taught will show the same lack of real conflict.

We turn now to considering some possible approaches to those conceptual issues discussed earlier in this chapter where conflict does exist.

(c) *Conflict and discussion*

After having students elaborate their views, a number of writers have suggested the next step to be one of providing experiences which are aimed at challenging these views.[22,24,25] Given the evidence outlined earlier of students retaining pre-instruction views after completing a physics course, there is little doubt that an exposition by the teacher will *not* challenge the views. Rather it is discussion about and reflection on observations which seem to run counter to childrens' views which is needed. Without real opportunity to consider how to make sense of an apparently conflicting observation, the child may well just dismiss the conflict as an anomaly.[26]

It follows that discussion about observations needs to take place in an environment which supports the acceptance of a variety of views, and the scrutiny and challenge of the views. Minstrell, mentioned in (b) above, makes a strong point about the classroom atmosphere that is needed. One specific technique which has been used to foster discussion and challenge involves a debating format.[8] Students are asked to predict the outcome of some event, such as the relative times for two objects of different weight to fall the same distance. The two groups resulting from the predictions (equal times, heavier is faster) then attempt to convince each other. Clement[22] has pointed to Galileo's *Dialogues* as an example of teaching through the use of alternative viewpoints.

(d) *Intelligible, plausible, fruitful*

Hewson[27] has argued the need for conflict, such as that described in the previous section, to have particular characteristics. It is not enough that students become dissatisfied with the view they hold. If it is to be replaced by the 'new' view being presented by the teacher, that new view must be intelligible, plausible and fruitful. We will explain what Hewson means by applying his arguments to what we are writing here.

To make the ideas in this chapter intelligible we should write in a way which means you can understand what we are trying to say. However, this is only the first step. You may find that our ideas, although intelligible, do not accord with your views of physics classrooms; our ideas may not be plausible. (You may find the literature from a flat-earth society intelligible but not plausible.) Even if our ideas are plausible to you, this will not mean that you accept and use them. For this to happen, our ideas will have to seem to you to offer some more utility in your classrooms than opposing ways of thinking about teaching and learning. That is, our arguments will have to be fruitful to you.

In the same sense as this, Hewson argues that students must see new ideas as intelligible, plausible *and* fruitful before they will be wholly accepted.

(e) *Changing students' views takes time*

This is an obvious corollary to what we have already said. The views children bring to classrooms are firmly held. It takes time for children to understand their own views, to consider alternative views and to reconcile conflicts.[10,28] All the evidence presented earlier makes it clear that you are very unlikely to have students understanding basic mechanics if you give a five-minute exposition about the logic of Newton's First Law and then move on.

(f) *Learning about learning*

Having students elaborate their views (as suggested in (a) above) necessarily involves them in passing consideration of their own learning. One attempt to change students' views about mechanics has deliberately sought for them to consider more directly their own learning.[8] Part of the strategy used had students coming to understand that they had views, and that these views were at odds with physics. This understanding of their own learning was an important part of the acceptance of scientists' views about mechanics by the students.

The students in this study were trainee teachers, not school children. However, one of us who is currently teaching a year 7 (age 11 years) secondary school science class has tried to translate the learning-about-learning approach into that context. Each student in the year 7 class has, as well as the usual note book, an exercise book called the 'thinking book'. In this book students write about a number of different issues, all of which are presented to them as issues with no right or wrong answer. Among these are responses to questions, demonstrations, experiments, etc. with one or two broad aims. These questions concern either childrens' views of real world phenomena or children's views of how they (as individuals) learn. The 'thinking book' responses are sometimes used in whole class discussions about these two broad areas. This is an approach that is being explored in a number of teaching areas.[29]

(g) *Qualitative mechanics*

When the precise mathematical formulations of mechanics are the sole focus of teaching, rote-learning of formulae often replaces understanding of concepts. One obvious strategy to prevent this is to teach physics without numbers, at least in the early parts of a sequence of teaching. Qualitative approaches have been used in laboratory work[22,30] and problem solving[31] in mechanics. The laboratory work has focused on qualitative predictions and explanations, and used these as the basis of class discussion or debate between pairs of students. Qualitative problems similarly focus on concepts and the relationships between concepts.

(h) *Language in classrooms and text books*

Our understanding of youngsters' views of mechanics give a new dimension to this problem. For example, take the statement 'a force will cause a body to move'. No matter how much we might say that everyone knows what we really mean ('a net force will cause a body to change its motion'), the fact remains that many of our students will have a form of the Aristotelian conception of motion. 'A force will cause a body to move' will reinforce this conception. Even more common is the suggestion that we 'overcome interia'. Not only is this incorrect, it may well reinforce aspects of an impetus view of motion—where the scientist's concept of inertia and a notion of some sort of internal force acquired through movement are ofter intertwined.

The issue of language is difficult and complex. Students use language which is meaningful to students; teachers use language which is meaningful to teachers. There are a range of important teaching implications to be derived from an understanding of language and its role in learning. We merely wish to draw attention to one of these implications which arises from considering the intuitive rules used by students. Language which is meaningful to teachers may, because of students' views of the world, have a quite different (even conflicting) meaning for students. If we are not sensitive to this, we can unwittingly reinforce the very views we want to change.

In summary

The beliefs children bring to the learning of mechanics are firmly held and difficult to change. This difficulty is well illustrated by reports of successful physics students retaining common pre-instruction conceptions of the world.[15,22,32] Many writers have suggested that it is more difficult to change students beliefs in this area of introductory mechanics than in any other area of science.

The evidence of successful students retaining pre-instruction views points to the fact that expositions by the teacher will by themselves rarely change student beliefs.

We do not yet understand well to achieve such a goal, but one necessary step is to allow students time to understand their existing views. While the multitude of constraints operating in school compel teachers to think in terms of what can be taught in one period, youngsters require a much longer time to develop ideas. Students, in terms of learning, operate on a different time-scale to teachers.

Discussion of observations and interpretations of these observations is a most useful teaching approach. It allows students to verbalize their views, teachers to understand these views, students the opportunity to consider alternative interpretations, and, most importantly, students the time and context to reconsider their own interpretations. The advocacy of such an approach carries with it an assumption of reconsideration of the nature of the dynamics which should be taught at junior secondary school. All that has been written above implies that teaching students to use the formula $F=ma$ is inappropriate unless students have been helped to an acceptance of a Newtonian perspective. Hence, whatever time is available in the curriculum for physics topics, ought to be used first for considering the difficult and abstract concepts involved. Giving prime importance to the mathematical statements relating these concepts will only continue to hide the clear inconsistencies between the beliefs of students and the tenets of physics.

One obvious source of observations for discussion is practical work. But again, the perspective we are arguing suggests practical work of a different form. It is not experiments to 'verify' Newton's Second Law of Motion which fit this purpose, it is experiments which give rise to observations which challenge aspects of common pre-instruction views. Further, if it is interpretations of the real world we wish to challenge, then there is an argument for using real world materials rather than specialized laboratory apparatus. The exercise involving prediction about and observation of falling bodies described in Example 3 in the introduction to this chapter will be more fruitful in stimulating the form of discussion described there than will be the measurement of 'g' with ticker timers. White[33] has written about practical work from a different perspective but in a way quite consistent with what is argued here. He represents a strong case for the use of everyday objects, rather than laboratory equipment so as to help link school science with daily life.

Reports of attempts to use these forms of approach to change student views of force and motion make it clear that it is not an easy task. However, it is also true that such approaches have been considerably more successful than traditional modes of physics teaching in terms of helping students confront and change their pre-instruction views.

Although not writing from this particular perspective, Warren[19] has described well the most powerful teaching lesson to be derived from these studies:

> The idea of force is of very great importance in elementary science, engineering and mathematics. It is obviously very widely misunderstood, not only by students, but also by highly qualified, mature adults. It is very hard to assess how intrinsically difficult the idea is, since it has been made very much more difficult in practice by the almost incredible confusion of approach, which has continued unchecked by any action by any professional body. Paradoxically, if we were generally to recognise that it is difficult and were to teach it accordingly, the subject would become more easy.

References

[1]Piaget, J. (1929). *Children's Conceptions of the World*. Routledge and Kegan Paul: London.

[2]Piaget, J. (1970). *The Child's Conception of Movement and Speed*. Routledge and Kegan Paul: London.

[3]Watts, D. M. (1983). A study of alternative frameworks in school science. Unpublished PhD thesis, University of Surrey, Guildford.

[4]Osborne, R. J. (1980). Force. Learning in Science Project, Working paper No. 16, University of Waikato, Hamilton.

[5]Watts, D. M. (1983). A study of schoolchildrens' alternative frameworks of the concept of force. *European Journal of Science Education* 5 (2), 217-30.

[6]Watts, D. M. and Zylbersztajn, A. (1981). A survey of some childrens' ideas about force. *Physics Education* 15, 360-5.

[7]Sjøberg, D. and Lie, S. (1981). Ideas about force and movement among Norwegian pupils and students (mimeograph). Centre for School Science, University of Oslo, Oslo.

[8]Champagne, A. D., Gunstone, R. F. and Klopfer, L. E. (1985). Effecting changes in cognitive structures among physics students. In *Cognitive Structure and Conceptual Change* (Eds L. H. T. West and A. L. Pines), Academic Press: New York and London.

[9]Peters, P. C. (1982). Even honours graduates have conceptual difficulties with physics. *American Journal of Physics* 50 (6), 501-8.

[10]Viennot, L. (1979). Spontaneous learning in elementary dynamics. *European Journal of Science Education* 1 (2), 205-21.

[11]Langford, J. M. and Zollman, D. (1982). Conceptions of dynamics held by elementary and high school students. Paper presented at the annual meeting of the American Association of Physics Teachers, San Francisco.

[12]Helm, H. (1981). Conceptual misunderstandings in physics. In *Perspective 3*. School of Education, University of Exeter, Exeter.

[13]Minstrell, J. (1982). Explaining the "at rest" condition of an object. *The Physics Teacher* 20, 10-4.

[14]Driver, R. (1983). *The Pupil as Scientist?* Open University Press: Milton Keynes.

[15]Gunstone, R. F. and White, R. T. (1981). Understanding of gravity. *Science Education* 65, 291-9.

[16]McCloskey, M., Carmazza, A. and Green, B. (1980). Curvilinear motion in the absence of external forces: naive beliefs about motion of objects. *Science* 210, 1139-41.

[17]Gardner, P. L. (1984). Circular motion: some post-instructional alternative frameworks. *Research in Science Education* 14, 136-145.

[18]Gunstone, R. F. (1984). Circular motion: some pre-instructional alternative frameworks. *Research in Science Education* 14, 125-135.

[19]Warren, J. W. (1979). *Understanding Force*. John Murray: London.

[20]Di Sessa, A. (1982). Unlearning Aristotelian physics: A study of knowledge-based learning. *Cognitive Science* 6, 37-75.

[21]White, B. (1983). Sources of difficulty in understanding Newton dynamics. *Cognitive Science* 7, 41-65.

[22]Clement, J. (1982). Students' preconceptions in introductory mechanics. *American Journal of Physics* 50, 66-71.

[23]McDermott, L. C. (1984). Research in conceptual understanding of mechanics. *Physics Today* 37, 23-32.

[24]Osborne, R. J., Bell, B. F. and Gilbert, J. K. (1983). Science teaching and childrens' views of the world. *European Journal of Science Education* 5, 1-14.

[25]Posner, G. J., Strike, K. A., Hewson, P. W. and Gertzog, W. A. (1982). Accommodation of a scientific conception: toward a theory of conceptual change. *Science Education* 66, 211-27.

[26]Rowell, J. A. and Dawson, C. J. (1983). Laboratory counterexamples and the growth of understanding in science. *European Journal of Science Education* 5, 203-15.

[27]Hewson, P. W. (1981). A conceptual change approach to learning science. *European Journal of Science Education* 3, 383-96.

[28]Gunstone, R. F., Champagne, A. B. and Klopfer, L. E. (1981). Instructions for understanding: A case study. *Australian Science Teachers Journal* 27 (3), 27-32.

[29]D'Arcy, P. (1983). Writing: A voyage of discovery starting from the inside moving out. *Learning about Learning Booklet* No. 13, Trowbridge, Wiltshire.

[30]Trowbridge, D. E. and McDermott, L. C. (1981). Investigation of student understanding of the concept of acceleration in one dimension. *American Journal of Physics* 49, 242-53.

[31]Champagne, A. B., Klopfer, L. E. and Gunstone, R. F. (1982). Cognitive research and the design of science instruction. *Educational Psychologist* 17, 31-53.

[32]Champagne, A. B., Klopfer, L. E. and Anderson, J. H. (1980). Factors influencing the learning of classical mechanics. *American Journal of Physics* 48, 1074-9.

[33]White, R. T. (1979). Relevance of practical work to comprehension of physics. *Physics Education* 14, 384-7.

CHAPTER 6

The Gaseous State

Marie Geneviève Séré

This chapter studies children's conceptions about matter in the gaseous state. Air is all around us and is an intimate part of our everyday environment, yet, as it is invisible, its properties are taken for granted and rarely appreciated or consciously considered by children before they study them in school.

Children are very familiar, however, with the word 'aire'.* It is even part of the vocabulary of very young children who use it to 'explain' very different observations, as Jean Piaget described in his book *The Child's Conception of the World*.[2] The word 'gas', on the other hand, is less known and less used by children. When they use it it means the kind of gas used in lighters, stoves and other sources of heat.

This chapter will focus on the properties children do attribute to gases. We present some results from children starting from the age of about 11, an age when they can start reasoning in more abstract ways. The results concern different gases: air of course, but also other invisible gases and coloured gases, because it appears that children do not generalize the knowledge that they acquire in a particular case.

In order to understand and interpret even simple experiments on gases, pupils must use fundamental physical dimensions such as quantity, volume, mass, pressure and temperature, to describe the state of a gas. We are going to indicate how children picture these dimensions prior to teaching. We shall also point out obstacles and difficulties they encounter when being taught.

---

*Romance languages, more than English, use 'aire' to mean breeze. The *Concise Oxford Dictionary* gives 'airless' as 'stuffy, breezeless, still'.

In this chapter, we will be considering the following:

(1)   images that children associate with air;
(2)   some qualities attributed by children to air and gas;
(3)   interpretations given by children of forces exerted by gases, especially the directions in which gas pressure acts; and
(4)   variations in magnitude of pressure acknowledged by children.

In documenting children's ideas we shall make use of our studies involving French children aged 11-13 years.[3] We shall also draw on the results of an interview study with English school children aged 12-16 about their ideas on pressure and atmospheric pressure.[1]

Images that children associate with air

To understand children's ideas about air before teaching, it is interesting to refer to the works of Jean Piaget who carried out interviews with children from the age of four.[2] Young children spontaneously use air in their explanations of thought, dreaming and memory, associating them with a circulation of air or of smoke (it appears that the word 'gas' has not been used by any of the children quoted by Jean Piaget).* For example:

Interviewer: How do dreams come?
A child, 6½ years: Because there is some wind.
I: Where does it come from, this wind?
C: From outside

Interviewer: What is spirit?
A child, 8 years: It's somebody who is not like us, who has no skin, no bones, who is like air, who cannot be seen.

Interviewer: What is spirit?
A child, 11½ years: It is air.
I: Why do you think it's air?
C: Because it cannot be touched.

A child, 7½ years: Thinking comes with air and smoke. ... Thinking attracts the wind and the smoke and all that gets mixed.

These sentences are not very precise, obviously, but give an idea of the way children use air in their explanations. For them, air is something which exists but cannot be seen or touched, something which circulates, gets in and out of places where matter is unable to go, something which makes things happen without itself being perceived.

---

*It's not actually surprising that children associate thought and air. Historically, it has been the same. Even in the seventeenth century, Descartes stated that the orders of the brain followed a sort of pneumatic circuit in the body, and that thought was transmitted through air circulation.

Our studies show that by about the age of 11, children know quite well where there is air.[4] In a simple question 'Is there any air in this open container?', 83 per cent of 11 to 12-year-old children gave the correct response. A slightly smaller percentage said there was air in a closed container.

In the case of more complex situations, as for instance a flat tyre, fewer children gave the expected answer. (Most children think that, since the air has been heard flowing out, all of the air has gone!) An important point to note is that for all these questions about motionless air, pupils' answers make reference to moving air. For instance:

There is some air in this open bottle, because air can *come in*.

There is no air in this open bottle, because air can always *go out*.

We also observed a child, during a teaching sequence, who in order to get a container full of air, suggested she would go to the playground and run holding the container facing the wind. Another girl thought that air did not exist when it was motionless, when she said that there was no air in a syringe, but that she could 'make some air' by moving the piston up and down. The presence of air was then obvious to her as she could hear it.

This association children make between air and movement also has implications for their understanding of heat. Most children are very good at describing the movements inside a large body of air,[8] for example when a window is opened to ventilate a room, or when there is a source of heat in the room. They are not surprised therefore that air is able to transport heat as the idea of convection relates well with the images of movement they have in mind. Indeed, some of them initially confuse air and heat, though it appears that this confusion is resolved with teaching.

They also imagine that air expands because, to them, air is everywhere, permeating everything, edging into the smallest corners, passing through any hole, always 'sticking' to the sides of a container. Their knowledge of the diffusion of two gases is more limited, however. Among a sample of 20 children of about 12 years old, more than half thought that two gases closed in a large container (in the question, the size of the container was that of a cupboard) don't mix. They said that they mix only at the boundary between the two gases. One of them suggested that the mixing was like a 'gradual range of colours'.

For children movement is also associated with living things. If they think of air in terms of movement do they also attribute other characteristics of living things to it? Some younger children do tend to talk as though air has feeling and volition.[7] For instance, they say that it is 'active only if it is disturbed, or annoyed'; air gets 'tired of pushing, and stops pushing'. All these statements reflect an elementary, animistic type of reasoning. We observed that this reasoning mostly disappears as the teaching proceeds. When older children say for instance that 'air tries to..., wants to...' it seems to be only a way

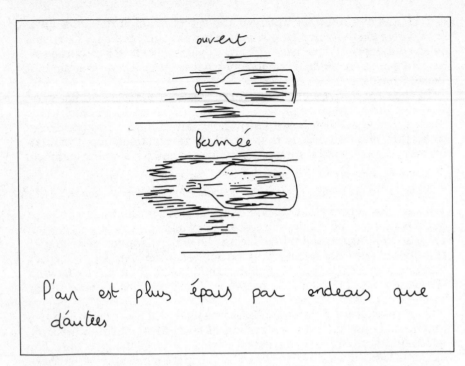

Figure 6.1:   A drawing made by an 11-year-old to describe the air in an open and in a closed bottle.

of speaking, which is also used by adults, and does not reflect an animistic view of air.

Even though it cannot be perceived we found that children did describe air, and when we compressed or expanded air in a container they attempted to describe the state of the pressure of the air. 'Normal air' (that is to say atmospheric air) they said was thin, not thick, or not as thick in every place (see Figure 6.1), flowing, or relaxed. Compressed air they described as being piled up, heaped up, shrivelled, shrunken, contracted, stuck, tight. Expanded air, they said, was normal, at ease, relaxed, enlarged, expanded or stretched.

Some properties of matter attributed by children to air and gas

We have just seen that in the mind of children air in motion is a reality. But what do they think of motionless air? Do they think of this as matter? To understand that air is actually matter, it is not sufficient to be able to recognize where it is present. It is important to know that it remains unchanged and that its quantity and mass are conserved in all the transformations it undergoes. We shall see further that this notion of conservation is essential in understanding other properties of gases. It is of interest, therefore, to know to what extent children acknowledge the fact that for gases, quantity and mass are preserved in the course of simple transformations.

The idea that air or a gas has a mass is not obvious to children. Indeed, some of them think that 'the more air there is, the lighter it is' when considering, for example, an inflated football or a floating object. The idea that air has mass is, however, a concept that children acquire easily. French children aged about 13, who were taught the idea, nearly all remembered it and were able to use it again after several months.

The idea that a coloured gas has a mass is less of a problem. Children seem to make this deduction from their observations. Certainly a coloured gas has more the appearance of matter than air.

We have presented a number of written tasks to children before and after teaching the topic of air, and have studied their ideas during the teaching sequence. The particular aspects which were focused on in the tasks included:

(1) moving bodies of air from place to place;
(2) variation in volume of air in a closed container at room temperature; and
(3) variation in temperature.

Moving bodies of air from place to place[4]

From the way children describe air, it is not surprising to note how difficult it seems to them to trap and, consequently, to transport air.

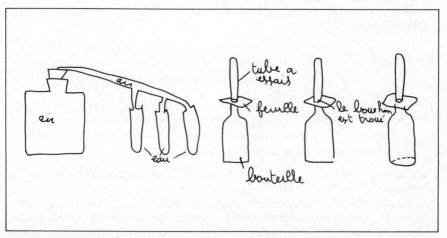

Figure 6.2: Two children's solutions to the problems of how to move air from one container to three other containers.

More than half the children, prior to teaching, believe this is impossible. When they carry out experiments, some of them soon understand
that in order to isolate, catch and transport air, they have to enclose
it. This is a very important development because children are now able
to think about quantities of air, measure them and study their
properties.

We have noticed that students who realize how important it is to
enclose air to keep it unchanged are more successful than others in
solving problems involving decantation. Figure 6.2 shows the solution
given by two students to the problem of how to decant air from one
container into three other containers.

Variation in volume of a closed container at room temperature[4]

We explored children's thinking about this by presenting them with
a syringe. We blocked the nozzle of the syringe, then we changed the
position of the piston and asked them whether the amount of air was
more, less or the same as in the previous position. Though the question is very simple, before teaching, only half of the children said that
the amount of air would remain the same; however, more of them gave
this answer if they were allowed to feel the sensation it produced on
their hands, or to observe a syringe full of coloured gas.

This further perceptual information seemed important in helping
children towards the view that quantity does not change in spite of
change in volume, although the particular aspect which convinced
each varied. It could be the resistance they felt on their hand when
holding the piston, the sensation on their finger as they closed the
syringe, or the colour of the gas which varied in appearance.

Those who gave correct answers tended to suggest either of the
following reasons:

(1) nothing gets in, nothing gets out. This is similar to the 'idea of
    identity' which Jean Piaget identified in children's reasoning
    about, for example, the conservation of a quantity of a liquid
    when it is decanted.
(2) If the piston is allowed to move backwards, it will come back
    to its original place again. This notion of 'reversibility', again
    identified by Jean Piaget in children's reasoning, was used less
    than the identity idea in this case.

Those who said that the quantity of air is not conserved tended to
confuse volume with quantity.

We suggest that the notion of conservation when volume changes
is an idea which is easily understood by 11 or 12-year-old children, as
long as their attention is specially focused on this point; maturation
alone does not appear to be sufficient for this idea to develop, it is
important to help it by appropriate teaching.

Variation in temperature[8]

Do children understand that the temperature of air, a gas or a vacuum can change? This idea of temperature is not a simple one. As other chapters in this book have shown, ambient temperature is a sort of reference in evaluating temperatures. But this temperature is actually that of ambient air. It is, therefore, interesting to find out how children realize that air is characterized by a temperature.

Before teaching, about one-third of the children aged 11-12 considered that *air cannot be heated*. A greater number, about two-thirds, considered that *gas cannot be heated*. Children aged 12 when individually questioned on this point gave two sorts of answers. For some of them, heated air is transformed into 'something else', carbon dioxide or a gas, for example. The majority did consider that air becomes 'hotter' than before without its nature being changed. However, they did not appreciate the range of temperature: $60°C$ for instance, seems to them a very high temperature, capable of causing burns. Teaching on this particular point does appear to influence children's ideas. The act of carrying out and commenting on activities in which air is heated seems sufficient to allow most children to believe firmly that air can have different temperatures.

Nearly all of the children acknowledge that the reading of a thermometer in an *empty container* (a vacuum) would not change, even if the enclosure is heated. Phillipe suggests, for example that:

> it will hardly show $10°$... even less... $0°$ if it does not touch the inner sides.

Another aspect of children's ideas which was explored was the question of whether there is more, less or as much air when it is heated? We explored this by asking if the mass of air in a *closed container* increases when heated. The question (shown in Figure 6.3) looks simple, and so it is to pupils who have never learnt anything before on this point.*

Before teaching, two-thirds of the children gave a correct answer, using the idea of identity mentioned above: mass does not change because 'nothing gets in, nothing gets out'. But children who have studied the variations of temperature of air (as we usually do in France at that age) tend to consider other factors. Less than half of them gave a correct answer, those who did still frequently used the idea of identity. However, others used the following kinds of ideas:

(1) Heated air is lighter than cold air. They infer from this statement that the quantity of air is lighter when it is heated.

---

*The answer to this question is not so obvious for a physicist who takes into account Archimedes law about the buoyancy force! We suppose that the correct answer for a child is that the mass of the jar is constant, and we mainly analyse the explanations of the children.

Nicole brings scales and a CLOSED jar which contains air only, into the garden. She puts the jar on the scales, the needle of which can move even for very small masses. She observes the position of the needle:

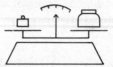

Nicole comes back after leaving this equipment in the sun for several hours. She observes the position of the needle.
Choose the drawing which shows the position of the needle.

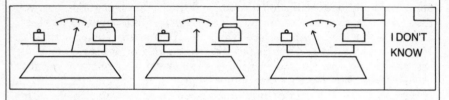

I DON'T KNOW

Explain your answer:

Figure 6.3: A written test question concerning conservation of air, asked before and after teaching.

(2) When the container is heated, pressure rises. 'It piles up air, more air is produced.' The consequences of this confusion will be referred to later in this chapter when we discuss ideas about pressure.

(3) 'There is more air because it expands.' We find this confusion of volume with quantity of air in the following remarks made by a student who explains the experiment shown in Figure 6.4.

P: Air is heavier... hot air makes a push of air.
I: Where does this air come from?
P: Heat is somehow the cause. By heating it, we have made it shrink a little allowing new air to be produced and grow. That's it?

If the same question is asked about an open container (which, when it is heated, contains a smaller quantity of air and has a smaller mass), correct answers are still less numerous, whether before or after teaching, because of the same difficulties. In the case of the open container, a further difficulty was identified: some pupils believed that the hot air which leaks out leaves a gap. Either this gap is immediately filled with the ambient cold air (they therefore believe that the

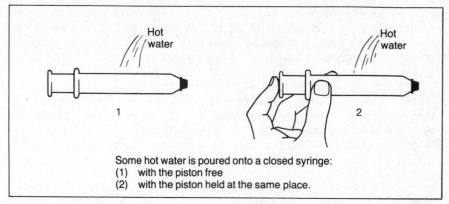

Some hot water is poured onto a closed syringe:
(1)   with the piston free
(2)   with the piston held at the same place.

Figure 6.4:   One of the activities carried out and discussed during the individual interviews.

quantity of air is constant), or this gap remains empty and there is a vacuum in the container. Children who give correct answers explain:

> Hot air goes up and gets out of the container.
> Air always gets mixed with the vacuum.

The consequence of all these difficulties is that to a certain number of children air is not the same everywhere, either in a container or in a room. A vacuum surrounds the source of heat when it is hot enough (this does not happen around a weak source of heat such as the human body), or the air is inhomogeneous, gathering towards the top of the container or in the most remote zones from the point where the heat is produced.

From these observations, we can conclude that children aged 11-12 experience various difficulties in understanding that a quantity of air and its mass are preserved when it undergoes transformations. They seem to be able to understand that the quantity of air is conserved when it undergoes transformations at constant temperature; however, they have difficulties in conceptualizing what happens when its temperature changes. It is important to give careful attention to these transformations when teaching because the conservation of quantity of air is an essential basis for quantitative thinking about amounts of air.

Interpretations given by children about forces exerted by gases

When do gases exert a force?

We know that a gas has the property of exerting forces on what it is in contact with, such as sides of containers, surfaces of liquids, and so on. These forces are always perpendicular to the surfaces and directed from the gas to the surface. That is the reason why it is sometimes said that 'air exerts a pressure' instead of 'air exerts forces', though pressure is never a vector. It is a scalar quantity which, together with the temperature, determines the state of equilibrium of the gas.

There are a lot of simple experiments and everyday experiences which, from a scientific point of view, demonstrate that gases exert forces whatever their state of pressure. Children, however, have other interpretations of these same experiences and do not always make the inferences that we would like them to. There seem to be three principal difficulties involved:[3]

(1)   For many children, gases exert forces only when they are set in motion. For instance, we interviewed 17 children aged 12-13 about what they felt when a sphygmometer was applied to their arm. As long as the armband was being blown up, they said that the air was pushing, exerting or producing a pressure. The flow of air was then stopped and the armband was left inflated. The 17 children, without an exception, denied that air was going on pressing, pushing, etc. even though the armband was obviously compressing their arm.

The same kind of thinking has emerged in talking to children about drinking orange juice through a straw. As one child said: 'Air *only* presses down on the surface *when* you suck.'*

All these children view forces exerted by gases in a dynamic way: there actually is a force only when air is moving itself or sets an object in motion.

Even when children appreciate that gases in equilibrium exert forces, they still try to establish a link between force and motion. Some of them use the idea that air is in perpetual motion (they may then not be far from understanding that gases are constituted of particles in motion). For others, the notion is merely imaginary. They suggest, for example, that the 'push' of the air does not all happen at once, that there is always a little air which moves after the 'push', like drops of water which fall after you have poured out a glass of water.

This result has important implications for teaching, for it shows that children only consider something happening during phases of motion. For them 'nothing happens' or air 'does nothing' in phases of equilibrium. The teacher, on the other hand, when teaching ideas about atmospheric pressure, is particularly concerned with phases of equilibrium.

(2)   For many children, gases exert a force only if they undergo a force, a push, or if they are heated. This means that, for children, an external cause is necessary for gas to exert forces.

---

*All the examples of this part concern air. We verified that the reactions of children are very similar when they are shown experiments with coloured gas.

When temperature does not change, they interpret experiments in terms of the transmission of movement through the gas, rather than using the idea of force. For instance, a child was commenting on an experiment in which two syringes were joined by a flexible tube and the movement of one of the pistons was immediately followed by the movement of the other, saying:

> If you push on this piston, the air that's there goes through the tube and pushes the other piston. ... Air edges to the second syringe and pushes the second piston.

If the air temperature is varied, children will also say that it is this change which causes the effect. For example, in talking about what happens when a test-tube is heated at the bottom (see Figure 6.5), a pupil said, 'hot air will push the air which is in the upper part... usually air doesn't push'.

(3)   For many children, gases exert forces in one direction only.

No change of temperature.   For many children, when there is no motion, there is no force, and when there is motion, they transfer the characteristics of this motion to the push, the thrust or the force. Thus, they tend to attribute unique direction to this force, that of the motion. For instance, for most of these children, air in a container does not exert any force against the inner sides. As a 12-year-old said: 'The air pushes only if it has a chance to succeed!' Another 12-year-old said that air pushes on the covering membrane but 'just a little bit' on the inner sides.

If there is a change of temperature.   In these cases, pupils tended to suggest that force or pressure would act only in one direction, usually the vertical direction. Many of them initially interpreted the experiments showing the expansion of air as a push upwards. However, it seems that the study of expansion helps the pupils to weaken the link

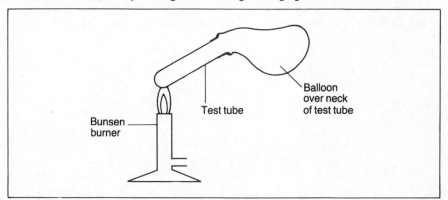

Figure 6.5:   An activity on the expansion of air carried out and discussed during the individual interviews.

in their thinking between force and motion, and to understand that gases can exert forces even though no motion intervenes as a cause.

All these results suggest that children can interpret situations involving the compression of gases rather well but have more difficulty interpreting phenomena involving atmospheric air or where a body of gas is expanded. In the next section we will outline children's interpretations of tasks which were designed to elicit their thinking about the action of compressed air and atmospheric air.

Compressed air

When air is compressed, it frequently happens that the movement and the resultant force go in the *same direction*. This happens in the case of the syringe, where the movement of the piston, the pressing force which operates on the finger blocking the nozzle, and the flow of air which occurs if the finger is removed, are all going the same way. Children, therefore, easily interpret these experiments, saying that there is a force (unique in their minds) or a push, or a pressure exerted by air. What is difficult for them is to recognize that this force, or push, or pressure still exists at the end of the experiment, when the state of equilibrium is reached.

But there are some cases in which the compression in a direction results in observable forces in *different directions*. How do the children recognize these forces? Some of them are not sure that they exist, and some of them acknowledge them but believe they are rather small in the directions different from that of the movement.

This was investigated using the 'problem of the ladybirds'. Children were shown the apparatus in Figure 6.6 and were asked: 'How can you send "sleeping gas" to both ladybirds at the same time?' Initially a small hole in the side of the syringe was hidden from view to find out whether the children could think of making one—if not, the interviewer pointed it out. The results of this task indicated that the ma-

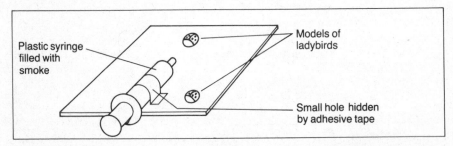

Figure 6.6:   Apparatus given to children to solve the problem: 'How can you send "sleeping gas" to both ladybirds at the same time?'

jority of pupils considered that the gas would come out mostly at the tip of the syringe. As one of them said: 'it goes past the hole (indicating the hole in the side) and through this hole'.

That children are unlikely to consider that a force acting in one direction on a body of gas can result in action in different directions has been reported also in the case of pressure in liquids.

In an interview with 84 English pupils aged 12-15, the pupils were asked to consider how the pressure on a fish in a tank of water varied with both depth and direction.[9] The majority of pupils (just over 50 per cent of those aged 12 and over 75 per cent aged 16) appreciated that the water exerted a pressure on the fish and that this increased with increase in depth. When asked to comment on the magnitude of the pressure acting horizontally on the nose of the fish, only a minority of pupils (about 10 per cent of those aged 12 rising to about 30 per cent aged 16) suggested that the magnitude of the pressure would be the same in all directions. Most of the pupils suggested that the pressure acting downwards would be greater than that acting horizontally. In comparing the pressure on the back of the fish with that on its nose one pupil said:

> Oh well, obviously the pressure on his back would (be bigger) because there would be no pressure whatsoever on his nose almost, because he wasn't moving to cause any water disturbance.

Here, the action of the water due to its weight is considered as acting in one direction only, the vertical direction. Pressure in the horizontal direction is considered to exist only when the fish is moving.

Atmospheric air[1]

In situations which involve the effects of atmospheric pressure, we often face equilibrium situations and it is difficult for children to recognize the existence of forces. That is the reason why in teaching experiments we aim at producing a difference in pressure in order to produce an observable effect. But how do children interpret such experiments?

To give an indication of this, we report on a study involving English secondary school pupils aged 12-16.[9] The pupils were presented with the four situations shown in Figure 6.7. Their answers to the questions about each task were probed carefully to find out how they were thinking and the different types of reasons given were categorized. It was found that similar types of reasoning were used in response to the different tasks and these are described below.

(1) *The atmospheric exerts a pressure which is observable only when there is a pressure difference*

In response to the question on 'washing-up', a student commented:

> And the soap would seal the bottom of the cups so no air could get in

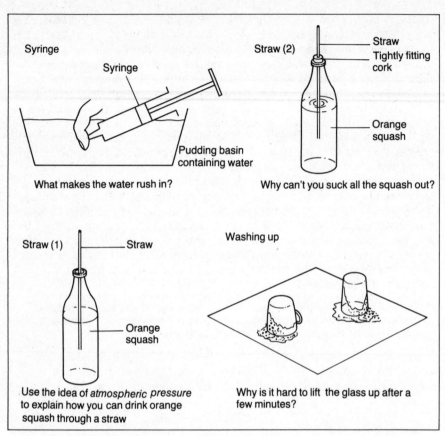

Figure 6.7: Some situations involving atmospheric pressure used in written test questions.

from the outside, so it would be hard to get the cups off, because there was a higher atmospheric pressure outside than inside.

This type of response which refers to the pressure of the air inside and outside the vessel, was used by only a small minority of pupils (about 10 per cent at age 12 increasing to about 20 per cent at age 16).

(2)   *The atmosphere exerts a pressure on surfaces*
In this type of response, pupils mention the pressure of the atmosphere pushing on surfaces but do not refer to pressure differences. For example, in response to the syringe question a pupil stated:

Well the water tries to fill the vacuum up... because there's air pressure here (on the surface of the water) and it pushes the water up into the syringe.

This type of reason showed no clear trends with age. It was used most frequently in response to the question about the straw (by about 25 per cent of the pupils of all ages).

The majority of pupils gave their answers to the questions in terms of what was happening *inside* the vessels without making any reference to atmospheric pressure *per se*. Three main types of reasoning were identified.

(3) *Vacuums suck or exert pressure*
In many cases, pupils explained their answers in terms of a vacuum or suction actively pulling. For instance, in response to the syringe question a pupil stated:

> There's nothing there... the vacuum pulls it up.

Or in response to the straw question:

> You suck on a straw and it creates a vacuum inside the straw and the orange squash is pulled up through the straw... (by) the vacuum.

Such responses indicate that these pupils do not appreciate that a vacuum, either total or partial, has no power by itself.

(4) *Spaces must be filled*
Another type of reasoning was used which also referred to vacuums. In this case, the pupils used the argument that 'nature abhors a vacuum'. For instance, in response to the straw question, a student said:

> A vacuum created in the straw. Something has to go in to fill the vacuum up.

(5) *Pressure of air inside sucks or pulls (dynamic view of air)*
An interesting type of response to some of the tasks given by up to a third of the pupils, referred to air inside the vessels actively sucking or pulling. In answer to the syringe questions, pupils said:

> Air's like pulling it up...
> The air in the syringe is wanting to suck water up.

Or in response to the question on washing up:

> The air inside the cup is sucking on to the surface—like stopping the cup being picked up... because the air is trapped under the cup.

Overall, about half of the pupils interpreted the tasks in terms of what was happening *inside* the vessels, either through the action of vacuums or of air actively sucking. This proportion did not decrease significantly with age.

In general, the results of this investigation show that children tend to interpret such situations in terms of a single agent, cause or force: a single push in the direction of motion producing the observable effect. In fact, their attention is mostly drawn to the motions and they tend to think of gases more in terms of their ability to transmit motion than to exert forces. The study also indicates the difficulty that pupils have in taking account of more than one interacting system (to see, for example, the water entering the syringe as the result of what is both inside and outside the syringe). Instead, they tend to focus on a single agent, whether it is the pressure of the air on the outside, the air on the inside sucking or the vacuum sucking.

Variations in pressure acknowledged by children

It is obvious that the word 'pressure' is complex and practically unknown in children before they have the opportunity in school to carry out experiments about gases. Therefore, the results given show what French students in the classes observe, select and take into account from these experiments, and how they organize their observations and knowledge in order to form a concept of pressure.

How children describe air at different pressures[6,7]

During individual interviews, even before talking with children about pressure, we asked them whether they could see a *difference* between two quantities of gas whose pressures were different.

When these differences of pressure are caused by differences in temperature, students only note that: 'It's hotter... it's cold.' When the differences of pressure are due to such properties as change of volume, for example, most of the children indicate that there is something different. We saw in the first part of this chapter the different properties that they use to describe air or gas. They sometimes say that in a hard, blown-up tyre, for example, that air is strong or powerful. We noticed also that it is mainly the students who succeed in giving correct explanations who use these terms. Before teaching, two-thirds of the students did not attribute the concept of pressure to the notion of air. For them, either there is no difference, or it is dirty, it smells bad, etc. However, after teaching, all the children are able to use the notion of 'piled up'.

When depressed air is in question, fewer children can notice a difference. The fact that air fills a larger volume than usual seems rather 'normal' to them.

We also asked some questions about *pressure*, and in so doing, asked pupils to make two sorts of comparison:

(1) comparing before and after a transformation;
(2) comparing inside and outside a container at the same time in an experiment

Without going into the details of the results, it can be noticed that:

(1) Comparisons inside/outside and after/before pose quite different problems to students. Results are generally very different. So it can be said that children treat these problems quite differently.
(2) Pressures larger than atmospheric pressure or increases in pressure always give better results than equalities of pressure or decreasing pressure.
(3) It also happens that students discern differences of pressure where there are none. Therefore, for the youngest students, the mere fact of corking or uncorking a bottle changes the pressure (Figure 6.1)

When you close the bottle, air is no longer free to move.

It's like a prisoner. So the pressure decreases.

From a pedagogical point of view, it is important to explain to students the identity of pressure, as a preliminary to the study of variations of pressure. Results are far better every time there is a concomitant variation: e.g. when the pressure increases in proportion to quantity (e.g. when a ball is inflated) or when the pressure increases according to temperature (as in the case of a tyre left in the sun).

How students form the notion of pressure[6,7]

The simplest problem for pupils seems to be the transformations at constant temperature. We shall discuss the cases of constant temperature and variable temperature separately.

Transformation at constant temperature

In deciding whether pressure of a gas varies, children use images of phenomena; they think about the quantities of gas concerned and they consider the forces involved.

Images. The notion of 'piled up' (or 'heaped up', 'tight', etc.) appears to be very useful. Of course, more tend to give an answer in terms of 'piling up' than using the term 'pressure'.

Evaluation of quantities of gas. It appears that many children base their evaluation of pressure on the quantity of gas observed. In the course of individual interviews, particularly, we saw children tending to relate pressure and density (without either pronouncing the word or having a clear idea of this notion!). For example, a student speaking about a syringe whose piston had been pulled said:

The air inside there is at very low pressure because you have sealed the container up and then expanded the volume. There was the same amount of air in a much increased volume.

Evaluation of pressure based on quantity is also made by certain children who consider that to each volume there corresponds a quantity of air which appears 'normal' to them.

> Air takes a certain amount of space, not more, not less. Here, there is too much air. There is pressure.

Evaluation of actions exerted by air. The physicist makes use of pressing forces in order to evaluate pressure. Do children do the same? In fact, many children do, since experiments aim at demonstrating the effects of forces so that they can infer the value of pressure. We saw in the previous section some 'traps' children meet when the balance between forces is disturbed.

Transformations at variable temperature

In this case, the number of dimensions necessary to interpret experiments increases. Even having a real knowledge about gas, children around 13 years old fail to integrate all these parameters. Their answers mostly depend upon the observations they select from experiments: and depending on which quantities they pay attention to they give different results.

Pupils' ideas about the effect of change in temperature on a body of gas were explored using the apparatus shown in Figure 6.8. In many cases, pupils suggested the pressure in the vessel would decrease as the volume decreases. For example, a 14-year-old said:

> Air is more contracted because it has been cooled. ... Pressure increases because there is less volume while the mass is constant.

When the same vessel was heated instead of being cooled, a pupil then argued in terms of 'pushes' instead of volume:

> The air in the tube tries to go out, it pushes on the balloon, it is stronger than the exterior air. Its pressure is bigger.

Reasoning based on volume contradicts that based on 'pushes' and in some cases students recognize this:

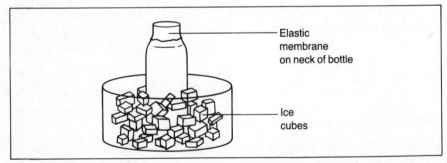

Figure 6.8: Apparatus used to investigate pupils' ideas about the effects of changing the temperature of a fixed quantity of air.

When air gets contracted, pressure is *higher* inside. I wonder... I don't know. ... Because, else... it must be *lower*, because, else, the membrane would not have been lowered. ... So I don't know if it is higher or lower!

Resolving this contradiction involved distinguishing between the phases of equilibrium and the transient period of disequilibrium and recognizing that at equilibrium the pressure inside and outside would be the same. Very few students succeeded in thinking about the situation in this way.

Some implications for teaching about air and air pressure

It appears that the status of movement and equilibrium are different. They are for the physicist, since different theories have been built to describe these two phases of experimental situations. They are also different for children. Children take little interest in equilibrium, yet readily suggest ideas to explain how and why air is set in movement or produces movement. So it could be fruitful to first study air in movement and the forces it exerts, then study motionless air, its characteristic parameters and the forces it exerts as well. That could help to differentiate forces (causes of the tendency to equilibrium) and pressure (a parameter characteristic of equilibrium).

On the other hand, children have to reason less in terms of properties of one quantity of air, and more in terms of interactions between two or several systems. It could be useful, therefore, to teach them that comparisons with 'outside' are necessary to interpret what happens 'inside' a container.

References

[1]Engel, M. E. (1981). The development of understanding of selected aspects of pressure, heat and evolution in pupils aged between 12 and 16 years. Unpublished, PhD thesis, University of Leeds, Leeds.

[2]Piaget, J. (1929). *The Child's Conception of the World*. Routledge and Kegan Paul: London.

[3]Séré, M. G. (1982) A study of some frameworks of the field of mechanics, used by children (aged 11 to 13) when they interpret experiments about air pressure. *European Journal of Science Education* 4 (3), 299–309.

[4]Séré, M. G. (1986). Children's conceptions of the gaseous state, prior to teaching. *European Journal of Science Education. (1986) 8*, (4) 413–425.

[5]Séré, M. G. (1980). Apprentissage, en situation de classe, de la notion de pression de l'air en sixième et cinquième. Secondes journées sur l'éducation scientifique. Chamonix. France.

[6]Séré, M. G. and Chomat, A. (1983). Analyse de l'influence d'activités de classe sur les représentations des élèves. Exemple: l'enseignement de la pression atmosphérique en sixième. Cinquièmes journées sur l'éducation scientifique. Chamonix, France.

[7]Séré, M. G. (1983). Premiers pas et premier obstacles à l'acquisition de la notion de pression. Working paper, LIRESPT, University of Paris VII, Paris.

[8]Séré, M. G. (1984). L'air et les gaz en classe de 5ème. Working paper, LIRESPT, University of Paris VII, Paris.

[9]Engel Clough, E. and Driver, R. (1985). What do children understand about pressure in fluids? *Research in Science and Technological Education. 3*, (2) 133–144.

CHAPTER 7

The Particulate Nature of Matter in the Gaseous Phase

Joseph Nussbaum*

Introduction

One of the central instructional goals of most junior high school science curricula is the understanding by pupils of the particle model of matter. For, in modern science, the fundamental notion that all matter is particulate and *not continuous* is of prime importance for all causal explanations of any kind of change in matter.

The early atomists of Greece and Rome visualized individual atoms racing freely through a void, colliding and rebounding, or jamming together and interlocking. They were able to rationalize this view by imaginative analogy with perceptive observation. As Lucretius (the first century B.C.) states in his poem, *On the Nature of Things*:

> Before our very eyes. Do but observe:
> Whenever beams make their way in and pour
> The sunlight through the dark rooms of a house,
> You will see many tiny bodies mingling
> In many ways within those beams of light
> All through the empty space, and as it were
> In never-ending conflict waging war,
> Combating and contending troop with troop

*The early work on this chapter was carried out with Dr S. Novick of the Israel Science Teaching Centre, The Hebrew University of Jerusalem. Unfortunately, he passed away too soon, leaving this and other significant projects unfinished. Any new idea in this chapter that the reader finds useful should be associated with his memory.

Without pause, kept in motion by perpetual
Meetings and separations; so that this
May help you to imagine what it means
That the primordial particles of things
Are always tossing about in the great void.[1]

However, as is well known, the atomistic view was not universally and whole-heartedly accepted in the scientific community until the dawn of this century. Although Hero of Alexandria (in the first century A.D.) systematically explained the unique properties of air in terms of particles separated by a void, the prevalent view up to several hundred years ago was that a complete vacuum was impossible.

These few observations from the history of the theory of matter give an indication that internalizing the particle model requires a difficult accommodation of people's naive preconceptions, and is not a model which is likely to be constructed quickly or eagerly by children.

In this chapter, we shall report on several studies which have revealed pupils' ideas about certain aspects of the structure of gases. We chose to concentrate on phenomena of gas behaviour, since it was mainly through the study of the behaviour of gas that scientists gradually evolved the particle model. It appears that many introductory science programmes tend to follow this historical line and introduce the model while examining the behaviour of gases.

After describing these studies and their findings, we propose an analysis of the potential sources of pupils' difficulties in this area. In the analysis, we attempt to trace the way alternative conceptions about gas behaviour evolve, and identify their possible philosophical and metaphysical foundations. Towards the end of the chapter we refer to a specific strategy that we devices and carried out to initiate and encourage the desired accommodation in pupils' ideas about the structure of gases.

Review of Selected Studies

Four selected studies, investigating pupils' understanding of the particulate nature of gas, will be reviewed in this section. These studies were conducted in three different countries involving pupils over a wide age range. The first three studies investigated pupils' conceptions at varying age levels; however, each individual pupil was assessed only once. Therefore, the dynamics of conceptual change which may occur within the individual pupils regarding the particle model was not directly investigated but inferred. The fourth study presents an attempt at following the dynamics of conceptual change in the same individuals while they participated in a structured set of lessons.

An interview study in Israel, 1978[2]

The purpose of this study was to investigate the extent to which 14-year-old (eighth grade) Israeli pupils were able to apply several aspects of the particle model in explaining simple physical phenomena in the gaseous phase. These pupils had been formally taught the model in their seventh grade physical science programme. This programme, entitled 'The Structure of Matter', included activities which involved gases, liquids and solids. By studying the various phases of matter, the pupils were able to learn about selected characteristic properties of matter, i.e. density, fluidity, compressibility, crystallinity, diffusion, phase change, decomposition, separation and mixing. A significant part of the programme was devoted to an interpretation of these properties in terms of particles or in terms of atoms and molecules.

We designed a 30-minute interview procedure to present some phenomena and to probe the various frameworks which the pupils used in interpreting them.

Interview content and structure
The interview was based on three phenomena and involved eight particular questions or tasks. Each phenomenon was the focus for probing the understanding of the following aspects of the particulate model of gases:

(1) a gas is composed of invisible particles;
(2) gas particles are evenly scattered in any enclosed space;
(3) there is 'empty space' between the particles in a gas;
(4) particles of a gas are in intrinsic motion, even when they are not pushed externally; and
(5) when two different gaseous substances interact to form a third substance we picture this as the joining together of different kinds of particles.

Phenomenon 1
A one-litre flask containing air and a hand evacuating pump were shown, and the operation and function of the pump were demonstrated. The pump was then connected and operated for a few seconds in order to remove some of the air from the flask (Figure 7.1). The pupils were then asked:

Task 1: Suppose that you had magic eye glasses with which you were able to see the air in the flask. Draw how it would look *before* and *after* the vacuum pump was used to remove some of the air.

Pupils responded to this task by either shading certain areas of the flask (apparently representing a continuous model) or by placing dots in certain areas of the flask (apparently representing a particulate model). This task examined *spontaneous application* of the idea of the

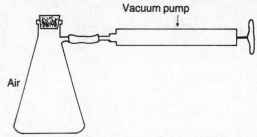

Figure 7.1: Apparatus for removing air from a flask phenomenon no. 1.

particulate nature of air and that particles of air are being evenly scattered.

> *Task 2*: Here are some 'before and after' sketches drawn by some pupils from another school [Figure 7.2] when shown the same phenomenon. Which drawing do you think is the best picture of the air in the flask before and after evacuation?

Pupils who drew a 'continuous picture' in Task 1 were first shown a page with various predictions based on a continuous model (Figure 7.2a). After responding to the drawings on that page, they were shown a second page containing the same predictions in terms of the particle model (Figure 7.2b). This task examined the ability *to recognize* the picture that best represents air being evenly scattered in a closed space and its particulate nature.

> *Task 3*: Explain what there is between the dots in the drawings (on the second page).

This task probed the idea of having 'empty space' between gas particles.

> *Task 4*: Explain why all these particles don't fall to the bottom of the flask and simply pile up there. What holds them up?

This task probed the idea of the intrinsic motion of particles.

Phenomenon 2
Two colourless liquids were presented in two stoppered flasks. The first (concentrated ammonia) was opened and a strip of orange indicator paper was held at its mouth. The strip turned blue. The first flask was closed, the second (concentration hydrochloric acid) opened, and the blue strip was held at its mouth. The strip turned red (Figure 7.3). The following questions were then asked:

> *Task 5*: What made the paper turn blue over the first flask and turn red over the second flask? Make a sketch. In what basic way are the two colourless liquids different?

This task probed the idea that vapours are made of particles and the idea that liquids are made of particles.

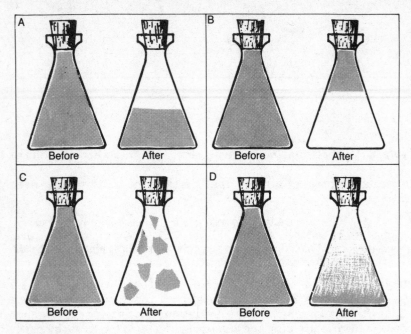

a. First page: a continuous representation of air structure

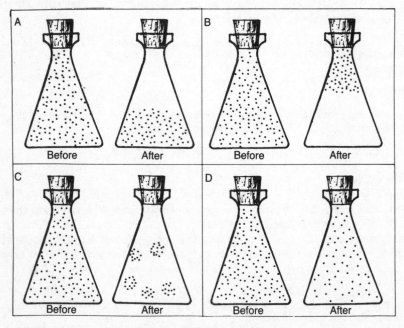

b. Second page: a particulate representation of air structure

Figure 7.2:   Diagram pages for task 2.

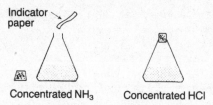

Concentrated NH₃   Concentrated HCl

Figure 7.3:   Apparatus for phenomenon no. 2.

Task 6: How does the substance rise from the liquid to the paper?

This task probed the idea of the intrinsic motion of the particles.

Phenomena 3
The two flasks containing colourless liquids were again used. A few drops of each liquid were placed in cotton-filled depressions in two small corks. These corks were simultaneously inserted in either end of a 30-cm glass tube. After about one minute, a white smoke ring appeared in the tube, closer to one end than the other (Figure 7.4). The pupils were then asked:

Task 7: What is the 'white substance' and how is it formed? Make a sketch.

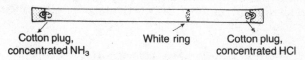

Cotton plug,   White ring   Cotton plug,
concentrated NH₃   concentrated HCl

Figure 7.4:   Apparatus for phenomenon no. 3.

This task probed the idea that a chemical change is an interaction between particles.

Task 8: Explain why the white ring does not appear in the middle of the tube.

This task probed the idea that particles have intrinsic motion and that different particles may have different speeds.

(Pupils' responses to the structured questions as well as to further probing were immediately recorded on sheets beside their drawings, together with pertinent general impressions. Responses were later categorized in terms of their relationship to the five aspects of the particle model listed above).

Findings of the interview study
The study sample (about 150 pupils) was drawn from nine urban schools which were chosen to represent the population variability. The varying responses, relating to the five aspects of the particle model

being probed in the interview, and their frequency (percentages) in the sample are given below.

Aspect 1:   Gas is composed of invisible particles
This proposition is the most elementary one in the particle model. We found that 64 per cent of the pupils *spontaneously* suggested that air is made up of particles. When asked to choose the best visual representation of the structure of air out of a given set of alternatives, 78 per cent chose the diagram which represented the particulate form of air. Is it fair to assume that those who chose the particle diagram as the best representation also have some basic understanding of other aspects of this model? The following findings show that this assumption is premature.

Aspect 2:   Gas particles are evenly scattered in any enclosed space
The task of explaining the 'space filling' property of gas in terms of evenly scattered particles is intended to force pupils to demonstrate that they have overcome the concept of continuity of matter and are thus able to think of the behaviour of individual particles. It was found that one out of every six pupils who supported a particle representation in Tasks 1 and 2 believed that the particles are not scattered evenly in an enclosed container but that they were concentrated in some part of a confined space. This response indicates a need found in a significant number of 'particulate' pupils to retain some sense of continuity in the structure of air.

Aspect 3:   There is empty space between the particles in gas
Only about 45 per cent of the particulate pupils (35 per cent of the sample) explained decisively that there was empty space between the particles; 16 per cent were unsure about the nature of the vacuum and they suggested this only after being pressed. These pupils initially answered that between the particles represented in the drawing there should be more particles. Among the pupils who showed no realization of empty space, many differing ideas were offered when they tried to explain what existed between the particles: 'Dust and other particles'; 'other gases such as oxygen and nitrogen'; 'the particles are closely packed—there is no space between them'; 'air, dirt, germs'; 'unknown vapours'; 'particles expand into empty space', etc.

Aspect 4:   Particles in gas are in intrinsic motion
Only about 50 per cent of the 'particulate' pupils (about 40 per cent of the sample) suggested that gas particles have intrinsic motion. Many of them did not attribute the space-filling property of gases (Task 4) to the intrinsic motion of the particles. Among other factors mentioned were: 'the particles want to rise' (i.e. an animistic property);

'the particles weigh very little and therefore rise' or 'air floats in space because of its low specific gravity' (i.e. the natural tendency of air is to float up into space—this is the natural place of air); 'If all the particles fell to the bottom, there would be a vacuum and this is impossible in air' (i.e. a vacuum is impossible—matter is always sucked into the vacuum to fill it up).

Aspect 5: The forming of a new substance from two different gaseous substances is pictured as the joining together of different kinds of particles

Only 50 per cent of the 'particulate' pupils (about 40 per cent of the sample) said that the white substance (ammonium chloride) was a compound made up of a combination of different particles. Generally, this response was not offered spontaneously, but only when pupils were specifically asked about the nature of the white substance.

The findings of this interview study indicate that a significant proportion of the sample failed to internalize important aspects of the particle model. The explanation we suggest for these findings is that pupils approach the learning of the particle model with a relatively stable alternative model in which matter is conceived as basically *continuous* and *static*. In school, pupils are expected to abandon this perceptually sensible model in favour of an abstract one developed by scientists to interpret the results of *their* research into the physical and chemical properties of matter. Indeed, a particle picture sometimes contradicts one's sensory perception of matter.

The text of 'The Structure of Matter' mainly reinforced the first aspect of the scientific model, namely, the existence of invisible particles. This is the simplest aspect of the model. Today, even young children hear about invisible things such as germs and viruses that affect their health. They know that the smaller the object, the harder it is to see it. Thus, the assertion about invisible particles of matter should sound quite plausible. This can be seen in the fact that over 60 per cent of the sample conveyed this particular aspect in their responses. However, it is only when the several aspects, and their relationships to each other, are understood, that the model takes on its true significance.

The aspects of the particle theory which were least assimilated by the pupils were those which were most in dissonance with their prior conceptions about the nature of matter. These aspects were: empty space (the vacuum concept), intrinsic motion (particle kinetics) and interaction between particles (chemical change).

A cross-age study in the USA, 1981[3]

This study attempted to find out how pupils' conceptions change as they grow older and as they are progressively exposed to additional relevant information in higher grades. Since the intent was to test a fairly large sample over a wide age range, it was necessary to replace the clinical interview with a paper-and-pencil test. A written test was developed which was based on phenomena used in the interview study described above. The tested pupils were asked to (a) complete a drawing, (b) write an explanation (free response), or (c) choose among a number of given explanations or drawings (forced choice). An example item from this test is presented in Figure 7.5. This study was conducted in Iowa City. The sample included 576 pupils ranging from elementary school through university. It was found that the percentage of pupils who provided elements of scientifically accepted ideas generally increased with age although in several tasks there was no significant increase beyond the junior high school level. Again, the majority of pupils claimed that air is made up of particles, but only a minority demonstrated the internalizations of the idea of empty space between particles (at best 50 per cent of an age group) and of intrinsic particle motion (at best 40 per cent of an age group).

A study of high school students in England, 1984[4]

This study was part of a national survey project in England. A sample of 300 pupils, 15 years old, were tested mainly by paper-and-pencil about some aspects of the particulate nature of matter. Most of the questions related to the gaseous phase. An example item from the test is presented in Figure 7.6. The investigators reported on the following findings:

(1) More than 50 per cent of the students used particulate ideas, without necessarily comprehending other essential elements of the model. The rest of the sample did not refer to particles in their responses.

(2) At best, one in five of all students gave partially complete responses based on accepted particulate ideas (this proportion increased to one in three for students who had studied physics or chemistry).

(3) At least one in three of all students used alternative particle ideas (mixed conceptions) such as particles expand and contract, particles get hot, particles melt, particles behave animistically.

(4) About one in four students gave macroscopic responses with no mention of particulate ideas—others were unclassifiable due to their unclear answers.

Conceptual change in individual pupils: A case study in the USA, 1982[5]

All previous studies provided an assessment of the understanding of individual pupils at a specific point in their conceptual development.

The air particles in the flask drawn in the middle of this page are pictured as dots. The air particles are spread out uniformly in the flask.

The following questions were asked in a science class:

. . . why don't all the air particles in the flask fall down on each other and stay at the bottom of the flask?

. . . why do the particles remain spread out even though there is space between them and they don't have anything to rest on?

Five pupils suggested different answers to these questions--

Task No. 7
Circle the name of the pupil whose answer you think is best. If you have another better answer, don't circle any names and write your explanation at the bottom of this page.

My own explanation:

_____

_____

Figure 7.5: An example question format from the test used in the cross age study, in U.S.A..

After many experiments, scientists now think that:

- all things are made of small particles
- these particles move in all directions
- they move faster the higher the temperature
- they exert forces on each other
- they are too small to see through a microscope

Use any of these ideas to help answer the following question:

Why does the pressure in car tyres increase during a journey?

Figure 7.6:   An example question format from the test used with high school students, in England.

This case study was unique in that an attempt was made to follow the dynamics of conceptual change during the course of a teaching unit. The pupils in this study were sixth-graders (12 year olds) in a university town in the state of New York. A series of ten lessons covering the particulate nature of gas was designed and applied (see Figure 7.7 for lessons content). Half of the lessons were videotaped enabling the investigators to trace conceptual change in individuals through their verbal participation in class discussions. Further information was obtained through pupils' worksheets which were collected and analysed.

This analysis showed that pupils do not easily give up their preconceptions and that they tend to assimilate new information into their previous conceptions, constructing a mixed conception (called alternative particulate ideas in the survey report). Two selected cases are presented.

Case 1 (Figure 7.8)
Before instruction began, Roger believed that the remaining air in an evacuated flask would remain along the edges of the flask 'trying to bust out' (i.e. relating some animistic nature to matter). After exposure to the idea of the particulate nature of air, he performed on

Lesson 1–2	Experiments with air and with specific gases (air occupies space; identi–fying O_2 and CO_2; air has weight, air can perform work: Lifting objects, moving objects), air is a mixture of different gases.	
Lesson 3	Exposing SAFs about the structure of air in a re-duced pressure situation. Pretending that they can use magic eye glasses, pupils imagine how air would look in the flask 'before' and 'after' partial evacuation of the flask.	Particles + Empty Space
Lesson 4	Conceptual conflict and change: discrepant event–air compression. Pupils 'invent' the particle idea for the structure of air.	
Worksheet 4	Draw and explain what you believe *now* about the structure of air in a reduced pressure situation (lesson 3).	
Lesson 5	Short discussion on some functions of various visual models.	
Lesson 6	Exposing SAFs about the mechanism of gas diffusion. Experiment: smell — what makes it travel?	Particle Motion
Lesson 7	Cognitive conflict and change: discrepant event: diffusion of bromine in air and in a vacuum.	
Worksheet 7	Draw the air and explain what made the balloon inflate.	
Lesson 8	Consolidating the particle model and making a list of claims representing aspects of the model.	
Lesson 9	Reenforcement of the idea that the kinetic behavior of particles is responsible for air expansion: (1) when heating; (2) when adding particles.	Reenforcing Particle Motion
Worksheet 9	Draw the air and explain what made the soap film rise.	
Lesson 10	Reenforcement of the idea that air pressure is dependent on the number and the velocity of particles.	
Worksheet 10a	True/False evaluation of statements representing SAFs and ScF.	
Worksheet 10b	True/False evaluation of statements representing SAFs and ScF.	

Figure 7.7: The teaching unit: Lessons and worksheet content.

a worksheet as shown in Figure 7.8. His drawing and commentary clearly indicate that, for him, air remained a 'continuous light and

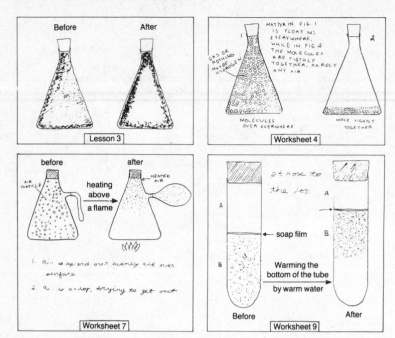

Figure 7.8: Case no. 3: Roger's performance at various points in a ten lesson unit.

clear stuff', but it now contained floating 'air particles'. For him, pumping out the air meant letting out this medium, the genuine air, leaving the particles on the bottom, like fish without water. In worksheet 7 he showed particles with space between them. However, he believed that air particles *rise* after they are heated (i.e. an assumed 'natural motion' of any hot air) and that they were 'trying to get out' (i.e. relating some animistic nature to the particles). This belief is repeated in worksheet 9. In worksheet 10a he related particle motion to vacuum suction. In worksheet 10b he gave a partial mechanical account of particle behaviour.

Case 2 (Figure 7.9)
Lisa demonstrated, in worksheet 4, that she still retained her belief regarding the continuity of air. She indicated a change in her conception in lesson 5 where she pictured odour as dots scattered all over the room with *space* between them. The idea of empty space is overtly suggested in worksheet 7. However, simultaneously, she retained the belief that air particles expand when the temperature rises (i.e. relating the bulk property of air to its particles). In worksheet 9, she demonstrated that she had discarded the idea that air particles expand when heated and had become capable of using a mechanical explanation for particle behaviour. In lesson 10 and worksheet 10 she continued to demonstrate an internalization of the mechanical view.

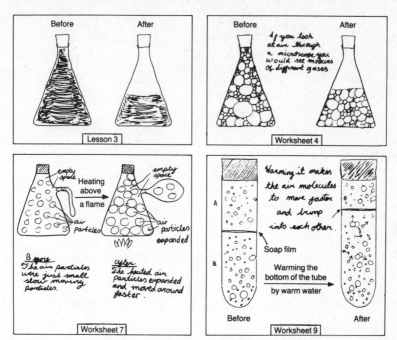

Figure 7.9: Case no. 2: Lisa's performance at various points in a ten lesson unit.

However, she still claimed at the end of the teaching unit that the vacuum exerts a suction force.

The complexity of the conceptual change dynamics appeared clearly in this case study. We saw how tenacious existing conceptions are and how they survive through many stages of instruction, and even when instruction is completed. Powerful preconceptions may survive and remain active helping the pupil assimilate new information. In this process, the scientific meaning of the information is distorted.

Sources of pupils' difficulties: analysis of concepts, theoretical constructs and metaphysical assumptions

In this section we propose an analysis of pupils' difficulties by studying the structure of knowledge in this area. In Figure 7.10 some of the primary concepts about the physical world are presented along with their interrelations. The concepts which were selected for this figure are 'common sense' concepts which evolve relatively close to direct experience with physical phenomena. Examples of such concepts with their interrelations are as follows: bodies may exert forces; volume increases with increase in temperature; matter appears as a solid, a liquid or a gas. Seeking understanding is a natural, spontaneous

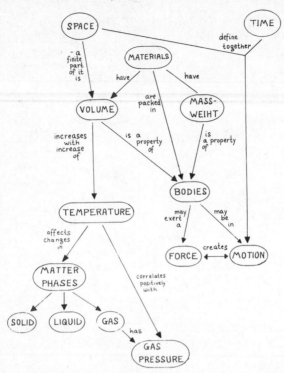

Figure 7.10:   A network of common-sense concepts and their perceived interrelationships.

feature of human beings. Thus, these 'common sense' concepts and the relations between them have always been the focus of intellectual inquiry and of physical investigations. In the course of the history of science, various theories regarding these concepts were proposed and held by various cultures and scholars,[1] the kinetic-particle theory being the one which is currently accepted by the modern scientific community. Thus its internalization by the pupils is often considered to be one of the most important objectives of science education today. A brief and schematic representation of this theory, as applied to the behaviour of gases, is added to the above set of 'common sense' concepts in Figure 7.11. The kinetic-particle theory is presented as an additional network of hypothetical notions which is connected by many links to the network of 'common sense' concepts. These hypothetical notions function in explaining the 'common sense' concepts and their interrelations. For example, pressure, which can be correctly sensed, is explained as resulting from particle collisions.

It is important to recognize that the concepts of the particle theory are intellectual constructs based on various assumptions which are beyond direct observation. One important assumption which can be found in the kinetic-particle theory is that the kinetic behaviour of the hypothetical particles is analogous in many respects to 'the

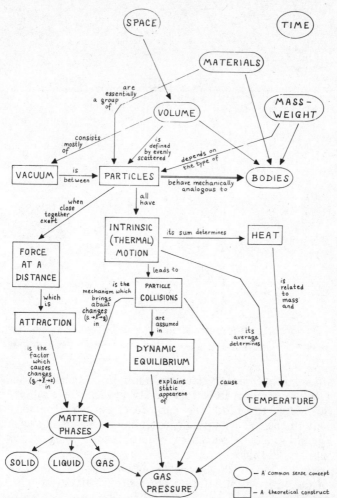

Figure 7.11: A combined network of common-sense concepts and some theoretical constructs of the particle-kinetic theory.

mechanical behaviour of bodies'. Superficially this assumption may sound as though it is simple and that it has clear implications, but this is not so. The mechanical behaviour of bodies has not just a single description and interpretation, rather it can be described and explained differently by alternative theories as will be shown below.

In assuming that particles behave like macroscopic bodies, the kinetic-particle theory refers specifically to the theory of Newtonian mechanics, which includes the concept of inertial motion in a straight line and at a constant speed as a fundamental characteristic (see Figure 7.12). The presumption of the idea of inertial motion requires the acceptance of 'limitless empty space' as a necessary notion. When we apply Newtonian mechanics to gaseous particles we envisage them

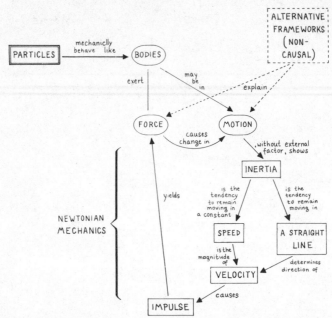

Figure 7.12: Some selected constructs from Newtonian mechanics. The existence of non-causal alternative frameworks is reminded.

moving in straight lines in a vacuum, bouncing into each other and the walls of the container and statistically creating a random motion. With this idea in mind we can describe and explain various phenomena in the gaseous phase, such as the 'space filling' nature of the gas in an enclosed container, gas pressure being exerted in all directions, gas diffusion, etc.

When we tell pupils that particles have instrinsic motion, can we assume that they think of particle motion within the Newtonian framework? This is unlikely. In many schools, pupils study particular ideas prior to Newtonian mechanics. Even when pupils have studied mechanics, as Chapter 5 indicates, Newtonian ideas about force and motion are difficult for most secondary school pupils to understand and use. Instead, we find pupils in schools, and even university students, using intuitive ideas or alternative frameworks which have characteristics of an Aristotelian way of thinking. The Newtonian framework and its rival frameworks are based on differing metaphysical assumptions. A common feature of all the alternative frameworks mentioned below is the assumption that there are 'non-physical', 'non-causal' factors that may create force and motion. These factors relate to the following notions (see Figure 7.13):

Animism. The relating of certain amimal characteristics to the behaviour of non-living objects. These characteristics include having intentions, desires and sometimes even phobias. Animism is prevalent

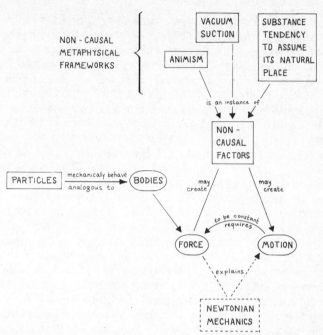

Figure 7.13: Some non-causal metaphysical frameworks. Newtonian mechanics as the alternative framework is reminded.

in magical thought, appearing in certain cultures and in young children.

Natural place of substances. This notion was prevalent during the classical period and through the middle ages. It was believed that every substance tended to move towards its natural place. A 'natural place' could be the centre of the Earth (downward) for some substances (soil, water) or away from the centre (upward) for others (air, fire). An example of this way of thinking is: 'Air is a substance which goes upwards because it is light and refined, more spiritual and less earthy and not because it has a relatively low specific gravity.' According to this notion substances move, if no barrier exists, towards their natural place because of their intrinsic tendencies, not as a result of interaction.

Vacuum is impossible. According to this notion 'nature abhors vacuum'. Therefore, if a vacuum is created momentarily it will immediately be 'filled' by nearby substances 'rushing in'. It is believed that the movement of these substances is caused by some 'sucking force' originating in the vacuum. Notice that as with the above notions, motion is not initiated by interaction between two material bodies.

Such notions were held by great scholars in the past who trusted their intuition and elaborated their theories on this basis. When we tell seventh- or eighth-graders that 'gas particles move', it is reasonable to anticipate that their spontaneous thought process with respect of motion and its factors will include at least some elements of these alternative notions. This was demonstrated by the findings of various studies described above. So far, in the above analysis, we have concentrated on alternative notions which pupils may have with regards to motion and its possible factors. There is another essential notion on which the particle theory is founded, i.e. the notion of 'empty space'. It was mentioned previously, the concept of empty space, as a natural part of the material world, is not easily internalized by pupils. We should recognize that the question of existence or non-existence of natural empty space was debated for centuries by philosophers. Realizing this, we may have a better understanding of the pupils' difficulties. This issue is rooted in the metaphysical dispute regarding the basic quality of 'space'. Nowadays, science accepts Newton's conception of space, which maintains that space is an entity that is independent of the various bodies of the world and thus the whole world should be limitless.* This conception was also held by the Greek atomists. However, the alternative conception which was defended vigorously by Aristotle prevailed as the dominant idea throughout most of Western history. Aristotle maintained that 'space' is not an entity by itself but is dependent and defined by the material bodies. According to him, 'natural empty space' is a meaningless notion. Matter must be con-

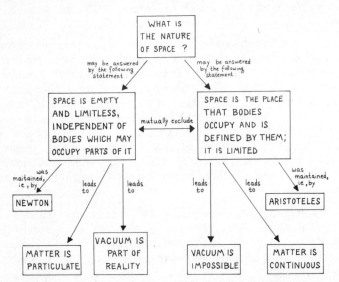

Figure 7.14: Differing metaphysical answers about the nature of space.

---

*Indeed, Einstein's conception of space is different, but it is applied only in advanced level physics.

tinuous and space only reaches to the edge of the *continuous* material world. The material world with its space is therefore limited. Figure 7.14 represents this dispute schematically.

The above analysis of the kinetic-particle theory and of its rival theories with their metaphysical roots should assist us in gaining a better insight into pupils' difficulties and the alternative frameworks within which they think.

Towards an effective teaching strategy

After reading the previous section, one may adopt a pessimistic view about the possibility of teaching the particle model *meaningfully* at the completion of the elementary or junior high school levels. The author does not take this view. The descriptions and arguments presented in the previous section were intended to arouse awareness and sensitivity to pupils' alternative beliefs regarding the structure of matter and its particulate nature. The lesson learned about the tenacious nature of pupils' preconceptions should motivate us to search for more effective teaching strategies. Based on our experience and on reviewing other people's research we arrrived at a suggestion of a strategy for initiating and encouraging desired conceptual change. Our proposed strategy is based on two basic assumptions.

The first states that major conceptual changes are initiated only as a result of some conceptual conflict between a person's previous conception and contradicting evidence—'a discrepant event'. There is nothing unique and innovative in assuming the above statement and other educators and psychologists have already proposed and attempted to apply it before. Our unique contribution is in adding the second assumption, i.e. unless pupils are very aware of the elements of their own existing conception they are unlikely to sense a genuine conflict. The implication is that if we want to enable pupils to benefit from conceptual conflict we must help them to expose and articulate openly their preconceptions. In the case of the particulate nature of gases,[6] we planned an 'exposing event' in which we encouraged all pupils to take an explicit position about the continuous or discontinuous nature of air. In this event the teacher demonstrates Phenomenon 1 from the interview study described on pp. 126–131 (Figure 7.1), and asks pupils to imagine how air would look through magic eye glasses. Then she/he initiates and guides group discussion in which usually all the answers shown in Figure 7.2a and some others are proposed by pupils. Most of these answers represent the view that air is continuous. In our experience, if this discussion is appropriately led, pupils gain an awareness of their own belief about the continuous nature of air. Most of them now realize that there might be alternative rational views of the nature of air, of which their own view is but one. The teacher then presses the question: 'what part of the container's volume is empty due to the missing air?' In other words, the question is: 'where on the drawing should we indicate an empty space which was filled earlier by the rest of the air?'

The 'discrepant event' is a demonstration of the compressibility of air. Air in a syringe is compressed down to half of its original volume. Then the pupils are asked what in the structure of air makes it compressible? Pupils start to realize that if air is continuous it is hard to explain its compressibility. In the next stage of the discussion pupils arrive at the suggestion that maybe 'air naturally contains empty spaces within its material', and that this feature makes it compressible. Accumulating experience with this approach indicates that even if only a small minority of the pupils spontaneously propose this idea, the rest of the group are well prepared and ready for its meaningful acceptance. Laying the cognitive foundation for the possibility of having 'a natural empty space' within air subsequently makes the idea of the particulate nature of air much more reasonable and internalizable. A more detailed description of this approach is found elsewhere.[7]

Here we gave a brief account of a possible teaching strategy. However, more work on improving strategies and activities for teaching the particle model has still to be done.

References

[1]Toulmin, S. E. and Goodfield, J. (1962). *The Architecture of Matter*, Harmondsworth: Penguin.

[2]Novick, S. and Nussbaum, J. (1978). Junior high school pupils' understanding of the particulate nature of matter: An interview study. *Science Education*, 62(3), 273–281.

[3]Novick, S. and Nussbaum, J. (1981). Pupils' understanding of the particulate nature of matter: A cross age study. *Science Education*, 65(2), 187–196.

[4]Brook, A., Briggs, H. and Driver, R. (1984). *Aspects of Secondary Students' Understanding of the Particulate Nature of Matter*. Children's Learning in Science Project. Centre for Studies in Science and Mathematics Education, The University of Leeds.

[5]Nussbaum, J. and Novick, S. (1982). A study of conceptual change in the classroom. A paper presented at NARST annual meeting, Lake Geneva, near Chicago, U.S.A.

[6]Nussbaum, J. and Novick, S. (1981). Brainstorming in the classroom to invent a model: A case study. *School Science Review*, 62(221), 771–778.

[7]Nussbaum, J. and Novick, S. (1982). Alternative frameworks, conceptual conflict and accommodation: Toward a principled teaching strategy. *Instructional Science*, 11, 183–208.

CHAPTER 8

Beyond Appearances: The Conservation of Matter under Physical and Chemical Transformations

Rosalind Driver

Introduction

Some of the more dramatic natural phenomena children experience in their daily lives involve chemical reactions in which the very nature of a substance appears to undergo an irreversible change. The process of burning is probably the most common of such experiences for children. Wood in a bonfire crackles and starts to glow, flames appear and smoke is given off; when the bonfire has burned down a small pile of grey ash is all that remains. Children watching a candle burn see a steady flame emerging from the wick and the wax 'disappearing'. Some will be familiar with coal or logs burning in their hearth at home or jets of gas burning in a stove. They are likely to have seen a sheet of paper catch fire and have probably watched the edge of the flame advancing across the sheet leaving a curled black fragile material in its wake.

These are the types of observations which children may have made from early childhood. When they have their first formal encounter with chemistry in the early years of secondary school students may be introduced to a wider range of fascinating phenomena: beautiful colour changes, exciting explosions, substances with unusual properties such as soft metals which can be cut with a knife. They see substances which appear to come and go as if by magic; clear liquids which produce a solid when mixed; dark crystals which give off a coloured gas when heated. It would be unusual for students not to be interested in studying these phenomena if only because of the element of surprise involved. Yet while it is the unpredictability of the events which appeals to younger students, chemistry is the subject which attempts to impose regularities on this diversity. Since the days of the alchemists chemists have questioned what it is through all the observble changes of matter that remains unchanged.

The view which we now present to children in school is that despite appearances matter does not come and go; that it consists of basic building blocks or atoms (around 100 different kinds) and that the diversity in observable changes is due to changes in the configurations of these basic building blocks.

One of the simplest changes which is often introduced to children early in their science courses is that of change of state. Typically children are asked to consider what happens when ice is heated and it changes to water and then to steam. Something which is solid and rigid is seen to change to a liquid which is 'sloppy' and takes the shape of whatever container it is put into. This in turn seems to 'disappear off' into the air. One the one hand children see these quite dramatic changes in physical properties, on the other they are told that the same building blocks (water molecules) are there in each case; that the observable changes are simply due to changes in their configuration and energy.

Later in their courses students may consider simple chemical changes such as the combination of substances with oxygen in the process of burning. Again the scientific interpretation given is in terms of the reorganization of basic building blocks, in this case the combination of atoms of oxygen with those of the material which burns.

It is worth reflecting briefly on the change in thinking that this involves for children in moving from reasoning which is perceptually dominated (where substances come and go and matter 'disappears') to conceptually dominated thinking, where despite changing appearances children accept that matter is particulate and that (within the range of phenomena they are taught at school) these component particles do not disappear, but just change their energy and configuration.

Although children in their secondary science courses may have been presented with such an interpretation of observed changes in matter, there is a question as to whether and to what extent they have been able to construct and use such a model in their own thinking. In this chapter we will be exploring aspects of this question by looking at the types of reasoning used by 11 to 16-year-old children about three types of changes: change of state, the process of dissolving and the process of burning. Studies of secondary school children's ideas about these phenomena have been undertaken in a number of countries including Britain, France, Sweden and New Zealand. Despite differences in language and in the science that is taught in school, common features do emerge in the types of ideas that can be identified in children's reasoning. Most of the studies drawn on in this chapter survey the ideas used by children at different ages and so give a 'snapshot' of the types of thinking used. A few studies have been conducted in the context of a teaching sequence and these give more information about the extent to which children's thinking changes as a result of organized learning experiences.

Change of state

During a change of state the outward appearance of a substance changes but from a scientific point of view we appreciate that it is still the same substance. Do school children appreciate this, and if so, what do they imagine is happening when a solid changes to a liquid, a liquid to a gas and vice versa?

These questions have been explored with New Zealand school students[1] aged 8-17. The students were interviewed to probe their ideas about what happens to water when it boils, when steam condenses and when ice melts. In a few cases students' responses suggested that the nature of the substance changed during these transforations (one suggestion was that water changes to air when it boils, air and steam being seen as the same thing). In most cases, however, the students appreciated that water and steam are basically the same substance:

> A vapour forms which is steam... it is water that has changed from a liquid state into a gas state (15-year-old)

or that ice is water in a solid form:

> The ice melted... when water is put in a certain degree it freezes... when it is warmed up again it melts back to water (13-year-old).

The majority of students gave an account of the changes referring only to observable macroscopic changes. From about age 13 some of the students described spontaneously what was happening in terms of particles or molecules. In describing what happened when water boils a 15-year-old said:

> It's when all the atoms in the water... the liquid are racing around really fast because they are getting hot and... some of them are going off in vapour because they are turning into a gas.

Among those who use molecular ideas that notion that molecules speed up on heating is used frequently. The idea that particles tend to move apart on heating is also quite prevalent:

> The element is heating the molecules in the water making them expand and move around faster and they move off into steam... [What do you mean by expand?]... They move further apart from each other (14-year-old).

This notion of particle separation is also commonly applied to the change of state from ice to water:

> They (the ice particles) are the same particles but they are in a different state... in the solid state they are kept together... in the water state they are spread out (15-year-old).

The use of particulate ideas in describing the three states of matter has been investigated with nearly 1000 Scottish 12 to 13-year-old students.[2] The investigators' purpose was to find out the extent to which the ideas on the particulate nature of matter taught in the Scottish Integrated Science scheme were understood.

As part of the study the students were asked to draw diagrams to show the shape, arrangement and spacing of atoms/molecules in a typical solid, liquid and gas. A selection of the students' drawings are shown in Figure 8.1. Nearly all the students' drawings showed particles in all three states, but about half of the drawings showed the particles in the liquid and gaseous state as smaller than those in the solid state. Interviews with some of the students indicated that this was not simply a question of a change in scale in their drawings but that it reflected an underlying view that molecular diameter decreases progressively from solid to liquid to gas. The spacing of the particles in the drawings was also studied. As many of the drawings in Figure 8.1 indicate, the majority represented the particles in the solid in an ordered way compared with a disordered arrangement in the liquid and gas. However, many show a noticeable increase in spacing between particles in the solid and liquid state. Whereas the ratio of molecular spacing in solids, liquids and gases is of the order 1:1:10, the authors of this study report that the children's drawings were remarkably consistent in showing molecular spacings in the ratio 1:2-3:5-8. (The mean separation of particles in a gas tends to be underestimated and that of particles in a liquid considerably overestimated.) Although the majority of students indicated that the particles in the liquid and gaseous states were moving, about a third indicated no movement in the solid state.

Many of the students' ways of thinking found in the Scottish study have also been identified in a survey of English 15-year-old students.[3] The students were asked a number of questions in which they were to explain certain phenomena using the idea that matter is made of particles. These questions were set in a written form to nearly 300 students and a smaller group were also interviewed. One of the questions asked students to use particulate ideas in explaining what happens to a block of ice as its temperature rises from $-10°$ C to $-1°$ C. The different types of responses given are shown in Table 1. The majority of students (about two-thirds) did use particulate ideas in their responses but only about a fifth used taught ideas. A marked feature in the responses was the tendency to transfer changes in macroscopic or bulk properties to the microscopic level; for example, suggesting that particles would melt, would get hot or change size.

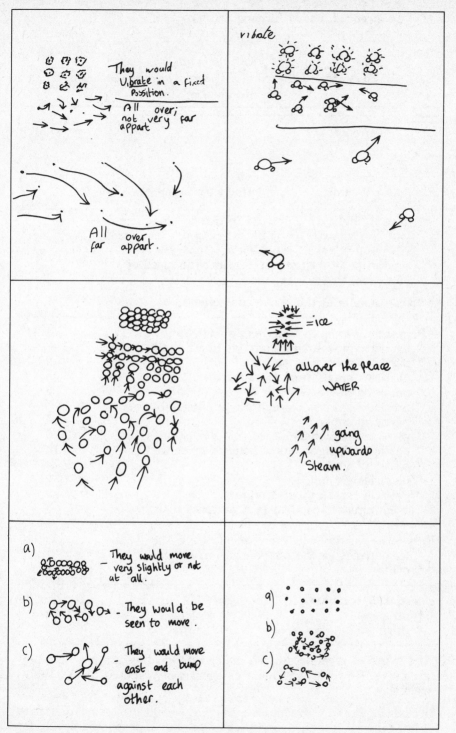

Figure 8.1: Drawings of 11 to 12-year-olds representing the three states of matter.

Table 8.1   Summary of the percentages of types of responses for the question on heating ice

Type of response	Percentage of total ($n = 294$)
Responses including components of the accepted answer 17	
* drawing indicating particle lattice and bonding, particles vibrate about fixed position, speed of vibration increases with temperature, average separation of particles increases with speed of vibration, thus ice expands	2
* one or more of the above components	15
Alternative responses in terms of particles[a] 48	
* particles move more freely (as in a liquid)	7
* particles sublime/evaporate	2
* particles break away from the ice	3
* particles collide within the ice (as in a gas)	3
* particles are free to separate (no bonds between particles implied)	10
* particles stationary in ice	3
* particles change volume (expand or shrink)	10
* particles melt	14
* particles get hot	2
* particles break up/disintegrate	3
* other alternative ideas (e.g. particles die)	3
Responses entirely at a macroscopic level..............................20	
* ice expands as the temperature rises	1
* other	19
Uncodeable responses 15	
* no answer	14
* other	1

[a]The types of responses listed under this heading are not mutually exclusive. However, the main categories of response are mutually exclusive.

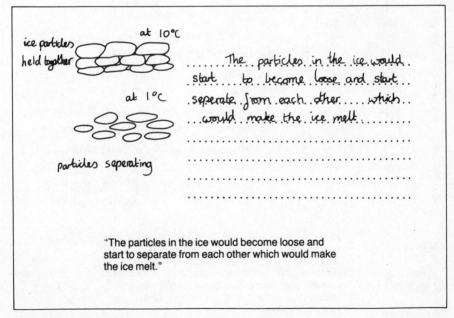

: : : : – at –1c

As the temperature rises the molecules hit each other faster thus making more heat. The molecules also become futher apart.

"As the temperature rises the molecules hit each other faster thus making more heat. The molecules also become further apart."

ice particles held together   at 10°C

at 1°C

particles seperating

The particles in the ice would start to become loose and start seperate from each other which would make the ice melt

"The particles in the ice would become loose and start to separate from each other which would make the ice melt."

Figure 8.2: Explanations given by 15-year-olds to the question on heating ice.

As the temperature rises the particles get smaller, so the ice melts.

When the temperature rises the particles start to turn from solid form and into liquid form because the heat melts them.

The strong association between particle separation and temperature was also noticeable (see Figure 8.2).

There was very little reference made to cohesive forces between particles (a point also noted in the Scottish study), and perhaps as a consequence, there was a tendency to see the ice melting as soon as its temperature started to rise (see Figure 8.3).

It is also worth noting that over 25 per cent of the students did not use particle ideas at all in their response: some simply described what would happen to the block of ice at the level of perceptual experience, others did not attempt a response at all.

These various studies show that most secondary school students will use particulate ideas in describing states of matter especially when they are prompted to do so. A number of aspects of the way these ideas are used can be identified including: lack of appreciation of particle motion or of cohesive forces between particles in a solid, a tendency to associate increased separation of particles with increases in temperature and, perhaps most significant of all, a tendency to

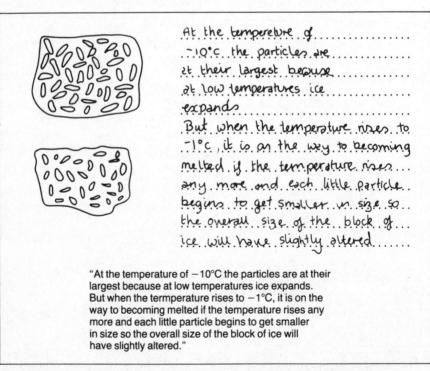

"At the temperature of −10°C the particles are at their largest because at low temperatures ice expands. But when the termperature rises to −1°C, it is on the way to becoming melted if the temperature rises any more and each little particle begins to get smaller in size so the overall size of the block of ice will have slightly altered."

Figure 8.3:   Response of 15-year-old to question on heating ice.

attribute bulk properties to the particles themselves. The interplay between the action of cohesive forces on the one hand and particle motion energy on the other was evident in very few students' thinking about solids.

The process of dissolving

Piaget and Inhelder studied children's ideas about the dissolving process as part of their investigation into the development of ideas of conservation of matter.[4] They asked children to predict what would happen in terms of changes in weight and volume when some sugar was dissolved in water. The investigators report that young children's reasoning is governed by perceptual experience; they predict that there will be no change to the weight or volume of the water since the sugar 'disappears' when it dissolves. Children over the age of 10 years may not be so influenced by immediate perception. They may, for example, argue that the sugar is still there but spread out in tiny bits. Although it cannot be seen, the children are basing their reasoning on the continued substantive existence of the sugar.

This general trend is seen in the responses of New Zealand secondary school students who were interviewed about a similar problem.* They were shown a teaspoonful of sugar dissolving in water and were asked 'what happens to the sugar?' Over 25 per cent of the students used the word 'melt' to describe the process, in some cases they considered the words 'melt' and 'dissolve' as synonymous.

> The sugar is dissolving... the water is sort of melting the sugar crystals (13-year-old).

Some denied that the sugar was still there when it was dissolved:

> No, it would have dissolved into the water... the sugar has just combined with the all the water to make that substance... the sugar and water is combined. (12-year-old).

This type of answer suggests that the student is considering that the substance 'sugar' is defined by its macroscopic properties, its hard crystalline structure. When it changes form it is no longer sugar. Other responses reflect this same idea by saying that the sugar is no longer there but that the taste remains.

Other students are less tied to perceptual features in their reasoning, suggesting that the sugar is still there:

> ... it's got rid of all the lumps and gone with the water... [Is it still there?]... Yes, but you don't see it because it is all mixed in (13-year-old).

---

*In this study the 15-year-olds were studying a science course, the 16- and 17-year-olds were taking a chemistry course.

Some students from about age 13 used particulate ideas in their explanations:

> Well it doesn't actually dissolve... it just gets broken up... into such tiny ones that you can't see it anymore (15-year-old).
>
> The sugar molecules all split apart and then their molecules just mix (15-year-old).
>
> ... sugar molecules are being pulled apart by the water molecules and diffusing them through the water (16-year-old).

Students' quantitative reasoning about the dissolving process was investigated with English students as part of a written survey.[5] Students aged between 9 and 14 years were shown a given mass of sugar being dissolved in a given mass of water in a glass and were asked to predict the mass of the solution. Nearly two-thirds of students of all ages studied predicted the mass of the solution would be less than the sum of the initial masses of the sugar and water.

A similar task was set to a large sample of English and Swedish 15-year-olds (including some who had studied chemistry and some who had not).[6] In this case the students were asked to say what the mass of sugar solution would be when 200 g of sugar was dissolved in 1000 g of water and to give their reason. About a third of all students predicted the mass of the solution would be the same as that of the constituents (nearly half of those studying chemistry gave this response). In some cases students' reasons clearly indicated that although the sugar had dissolved it had not disappeared:

> If you add two substances together and there is no chemical change only physical, the mass of the sugar will be the same and the water has the same mass. The sugar may appear to disapear but its their and therefore so is its mass.
>
> Not one of the two substances could have gone anywhere else except in the pan... even though the sugar cannot be seen it is still present.

In some cases students offered little more than algorithmic addition as a response stating simply:

> $200 + 1000 = 1200$

Over half the students predicted the solution would have less mass than the constituents. A number of different types of reasons were given for this.

(1) *Sugar disappears when dissolved*. Many responses of this kind suggested the mass of the solution would be the same as the original mass of the water:

> because sugar does not do anything to water... it just dissolves in to noting at all.
>
> when the sugar desolves into the water the sugar has no mass so it is just like the 1000 g of the water.

(2) *Mass and volume confused.* In some cases students' reasons suggest they are responding in terms of whether the level of the water will go up when sugar is added: in other words they are equating mass (in grams) with volume:

> because the sugar has dissolved by just making the mass a bit bigger.

This type of reasoning may be used even when students are using particulate ideas:

> the sugar goes into the space between the molecules of the water to form a solution therefore the mass is unchanged.

Molecular ideas are also used in the following example where the student is imposing changes occurring at the macroscopic level to those happening at a molecular level:

> the sugar crystals will dissolve in the water and their molecules will become a less complicated structure and will be lighter than before.

(3) *Sugar is still present in solution but is 'lighter'.* Reasons of this kind suggest that students are thinking of mass in terms of the weight of a solid acting on a surface. Since the sugar is dispersed in the water its 'weight' cannot therefore act in the same way as when it is in the solid state.

> Because when the sugar has dissolved there is no weight left of the sugar (because the granules have dissolved), so only the weight of the water can be weighed.

In the following example the student is suggesting that matter in a liquid form will weigh less than in a solid form:

> the sugar will decompose and form a liquid with the water and so will weigh less.

The responses given to this question suggest that just because students do not conserve mass does not mean that they necessarily think the sugar has disappeared.

What is apparent is that they have various connotations for the word 'mass' including associating it with ideas of volume, density, solidity and the pressure acting on a surface.

When children are encouraged to think about what is happening in this phenomenon from various points of view (as happens in an interview), they may go beyond their initial perceptually based response and convince themselves for various reasons that the sugar is still present in solution. This happened in the following interview with an 11-year-old girl who was asked whether a solution in water would be heavier, lighter or weigh the same as sugar and water before they were mixed.[7]

P: I think it might be lighter.
I: It might be lighter. That's interesting. Why do you think it might be lighter?

P: Because it's all dissolved away.
I: Um...
P: Into the water the sugar and there's no traces of it being there.
I: Dissolved away into the water...
P: Yes.
I: Um: and how does that affect the weight do you think when it's dissolved away into the water?
P: Because there's no weight in... er... the sugar in there. I don't think.
I: There's no weight in the sugar. Do you think there's any sugar in there?
P: Yeah, but it's dissolved.
I: But you think the weight has now gone?
P: No: I think its there.
I: You think it's the same?
P: Um...
I: Well some children tell me what you told me at first, that it loses weight when it goes in the water. Why do you think they tell me that? That the weight goes?
P: 'Cos there's no trace of it or anything.
I: I see, that's interesting.
P: It'll still be there though because it's just dissolved into the water, but it'll still be there.
I: Um...
P: 'Cos if you evap... um... put that on a Bunsen burner on the wire through to evaporate and you get the sugar, 'cos we did that before.
I: Did you.

Responses of this type suggest that students may have the information or knowledge of experiences from which to construct a view of matter as a conserved quantity but that this idea has not yet been put together in an immediately retrievable form.

The process of burning

In a study of secondary students' thinking about the burning process the ideas of a group of 11 to 12-year-olds were investigated both before and after teaching.[8] First we will look at the kinds of intuitive ideas used prior to teaching.

Pupils' intuitive ideas

When the children were asked to say what happens to a splint when it burns, most of them gave a description of what they observed in terms of the flame, the smoke and the ash left without suggesting any mechanism. Some referred to the flame 'eating' the wood, others to it 'dissolving' or 'melting' the wood.

A bunch of glowing splints were shown to the same children and these were blown gently, causing them to glow more intensely. The children were then asked to explain why blowing on a fire makes it burn more fiercely. Nearly a third of the children indicated in their answer to this question that they appreciated that air or oxygen was needed for burning, although the function they suggested for the air varied:

> because the fire needs oxygen to eat away.
> ... the fire likes air.

When asked whether a match would burn in outer space the answers given reflected the close association made by some of the children between air and gravity. About 20 per cent of the children gave a response similar to the following:

> It wouldn't burn because of the lack of gravity in outer space.

Other studies, including those described in Chapter 5, have shown that children tend to associate air with gravity. In some cases they 'explain' the pull of gravity as being due to air pushing down on objects. In other cases the students' ideas about air are less substantive—it is seen as the necessary medium for 'action at a distance', a medium for the transmission of a force including gravity and magnetic forces. (In this sense students are using the term 'air' much as scientists used the term 'ether' in pre-relativistic physics.)

Some used ideas which reflected a 'contagion' view of fire and flame when one part touches another part. Blowing is seen to help this process:

> Because it blows the flame on to the parts where it is not lit.

In commenting on the ash that remains some of the children spontaneously referred to this as the incombustible material in the wood, and when the children were asked to compare the weight of the ash produced with the original weight of the splint, the majority said it would be lighter. Two main types of reasons were given. One focused on the smoke that was given off, arguing that something in the wood disappears:

> It will be lighter, because when the splint burns and a lot of the wood matter changes to smoke and so just ash remains.
> because the smoke (carbon) is coming out of the wood.

In some cases no mention was made of where the matter is going to:

> Because when you burn it into ash, some of it will disapear and that is why I thought it would get lighter.

The other reason focused on the change in appearance of wood and ash arguing that a powder is lighter than a solid.

Before being taught, a third of the children suggested that the weight of the ash would be the same as that of the splint using a type of conservation reasoning (it is the same splint even though it has changed in appearance):

> because it is the same weight to begin with but the splint ashes are still the same because it is the same as it was before but looks different.

(This type of reason was given by very few pupils after teaching.)

In general, what we see in these responses is a *prototypic view* of burning: a view which is based on children's observations of fires, matches, splints, etc., burning. The general features incorporated in this view are:

(1)   burning involves things going red and a flame appearing;
(2)   oxygen (or air) is needed (its function may not be clear, it may even be seen as being 'burnt away' in the process);
(3)   things get lighter when they are burnt;
(4)   burning drives off the smoke or parts of the material are driven off as smoke; and
(5)   solid residues or ash are the incombustible bits left behind. (These are often grey black in colour and in powder or crumbly form.)

Similar ideas have been reported in a study with 11 to 12-year-old French children.[12] The authors suggest that when substances are in contact with a flame children see one of two types of things happening. The substance may remain the same but change into another form; children tend to view the burning of alcohol or of wax in this way, describing what happens as 'melting' or 'evaporating'. Alternatively, they see the substance as burning and changing into another substance such as ash, smoke or carbon—the prototypic view of burning.

These are the types of ideas which were used by children who had not been taught in any formal way about the chemical process of burning. We will now turn to consider the ideas used by the English children after a unit of work in which the following ideas were presented and discussed in the context of practical demonstrations:

(1)   air is a mixture of gases with oxygen as one component;
(2)   oxygen is required for burning;
(3)   when a substance burns it combines chemically with oxygen;
(4)   products of combustion may be solid, liquid or gaseous; and
(5)   the total mass of the products is the same as the mass of the constituents.

We will look at two aspects of students' thinking in the next sections: the role of air or oxygen in burning and the conservation of matter in burning.

The role of air/oxygen in burning

It appears that students do not have difficulty in appreciating that air or oxygen is needed for burning to take place. After teaching, the group of 11 to 12-year-olds all used this idea in saying whether or not a match would burn in outer space and in explaining why a candle goes out after it is covered with an inverted jar. Most of the children also appreciated that air was a mixture of gases and that oxygen is one component of the mixture.

Although the majority of children appreciated that air or oxygen is needed for burning to take place, few of them understood that in this process oxygen combines chemically with the substance which burns.

In discussing what happened when the inverted jar is placed over a burning candle a number commented that they think of the air or oxygen as being 'burnt away', and suggest that the candle will go out:

because the candle has burned up all the oxygen it needs to burn.

because the air which is enclosed in the jar is burned up.

The same children, after teaching, were asked to say why carbon burns but copper oxide (also a black powder) does not. Despite the fact that the children had recent experience of burning carbon and had burned copper to produce copper oxide, only a small proportion of the group said that the copper oxide would not burn because copper and oxygen had already reacted. The most common response given by nearly half the group was that copper oxide contains something which will not burn or which stops it burning (reflecting an aspect of the prototypic ideas about burning outlined earlier).

Although the majority of the children appreciated that air is necessary for burning, many did not consider it to be actively involved in the process, a finding which has also been reported for secondary school students in New Zealand.[9]

The difficulty students have in appreciating that burning involves chemical combination is also reflected in their responses to questions which ask about changes in mass on burning. A question about the burning of iron wool which has been used with both the group of 11 to 12-year-olds and in a survey of 15-year-old English students[10] is shown in Figure 8.4. The 15-year-olds surveyed were divided into those who had studied chemistry for the previous two years and those who had not. The same types of reasoning were identified in the answers given by both age groups, although the proportions using the different reasoning differ with age and with the amount of relevant teaching. The types of reasons given are summarized in Table 8.2.

About a quarter of the 12-year-olds predicted that the iron wool would get heavier, but only a few of these gave the reason that the iron combines with the oxygen:

pan P will get heavier. ... The ash would have encountered oxygen while burning and the oxygen would add to the weight (12-year-old).

More suggested the increase would be due to physical changes including the addition of soot from the flame. A confusion between weight and density was also apparent in the answers:

Pan P would be heavier than pan Q. ... When the iron wool was first on the scales there was air going through it but now it is a powder and it is in small parts it is heavier (12-year-old).

Over a quarter of younger students suggested that the weights would remain the same before and after the iron wool was heated arguing

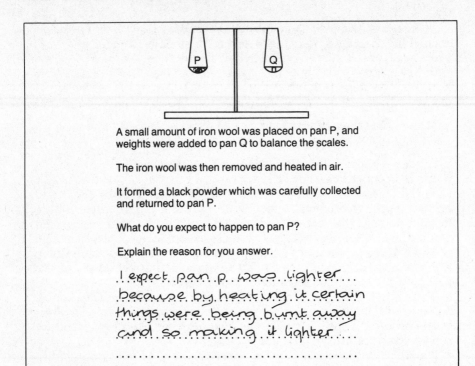

A small amount of iron wool was placed on pan P, and weights were added to pan Q to balance the scales.

The iron wool was then removed and heated in air.

It formed a black powder which was carefully collected and returned to pan P.

What do you expect to happen to pan P?

Explain the reason for you answer.

I expect pan p. was. lighter ... because. by. heating. it. certain things were. being. burnt. away and so. making. it. lighter. ....

Figure 8.4: The iron wool question and the response of a 15-year-old.

that it is still the same iron wool (a similar type of reasoning as that which was used in describing the burning of a splint).

> It would stay the same... because if it was burnt it would still all be there in powder form (12-year-old).

> it would stay the same because the powder is in the wool but heated up so there is really no difference (15-year-old).

Although we may judge this response to be incorrect it does indicate that students are thinking of something being conserved despite changes in appearance.

The idea that the iron wool gets lighter on heating was the most popular response of students of all ages. Some, especially the younger students, suggested that something would be burnt away or burnt out of the wool:

> Pan P will move up because it isn't as heavy as it was before, because some things will have been burnt out (15-year-old).

Most of the reasons given for the weight loss were in terms of either gas or smoke being driven off or the ash or powder that was left being lighter than the iron wool. About a quarter of the students gave the reason that gas or smoke would be given off (and this reasoning was

Table 8.2. Summary of types of responses to the question on the burning of iron wool

Type of response	% responses			
	Age 12 (post-teaching) n=48	all n=765	Age 15 C[a] n=224	non-C[a] n=541
Gets heavier	21	27	48	16
Iron combines with oxygen	0	15	42	4
Physical changes	23	10	6	9
soot from flame	14			
gas from flame	12			
heat from flame				
powder more 'solid' than iron wool				
powder more 'solid' than iron wool (which has a lot of air spaces in it)				
Other	6	2	0	3
Same	6	7	5	8
e.g. All returned to pan still the same iron, only change in appearance				
Gets lighter	44	52	41	56
Iron burnt away/lost on heating substances burnt out	15	4	2	5
Gas/smoke driven off	2	21	19	22
Ash/powder 'lighter' than iron	27	22	10	26
Oxidizes and loses weight iron displaced by oxygen	0	5	10	3

C[a], students studying chemistry for previous two years; non-C[a], students not studying chemistry for previous two years.

as prevalent among those who had studied chemistry for a number of years as for the younger students).

A similar proportion argued that ash or powder would be lighter than the iron wool:

> It would get lighter because powder is lighter than the iron wool (15-year-old).
>
> I think pan P would now weigh less because it is now powder and it was iron wool which is more solid than powder (12-year-old).

Both these responses reflect the connection which students tend to make between weight and solidity: powder, being less solid than iron wool is, therefore, lighter.

Overall, nearly half of the students of all ages suggested that the weight would decrease (this proportion did not change with age nor was it noticeably influenced by whether students had studied chemistry). The arguments used reflect the students' continued use of prototypic ideas about burning in which a solid is changed to an ash and smoke is driven off.

It is interesting to note how taught ideas about the role of oxygen in burning are assimilated into this scheme by students who have studied chemistry; these students tend to use such reasoning as 'iron oxide is produced which is driven off as smoke' or 'oxygen displaces the iron thus leaving an ash'.

A number of the features of students' thinking about burning are also encountered in their ideas about rusting. If you ask students, prior to teaching the topic, to predict what will happen to the mass of a pile of iron filings if it is left out in the air until the filings turn rusty, many are likely to predict a mass loss. The powdery rust is seen as being less substantive than the iron filings; the rust is even seen as 'eating away' the iron. These ideas are still evident even after teaching.

In the same survey of English 15-year-olds[10] students were asked to say how the mass of some nails would change when they became rusty. About a third of the students predicted the mass of the nails would increase, a third said it would stay the same and a third said it would decrease. Only a minority argued that the mass of the nails would increase because the nail combines with oxygen from the air forming iron oxide or 'rust'. Some (just over 10 per cent of those studying chemistry) argued that the mass would increase because the 'weight of the rust is added to the weight of the nail'. There is no indication in their responses that the iron from the nail is involved in producing the rust.

Some students said that the mass of the rusty nails will be the same as before arguing that nothing has been added or taken away:

> rust is part of the nail. It has not been formed by another substance.
>
> rust is iron that has been transformed.

In some cases students do recognize that rusting involved a reaction between iron and oxygen in the atmosphere; however, they argue that:

> The iron had only reacted with the oxygen of the air which does not weigh anything.

> The iron had only oxidized, reacted with oxygen, nothing disappears and oxygen weighs nothing.

Of the third of students who suggested the rusty nails would weigh less, most argued in terms of the rust eating away the nails. Some used the argument we have noted previously that the rust, which is a powder, is less solid than the iron nail and so weighs less. As with the previous question there are students who use taught ideas about oxygen but adapt them to their intuitive notions of rusting, giving reasons like:

> the oxygen dissolves some of the iron.

In general, we see the tendency of students to maintain their prototypic views about burning and rusting despite instruction. Burning is a process where the weight of the substance which is burnt is reduced and smoke or other combustible parts are being driven off. When this idea is in conflict with the view of burning introduced in school in which the products of combustion may be solid and can weigh more than the initial substance, a large proportion of students appear to be influenced in their thinking by perceptual features and to maintain some aspect of their prototypic thinking.

A number of other features of the students' ideas have also been identified here, including problems in conceptualizing weight, specifically the tendency to think of a powder as being lighter than a 'solid' substance, and appreciating that oxygen, air or gases in general are material substances and have mass (or weight).

This latter point has been explored with English children in the age range 11–16.[11] Children were asked to predict what will happen to a pair of scales, originally balanced with containers on both sides, when more air is pumped into one of the containers. Overall the majority of children in this age range appreciated that air has mass. However, nearly 50 per cent of the younger children and 25 per cent of the 15-year-olds suggested that increasing the amount of air in the container makes that side of the balance go up. Some suggest that this is 'because air is very light' or that 'air makes it lighter'.

Others argued that air has a tendency to rise:

> The air will rise inside the container so the container will rise (12-year-old).

> ... air is very light and it makes things rise (11-year-old).

> because, like a balloon, when air is put in it it rises (11-year-old).

Although it is only a minority of students who, in this context, did not appreciate that air has mass and hence weight, responses to questions about the role of air or oxygen in burning suggest that appreciating the substantive nature of air or oxygen is a problem when it comes to understanding weight changes when substances burn.

Conservation of matter during combustion

The ideas students used about the process of dissolving indicated the extent to which their thinking tended to be dominated by perceptually obvious features. A similar pattern emerges when students are asked about combustion in a closed system.

In the study with 11 to 12-year-old English students, two questions were asked which probed this issue. One of the questions showed a cartoon of an astronaut shut inside his space craft smoking a cigarette prior to lift-off. The students were asked whether the space craft (with all the things inside it) would be heavier, lighter or the same weight after his smoke. In their answers some students suggested it would be lighter because the smoke or ash would be lighter than the cigarette or because the smoke produced is weightless. The argument of oxygen being burnt up was also used:

> because a cigarette has to burn oxygen as well as tobbaco this means that some oxygen has disappeared.

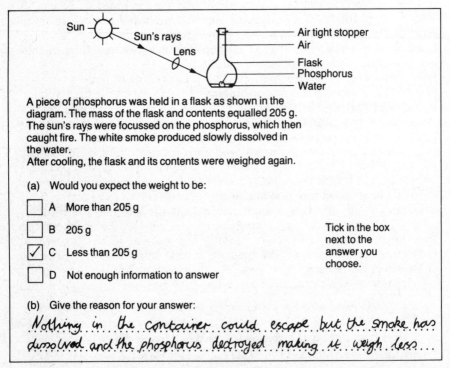

Figure 8.5: The burning phosphorus question and the response of a 15-year-old.

Table 8.3. Ideas used by 12 and 15-year-olds in response to the phosphorus question

Type of response	12-year-olds (post-teaching) n=48	% students		
		15-year-olds		
		C^a n=221	non-C^a n=555	*All* n=776
Same weight.........	46	43	22	30
Conservation reasoning nothing gets in or out	29	41	21	29
Other, e.g. phosphorus/smoke weighs same when dissolved	17	2	1	1
Loses weight.........	31	33	33	30
Oxygen used up	4	4	5	5
Smoke lighter than solid	4	18	15	16
Smoke loses mass when dissolved	10	11	10	10
Other	12			
Gains weight	17	4	8	6
due to extra weight of smoke				
Other	6	15	22	21
No response	0	5	17	12

C^a, students studying chemistry; non-C^a, students not studying chemistry.

Most students argued that the space craft would be heavier because of the smoke produced or the extra weight of combustion products. Only a small number (about 10 per cent) argued that the weight did not change:

> because nothing has gone out of the space craft even when the cigarette has burned.

It appears that, instead of considering the complete system, students are focusing on component aspects; the burning down of the cigarette or the production of smoke in thinking about weight changes.

We find the same types of ideas being used in response to another similar question, shown in Figure 8.5, involving the comparison of the mass of a sealed flask and its contents before and after the contents had been burned. This question was also set to 15-year-old students[10] and the types of answers given by the students of both ages are summarized in Table 8.3.

Again we see familiar ideas returning: loss in weight due to oxygen being used up, smoke being lighter than a solid, or substances losing weight when dissolved. It is perhaps interesting to note the similarity in the prevalence of these ideas between the younger and older pupils and between those who do and do not study chemistry.

Although only a minority of students gave answers to these questions which indicated that they conserved mass, it may be misleading to suggest that the majority of secondary students think that matter does 'come and go'. As with the dissolving problem, the issue appears to be what aspect of the problem students are focusing on in considering their answer. We may not be able to infer that students do not conserve mass in a chemical reaction, but what we can say, however, is that other more obvious perceptual features such as those identified in this section tend to dominate students' thinking and govern their responses.

Conclusions

A number of points emerge from these studies about childrens' understandings about the nature of material substances. Students of secondary school age have no difficulty in appreciating the substantive nature of solids and liquids and the majority of older students appreciate that gases too are substantive. To students, what counts as evidence for this is complex. How the amount of substance is measured is even more problematic. The notion of mass has various connotations for students including volume and weight. The weight of a substance, however, which is often informally used in classrooms as an alternative to mass is seen by children to vary with circumstances. For example, weight is seen to be associated with notions of density— a substance in a powder form is considered to weigh less than in a solid form. Weight is also influenced by buoyancy effects—air is considered to be weightless not because it is not substantive but because it is thought of as 'staying up' rather than 'pressing down' on surfaces.

These factors may interfere with students' attempts to construct a view of amount, substance or mass. Behind such a view is the idea that there is something which exists unchanged despite changes in physical appearances. When such changes are quite substantial, as in a change of state or when substances dissolve, it is all the more difficult for students to appreciate that the changes are in some sense reversible and hence to construct for themselves the idea of the continued existence of the component substances.

Perceptions are immediate and influential: constructing for oneself the idea that something is still there even though it cannot be perceived requires drawing on knowledge outside the event itself—appreciating that sugar is still there even when dissolved may involve thinking about what the solution would taste like, or what would happen if the water were evaporated.

Initially when children are first beginning to think about these kinds of transformations, such ideas require imagination on their part in moving away from the perceptually obvious focus of the situation to think about other less obvious aspects of it. The tendency of students to focus on limited aspects of the tasks where substances were burnt in a closed system is further evidence for this perceptually dominated way of thinking. Eventually some students develop a notion of substance as being conserved and therefore do not need to make such an imaginative effort when the idea is required in the future. It is probable that the extent to which such an idea is readily accessible to a student will depend on the amount of use that has been made of it previously.

It may be, as Piaget suggested, that the construction of the idea that matter is particulate supports the development of conservation of matter: changes in appearance can then be modelled in terms of rearrangements of indestructible particles. Certainly the majority of secondary students who are introduced to the model, use the idea that matter is particulate rather than continuous. When they use particulate ideas, however, they tend not to think of the particles as unchanging in themselves but often assume that the particles have the same bulk properties as the parent substance. Thus particulate ideas in themselves are not necessarily consistent with ideas of the conservation of matter (since the particles may melt, shrink, etc.).

Here we are seeing at a microscopic level an assimilation of particulate ideas into the views of the properties of matter that students already have.

This tendency to assimilate new ideas into already existing ways of thinking was clearly evident in the studies of students' ideas about burning and rusting where prototypic notions clearly influenced students' thinking about phenomena even after teaching.

The construction of what happens during a chemical reaction

requires an appreciation of atomicity of matter and its indestructibility. A general pattern in children's understanding of chemical changes has been proposed by Andersson,[6] who suggests that the following features can be identified in the development of children's thinking in this area:

(1) *That's how things happen*:   children are unquestioning about a chemical change whether it is the rusting of iron nails or the burning of a splint.

(2) *The displacement of matter*:   children argue that a change occurs, a 'new' substance appears simply because it has been moved from another place; the smoke formed when wood burns is seen as having been driven out of the wood by the flame.

(3) *Modification*:   in this case a new substance is seen as the original substance but in a new form. Some of the children talked about the burning of a splint in this way saying the ash was still the same splint but in a different form.

(4) *Transmutation*:   here the original substance is considered to be transformed into a completely new substance.

(5) *Chemical interaction*:   in this view, substances are seen as being composed of atoms of different elements. New substances can be formed by the dissociation or recombination of atoms in the original substances.

Although the chemical interaction view is the one which is introduced in teaching it appears that other views and interpretations of chemical changes are quite prevalent in students' reasoning.

It is possible that students have constructed ideas about atoms and molecules, and their symbolic representation in the way intended in science lessons, but when presented with a physical phenomenon to explain, students tend not to see these taught ideas as relevant using instead their intuitive ideas based on experience. The issue which needs to be considered is not just whether students understand the theoretical ideas or models they are exposed to in teaching but whether they can use them or see them as useful and appropriate in interpreting actual events.

References

[1]Cosgrove, M. and Osborne, R. (1981). Physical change. Working paper No. 26, Learning in Science Project, University of Waikato, Hamilton, New Zealand.
[2]Dow, W. M., Auld, J. and Wilson, D. (1978). *Pupils' Concepts of Gases, Liquids and Solids*. Dundee College of Education: Dundee.
[3]Brook, A., Briggs, H. and Driver, R. (1984). Aspects of secondary students' understanding of the particulate nature of matter. Children's Learning in Science Project, Centre for Studies in Science and Mathematics Education, University of Leeds, Leeds.
[4]Piaget, J. and Inhelder, B. (1974). *The Child's Construction of Quantities*. Routledge and Kegan Paul: London.

[5]Driver, R. and Russell, T. (1982). An investigation of the ideas of heat, temperature and change of state of children aged between 8 and 14 years. Centre for Studies in Science and Mathematics Education, University of Leeds, Leeds.

[6]Andersson, B. (1984). *Chemical Reactions*. EKNA Group, University of Gothenburg, Gothenburg, Sweden.

[7]Holding, B. Investigation of schoolchildren's understanding of the process of dissolving with special reference to the conservation of matter and the development of atomistic ideas. Unpublished Ph.D. thesis, University of Leeds.

[8]Knox, J. (1985). A study of secondary students' ideas about the process of burning. M.Ed thesis, University of Leeds, Leeds.

[9]Schollum, N. (1981). Chemical change. Working paper No. 27, Learning in Science Project, University of Waikato, Hamilton, New Zealand.

[10]Driver, R., Child, D., Gott, R., Head, J., Johnson, S., Worsley, C. and Wylie, F. (1984). *Science in schools: Age 15. Research Report No. 2*, Assessment of Performance Unit, Department of Education and Science, London.

[11]Miller, S., Robinson, D. and Driver, R. (1985). Secondary students' ideas about air and air pressure. In *Learning, doing and understanding in science.* (Eds. Bell, B., Watts, D. M. and Ellington, K.) SSCR: London.

[12]Meheut, M., Saltiel, E. and Tiberghien, A. (1985). Students' conceptions about combustion (11–12 years old). *European Journal of Science Education.* (In press). 7 (1), 83–93.

CHAPTER 9

The Earth as a Cosmic Body

Joseph Nussbaum

In our experience when groups of science teachers are presented with the question 'What are the most essential ideas which form the Earth conception?', they usually spontaneously propose a list of ideas similar to the following:

(1) the Earth is round;
(2) the Earth revolves on its axis and this makes day and night;
(3) the Earth is part of the solar system, the Earth travels around the Sun;
(4) the Earth is huge, its diameter is about 13,000 km;
(5) the Earth's axis is tilted and this causes the different seasons;
(6) the Earth has a molten core and a cold and solid outer crust;
(7) the majority of the Earth's surface is covered by oceans; and
(8) the Earth exerts a gravitational force and this causes objects to fall.

A list such as the above exemplifies the results of a 'subject matter approach' to the task of concept analysis (as opposed to a 'cognitive approach' which is described below). In a subject matter approach the task is conceived as extracting the important relevant ideas from science text books which represent the mature state of the discipline. The danger of this approach is that it focuses attention on advanced aspects of the concept while the identification and characterization of its very essence is neglected or taken for granted. And thus this essence is apt to be inappropriately treated in instruction.

Although most of the ideas above are indeed relevant and important, they are much more advanced than those few which form together the basis of the Earth concept, i.e. the Earth we live on is a sphere surrounded by unlimited space. This chapter will attempt to show that this basic idea is not self-evident, especially for young children.

An alternative approach to concept analysis is 'a cognitive approach' which focuses on the cognitive demands that the learning of the concept presents. One of the methods that is useful in undertaking a cognitive approach to concept analysis is to contrast a concept with its antithesis and characterize their antithetical aspects. This method may help avoid the possibility of ideas seeming deceptively self-evident. Thus, with regard to the Earth conception, the question asked is: 'What are the essentials which form the *most primitive* concept of the Earth?'

The first most primitive idea is that the Earth is *flat*, extending *infinitely* sideways and downwards. It should be recognized that an assertion about the flatness of the Earth immediately implies another assertion about the nature of *sky* and *space*. Those who possess a notion of an infinite flat Earth also believe that sky (whatever its substance may be) is horizontal, paralleling the Earth (remember the drawings of the Earth and sky by young children). If they speak about space they maintain that this space is limited at its bottom, where the infinite flat Earth is (not excluding possible limits in other directions as well). Thus, it is very important to note that (1) the flatness of the Earth and (2) the horizontal feature of the sky and the limiting function that the Earth serves in relation to space, are two ideas which are mutually implied and mutually dependent. A third idea which is essential to the primitive notion is that (3) the directions in which falling objects travel at different locations on the Earth, all form *parallel* lines (compatible with some absolute up-down dimension). These lines are vertical-perpendicular to the flat Earth's surface. These three essential ideas which together form a coherent (though primitive) conception of the Earth are represented visually in Figure 9.1.

The transition from the most primitive conception of the Earth to the scientific one requires simultaneous change in each of these three ideas. As the child changes his or her idea about the *shape* of the Earth, from a flat model to a *spherical* one, ideas about the features of the sky and space are changed along with it. Sky ceases to be horizontal and space 'loses its bottom', becoming 'spread out' evenly in all directions. The flat Earth, which has served as the infinite solid boundary limiting space at its bottom, changes by 'curving' and

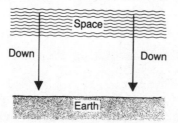

Figure 9.1: The three essential ideas which form the most primitive conception of the Earth.

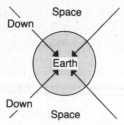

Figure 9.2:   The three essential ideas of the scientific conception of the Earth.

'shrinking' and becoming a *finite* spherical body embraced by *infinite* space. The transition from believing that cosmic space has a solid bottom (i.e. the Earth) to believing in a completely 'open' space that is evenly spread out in all directions, is a significant cognitive leap which is even greater than the transition from a flat model to a spherical one for the Earth. As the child accepts the spherical model for the Earth, 'fall' directions (i.e. the direction of the Earth's gravitational field) become radial directions, and up-down lines at different locations on the Earth are no longer parallel (see Figure 9.2).

The idea that up-down directions are not *absolute*, pointing to 'space's bottom', but are determined by the Earth's centre as the frame of reference, is central to the scientific conception. At this point, resolving the issue of what makes all objects fall toward the Earth's centre may not be crucial to the notion of the Earth as a cosmic body, for one can believe like Aristotle that:

> ... in fact, the true explanation of this motion [falling of objects] is that
> all heavy things have a natural tendency to move towards the centre of
> the earth.[1]

On the other hand, one might hold the Newtonian explanation that the Earth and other objects mutually exert a gravitational force resulting in what we perceive as the falling of objects toward the Earth's centre. Both explanations will meet the demands imposed by a notion of the Earth that is based on the three above ideas.

I hope that the sections which follow will convince the reader that these three ideas are in fact the most essential elements of the Earth conception.

Cognitive difficulties in acquiring the scientific Earth conception

What cognitive difficulties do pupils encounter in discarding their primitive notion of the Earth in favour of accepting the scientific notion? The basic cognitive difficulty most probably involves the general phenomenon of children's 'egocentrism', described by Piaget.

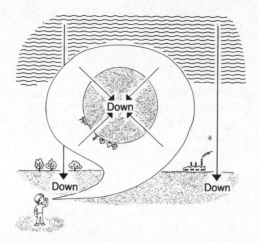

Figure 9.3: The cognitive demand in conceptualizing the Earth as a cosmic body—overcoming an egocentric frame of reference.

This is childrens' strong tendency to interpret reality only according to the way it is perceived from their own perspective (their *egocentric* frame of reference). The only way for people to conceptualize the Earth they live on as a huge sphere in space, is to visualize how their immediate surroundings would look from outer space. Hence they must overcome what their immediate perception 'tells' them regarding the three essentials of the Earth concept: the 'flat Earth', 'horizontal sky' and 'bottomed space', and 'absolute-parallel up-down directions'. Figure 9.3 represents this difficulty visually.

In terms of Piaget's theory, the mental operation that is involved in the process of developing the scientific Earth conception is imagining reality as it would be seen from different perspectives, i.e. overcoming the egocentric view. Thus, an indication that a pupil has meaningfully attained the scientific Earth concept will be his or her ability to operate cognitively on an Earth model without showing any signs of interference by egocentric thinking.

Probes to investigate children's conceptions

An interview procedure was developed with the aim of revealing the child's version of the Earth concept.

It was decided to start the interview with a set of questions in the absence of any visual Earth model, as we observed that visual props could provide the child with some cues that would interfere with the spontaneity and authenticity of his or her natural thinking. This set of questions included the following: 'What is the shape of the Earth? How do you know that the Earth is round? Which way do we have to look in order to see the Earth? (This question, though seemingly trivial, was found to be very useful as will be shown later in the discussion of the results.) Why don't we see the Earth as a ball? What does one have to do in order to see the Earth as a ball?' At this point the child is presented with a large globe and a removable figure of a girl stuck onto it, together with pictures in a booklet. The basic tasks common to nearly all the assessment items involved *predicting* directions of imaginary free-fall occurring at different points on a model of the Earth and *explaining* these predictions. Three examples of such problem situations are given below:

Problem 1: Water in bottles

I: [refers the child to a figure in the interview booklet—Figure 9.4a]...
Suppose this is a picture of real Earth. These two bottles [pointing at the two bottles on the North Pole] belong to a girl who is standing on this part of the Earth [interviewer simultaneously sticks the figure of the girl to the globe on the land of Greenland]. One of these bottles is closed and is half-filled with water. The other bottle is open and is empty. Take the blue crayon and draw some water in the opened bottle so that the water in the two bottles will be at the same level. [The child draws water in the opened bottle.] Suppose this girl has travelled with her two bottles from where she was before to this country [interviewer removes the figure from Greenland and sticks it to the globe on the land of Chile]. She put her two bottles on the ground next to her. Think abount the way the water will be in the bottles on this part of the Earth. Draw some water in the way it would be in the bottles on this part of the Earth.

The common responses to the above question are shown in Figure 9.4b,c. The response depicted in Figure 9.4b can be taken as a clear indicator of some egocentric thinking. What about the response illustrated in Figure 4c? Can it be taken as a clear indicator of the opposite conception, namely a scientific conception of Earth?
    A second step was designed to probe this question in order to detect those who remain egocentric although their overt response masks this. Those who responded as shown in Figure 9.4c were asked further:

One child with whom I spoke before thought that if the girl left the open

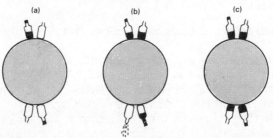

Figure 9.4:   A problem situation: predicting water position in the empty bottles (a) and two common alternative responses (b and c).

bottle for a while here [on the land of Chile], then she would not find any more water in the open bottle when she came back. Do you think that child was right or that he was wrong? Why would the water drip or not drip out of the open bottle?

Interestingly, this second question affects some of the children whose overt response was correct (Figure 9.4c) and they agree with 'the child', contradicting their previous response. They are willing to draw what they believe would happen to the water in the opened bottle, and their drawings look like that in Figure 9.4b. Their explanation is that the bottles are upside down and that there is no cork to stop the water in the open bottle from flowing out. It is possible that some of those who responded in this way reached a 'scientifically correct' solution, not because they have really operated conceptually rather than egocentrically, but because they have managed to isolate a narrow frame of reference including the figure and the line of the ground under it (Figure 9.5). In responding to the question, they did not use the whole Earth model as their frame of reference but referred to a 'familiar' segment of the model, ignoring the rest of it.

These children may merely be demonstrating an ability to rotate the picture mentally in order to solve the problem egocentrically. The above interpretation suggests that there may have been two subgroups who offered the response shown in Figure 9.5; those whose response evolved from a basically egocentric frame of reference (and whose ability to rotate the picture mentally and then solve it egocentrically helps to fool the adult observer) and those whose response evolved from the scientific point of view.

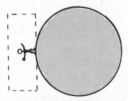

Figure 9.5: A segment of the Earth model when used as a narrow frame of reference allows egocentric children to give an apparently correct response.

Problem 2: The fall of rock

I: [Referring to a picture in the interview booklet (Figure 9.6a]... Suppose there are seven people standing at different places on the Earth. Each of them is going to drop a rock from his hand. Draw for each person the line that shows the way the rock is going to fall. [The child is asked first to draw lines for persons one through five only, leaving out positions six and seven.]

The responses up to now might be either as in Figure 9.6b or as in Figure 9.6c. The response illustrated in Figure 9.6c confronts us with

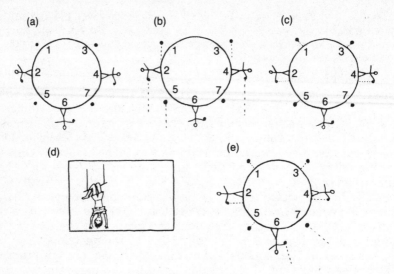

Figure 9.6: A problem situation presented in 'two steps' to detect 'hidden' egocentric views.

The child is shown (a) and asked to draw, for positions 1–5 only, lines representing how rocks would fall. Two common alternative responses are given in (b) and (c). If the answer was as in (c) then (d) is shown and the child is asked why the boy's shirt comes to the boy's face. (d) affects some of the children who first responded correctly (c) and they see persons 6 and 7 as standing upside-down. Hence they later predict falls to be shown as in (e).

the same difficulties of interpretation as mentioned above. Before they continue with person six, children who responded as in Figure 9.6c are presented with a picture card, shown in Figure 9.6d.

I: What do you see in this picture? What is happening to the boy's shirt? Why? [Children usually answer that the shirt comes down to the boy's face because he is too skinny.] Let's return to the picture of the Earth. Suppose person number six was too skinny and he didn't have a belt; do you think that his shirt might fall toward his face in the same way? Why do you think that the shirt of person six would/would not fall toward his head? Now remember that persons six and seven are going to drop a rock from their hands. Draw the lines that show the way their rocks are going to fall.

Some of the children who at first responded as in Figure 9.6c, now answer that the shirt of person six would come toward his face since he stands upside down on the Earth. When asked to draw lines showing how the rocks would fall for persons number six and seven, these children usually responded as in Figure 9.6e.

It is seen that such stories and pictures influence these children by suggesting to them (by the use of the story in the first example, and by the use of the picture card in the second example) a very clear egocentric perception of the problem situation. The child is forced to make a choice, to agree with this implicit suggestion or to reject it. Those who readily accept the cue and changed their mode of response were probably essentially egocentric to start with. What about those who reject the cue? Does their rejection demonstrate an operation from the scientific point of view? Or, have they remained egocentric but, despite the attempts to present them with tempting egocentric cues, they still managed to isolate and relate to a segment of the Earth's surface in their response? A new kind of interview task is needed here. This is introduced in the next interview stage and requires the child to predict the directions in which objects fall in imaginary holes dug into the Earth.

Problem 3: Direction in which objects fall in holes dug into the Earth

The child is asked first whether or not he or she believes that it is possible to dig such holes into the Earth. Supposing that it is possible to do so, he or she is then asked to predict what would happen if a person dropped a rock through such a hole (Figure 9.7). In order to make sure that the child perceives the problem situation three-dimensionally, the interviewer presents each problem using three visual aids: the picture in the booklet, the globe with the movable figure of a girl, and a styrofoam ball containing similar holes into which a pencil could be inserted for emphasizing the direction of the holes. The purpose of this type of question is to force the child into a more clear-cut choice between using the Earth's centre as the point of reference for the 'down' direction or using the Earth's surface as a sort of egocentric point of reference. This new type of question further enhanced the interviewer's ability to differentiate between the various notions held by the children.

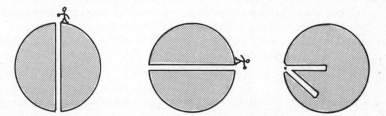

Figure 9.7: Drawings used with tasks demanding predictions of fall directions *inside* the Earth.

The administration of the interview

The interview content, described above, was applied in a sequence of interview studies carried out in New York[2] and California,[5] in Israel[3,6] and in Nepal.[4] The basic procedure and style presented above was used only in the pioneer study by the author, but the various modifications introduced in the procedure in later studies did not depart from the basic underlying rationale. The interviews were administered in the various studies to children of 8 to 14 years of age.

It should be emphasized that children rarely stated their notion explicitly and elaborately. In most cases it was because the children themselves were not fully aware of their own belief sets. Elements of children's notions were exposed through their responses to the interview tasks. When a child's total performance was reviewed and analysed, attempts were made to reconstruct from the exposed elements a coherent conception or *notion*.

Children's notions about the Earth

Five qualitatively different *notions* (belief sets) about the Earth were found to be held by different children in the sample groups. These five notions may not be the only ones that were held by the sample groups: needless to say, they may not be the only ones prevalent among children in general. However, the various studies by the author and others repeatedly found the same types of notions to be held by children of different ages and of different ethnic origin. Indeed the frequency of the prevalence of each notion varied from group to group, as will be described later in this chapter.

Notion 1

The Earth we live on is flat and not round like a ball.

Children who hold this notion do not state it explicitly at the start. They begin like all the others by answering that the Earth is round like a ball. However, a brief verbal probing reveals that they do not really believe we live on the surface of a huge ball. Rather, they believe that the Earth is basically flat. It would be a mistake, however, to infer that their answers are meaningless to them. Each child hears about the Earth's spherical shape from different sources. Failing to understand its real meaning, the child attempts to make some sense of it for her/himself.

Various examples of this sort are the following:

(a) Daryl (8 years) was asked, 'Why do people say that the Earth is round like a ball?' His answer was, 'Because sometimes roads go in circles around trees in parks' (Figure 9.8a).

The child believes the Earth we live on is flat and . . .

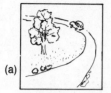

(a)

. . . the Earth's roundness
is just the roads' curves

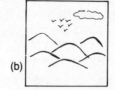

(b)

. . . the Earth's roundness
is just the mountain's shape.

(c)

. . . the globe represents
some other planet in
the sky.

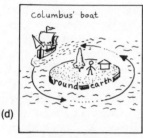

(d)

. . . is surrounded by ocean.
This is what enabled Columbus
to go around it.

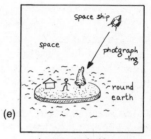

(e)

. . . is surrounded by ocean.
The round shape of this flat
Earth is seen in photographs
taken from space.

Figure 9.8: Representative answers to questions by children who hold notion I concepts of the Earth.

(b) Chris (8 years) answered the same question as follows: 'Because the Earth is round on hills and mountains' (Figure 9.8b).

(c) Constantine (8 years) answered the question, 'Which way do we have to look to see the Earth?' by saying, 'We have to look up to the sky.' Further probing revealed that he believed that there are two Earths. The one he lives on is flat, and the other, which is round like a ball, is a kind of planet in the sky (Figure 9.8c). He explained that the globes are models of that round Earth which can be seen in the sky. To the question, 'What kinds of things are on the Earth?' he answered, 'There are astronauts over there.'

(d) Dan ($12\frac{1}{2}$ years) said that the Earth is round and that Columbus was the first one to discover this by his trip around the world. Dan drew the Earth as round but his other performances indicated that he believed in a flat Earth that constituted the bottom of the cosmos. This flat model could not allow a journey around the world, and only after further probing did this child make his ideas clear. He believed that the world was flat and

round and surrounded by a big ocean. Columbus' boat travelled
around the world and finally returned home (Figure 9.8d).

(e)   Sarah (10 years) explained that the Earth was round and flat
and surrounded by an ocean (like Dan, above). Only from a
space ship could one see all of it at once and thus see the round
shape of the Earth (Figure 9.8e).

The above examples demonstrate how the meaning of a piece of
scientific information about the Earth's shape may undergo major
change and distortion by students while they attempt to attach some
meaning to it to make it compatible with their strong belief that the
Earth is flat.

When children of this category (flat Earth) were asked later in the
interview to predict falls in pretent situations on *given* round Earth
models (a globe and drawings in the interview booklet), they predicted
that objects would fall off the Earth when dropped from anywhere in
the southern hemisphere. When they were asked, 'Where will the
object fall towards?', they answered, 'Down'. They drew a line on the
picture to show this direction. When they were asked further, 'What
might be down there?', they answered that there is ground or an ocean
down there. When they were asked to draw what they meant, they
drew brown ground or blue ocean 'below' the Earth.

Leonidas (9 years) told the interviewer that astronauts saw the
Earth as a ball. He knew that the Earth is larger than Mars. He
could identify places on the globe. Leonidas had a book entitled
Space Dictionary and this was his main source of information. He
was asked the entire sequence of questions cited above. After he
drew 'ground' below the Earth, the interviewer said 'Suppose you
and I were in this picture. Draw two persons in the place where we
would be.' Leonidas drew two figures on the 'ground' below the
Earth (Figure 9.9a).

The reader may rightly raise the question what a spherical model

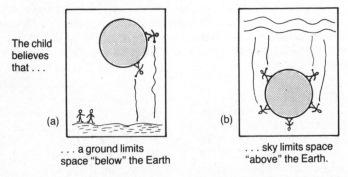

The child
believes
that . . .

(a)   (b)

. . . a ground limits   . . . sky limits space
space "below" the Earth   "above" the Earth.

Figure 9.9:   Further representative answers to questions by children who
hold notion I concepts of the Earth.

carrying small figures of people may mean to children who maintain that the Earth is flat? I have no answer to this question, but I would make the point that they are all willing to 'play the game' with the interviewer. So they take the spherical shape with the figure standing on it as a strange situation to which they have to add their familiar 'safe ground'.

Another task, indicative of notion 1, is the following. A child was provided with a picture of five people standing on different parts of the Earth, and was told that each one was going to throw a ball up to the sky. The child was then asked to draw lines showing the direction of each throw and to draw the sky in its proper place. Figure 9.9b shows a fairly typical performance of this task.

Diana (8 years), who performed as shown in Figure 9.9b, was asked 'Why didn't you draw a line for the fifth person?' She answered: 'Because this person cannot throw the ball up to the sky.' She was then asked 'What does he have to do in order to be able to throw it up to the sky?' Diana replied: 'To go to some other place.'

Diana's drawing and responses demonstrate another aspect of notion 1. While on the previous task, described above, the child responded by limiting space at its 'bottom', with oceans or ground, here the child limits the space 'above' the Earth by drawing the sky. Establishing horizontal ground 'below' and sky 'above' the Earth's model is really an act of mental reconstruction of reality from a clear egocentric point of view.

Notion 2

Children whose ideas are classified under this notion believe that the Earth is a huge ball composed of two hemispheres, as illustrated in Figure 9.10. The lower part is solid and is made up basically of soil and rocks. People live on the planary part of the 'lower' hemispheric surface (Figure 9.10a-c). The 'upper' hemisphere is not solid; it is made out of 'air' or 'sky' or 'air and sky'. Sky may be conceived as paralleling the flat ground at the 'top' of the upper hemisphere (Figure 9.10b). It may also be conceived to have a shape that covers the flat ground and touches it at its round edge (Figure 9.10c). Children in this category would claim that we live *inside* the Earth and that it is impossible to live upon it.

Nancy (9 years) was asked: 'You have said that the Earth is round like a ball. Where is that ball?' She answered: 'We are inside the ball'. Asked to explain what she meant, she said 'The Earth is flat, but what is round like a ball is the sky.' Voluntarily she drew a picture of what she meant (Figure 9.10a).

In this notion category, the sun, the moon and the stars may be conceived to exist *inside* the ball, *upon* the ball's surface or *outside* the ball. Outside the Earth there is *space* which is empty even of air

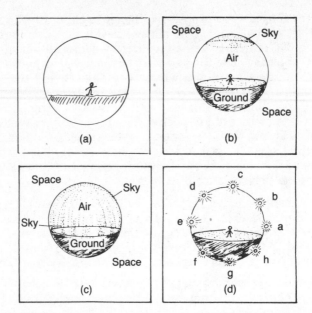

Figure 9.10: Illustrations for various ideas within the framework of notion 2.

according to one version, or which contains 'oxygenless air' that people (astronauts) cannot breathe.

This notion is a significant advance over the first one. Indeed, while it is still 'primitive' from the scientific point of view, it should be noticed that this model represents a relatively elaborated mental construction that the child has produced in attempting to accommodate his or her cognitive structure to fit the scientific information encountered. With all its incorrectness it may be seen as an elaborated model because, unlike the first one, it includes the idea that the Earth we live on is a *finite body surrounded by space*. This conceptual advance over the first notion allows the child to propose relatively more sophisticated explanations of various phenomena. Scientific correctness need not be a criterion of sophistication. The following may serve as an illustration.

Igal (12 years), whose notion is represented by Figure 10d, says that the sun travels across the sky and then slides down below the 'solid Earth' and subsequently rises again. By constructing this picture, Igal attaches meaning to a statement like—'At night the sun is below us, behind the Earth'—that he might have heard from some authoritative source. This picture also provides some explanation of volcanic phenomena, since Igal now 'really understands' what they mean by saying that 'there is a big fire deep down, underneath the ground'—the sun at position g in Figure 9.10d.

Notion 2 represents a very significant but only partial accommodation of the cognitive structure towards the scientific model. Notice that it still includes the belief that all of the countries are spread out on the huge flat disc of the solid Earth. When these children are presented with the task of predicting free fall in various places on a round model, they respond as shown in Figure 9.6b. However, they might add explicitly that the persons should not have been drawn there because it is impossible to stand on the Earth from outside. If these children are asked 'will the rock keep on falling forever or will it stop somewhere?', they respond that it would fall forever unless it hit some planet or star. Hence, 'down' directions are considered in this notion as *absolute* in cosmic space, unrelated to the Earth. These directions are compatible with the egocentric perception of what is 'downward'.

Notion 3

Children who hold notion 3 have some idea of an unlimited space that surrounds the spherical solid Earth. However, their thinking is still partially 'primitive'. They do not use the Earth as the frame of reference for up-down directions, rather, they assume the existence of absolute, Earth independent, up-down direction in cosmic space. They draw objects falling off and away from the Earth and in this respect resemble children holding notions 1 and 2. A sample task which differentiates notion 3 children from those possessing notions 1 and 2 is the following. The child was asked to predict the way rocks would fall as they were thrown *straight up* by several people, each standing in a different place on the globe.

After the children drew the lines, they were asked to draw in the sky using light blue shading. Notion 3 children drew the lines showing the path of the thrown rocks as 'obeying' some absolute up direction independent of the Earth model (Figure 9.11a). However, at the same time they drew sky all around the Earth model. In another task, mentioned above (Figure 9.4), children in this category predicted that an open bottle in the southern hemisphere would not hold water; the water, it was predicted, would drip and fall 'down' away from the

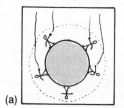
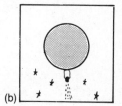

Figure 9.11: Representative responses of children possessing notion 3. (a) Rocks thrown 'straight up' with sky surrounding the Earth; (b) water falling from the southern hemisphere towards the southern sky.

Earth. To the question 'where is the water falling towards?', they answered: 'To the sky' or 'To space' (Figure 9.11b).

Notion 4

Children who hold this notion demonstrate some understanding of all the elements of the Earth concept. They seem to believe that we live on a spherical planet, and they know that there is space all around the Earth. They use the Earth as the frame of reference of up-down directions—namely, up-down directions are toward and away from the Earth. Some of them might even explain falling toward the Earth as being caused by *gravity*. However, all these 'correct' predictions apply to situations of free-fall upon the Earth's surface. They seem to relate to the Earth as a whole and do not relate up-down directions to the Earth's centre. For example, consider the way in which children who hold notion 4 typically respond to this interview question:

> Suppose that somebody dug a hole straight down through the Earth. Now, he is going to drop a rock into this hole. Draw the line that shows the way the rock will fall.*

Children who hold notion 4 usually respond to this question by predicting that the rock will fall all the way to the other side of the hole. Some of them add that the rock would come out of the hole and land next to it on the ground (Figure 9.12a), others say that the rock would stay floating at the opening of the other side of the hole (Figure 9.12b). For comparison consider a response typical to children holding notion 1 (Figure 9.12c) and one which is typical to children who hold notions 2 or 3 (Figure 9.12d).

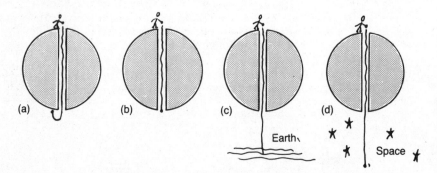

Figure 9.12: Predictions of a free-fall through the Earth typical to notion 4 (a or b) or typical to notion 1 (c) or 2 and 3 (d).

---

*The scientific answer that the rock would fall back and forth forever if there was no air resistance is not anticipated here. At this point, any response that considers the Earth's centre as the lowest point of the Earth will be satisfactory.

The child relates up-down directions to the
Earth's surface but not to the Earth's centre.
He believes that the rocks would fall . . .

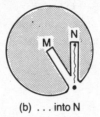

(a) . . . into K   (b) . . . into N

Figure 9.13:   Representative answers given by children who hold
notion 4.

In another task the children were asked: 'Suppose there are two
holes dug into the Earth, both start from the same point on the
ground, but inside each go in different directions. Someone is going to
drop a rock at the common opening to the two holes (Figure 9.13a).
Will the rock fall into K or into L?' (in Figure 9.13b. '... into M or into
N?').

Children using notion 4 said that the rock would fall into hole K
(Figure 9.13a) or into N (Figure 9.13b). They believed that objects
should always fall towards the Earth. However, once their objects
'entered' the pretend holes in the Earth they revealed that they did
not relate to the Earth's centre but to some absolute (Earth independent) 'down' direction. Therefore, they consider K (or N) to point
downwards more than L (or M). Observing Figure 9.13b, these
children mentally rotated the figure and thus N was perceived as
pointing straight down.

Notion 5

Children who held this notion demonstrated a satisfactory and stable
notion of the three aspects of the Earth concept: (1) a spherical planet,
(2) surrounded by space, and (3) with objects falling to its centre. For
example, Brigitte (8 years) was asked to predict what would happen
in the hypothetical situation shown in Figure 9.14a. The information
provided was that the person was going to drop the rock. Brigitte
drew a line from the rock down to the Earth's centre.

I: Why didn't you continue the line?
B: I don't think that the rock would continue to fall, because from here
     on it is going up.

William (9 years) performed this task in a similar way, but answered
the last question somewhat differently:

The rock would fall to the middle because gravity pulls it there. It won't

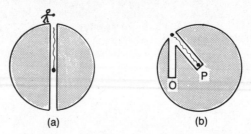

Figure 9.14:   Representative answers given by children who hold notion 5.

continue to fall because there is nothing that pulls it further [Figure 9.14a].

Timmy ($8\frac{1}{2}$ years) was asked to predict into which of the two holes a rock would fall (Figure 9.14b). He predicted that the rock would fall into hole P. When asked why, Timmy responded:

Because P is going straight down but O is slanted.

Similarly, he said that L and M were straight down while K and N were slanted (Figure 9.13).

These examples demonstrate that children who hold notion 5 possess all three necessary aspects of the concept. They can overcome immediate perceptual distractions and respond consistently in a mode which is compatible with the content of a scientific Earth conception.

Summary

The five notions described above are presented visually in Figure 9.15. They are ordered in a way that suggests the existence of conceptual progression from notion 1 (the most egocentric, 'primitive' one) to notion 5 (the most 'decentred', 'scientific' one). The three essential elements of the Earth concept are presented as three variables or dimensions. This is to say that each element takes at least two alternative forms (for example, 'shape' may be flat or spherical).

Although each dimension has two conceptually opposite forms, it does not appear in the five notions as dichotomous (either-or). Rather, it appears in several alternative forms, representing various levels of intensity and explicitness of the alternative extremities of the dimension. For example, the flat shape is very explicit and intensively expressed in notion 1. It is expressed only partially but yet quite explicitly in the flat part of the solid hemisphere in notion 2. It is expressed implicitly and partially in notion 3, where the assumption is made that people can stand and function only on 'top' (the minimally curved part) of the Earth. On the other side of the dimension, the spherical shape is expressed very explicitly in notions 5 and 4, and less and less so in notions 3 and 2, respectively.

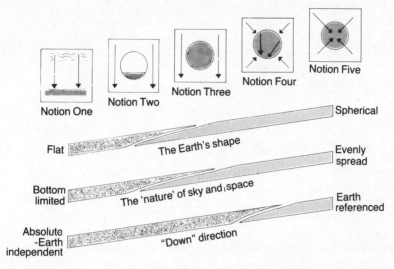

Figure 9.15: A schematic representation of the five alternative notions about the Earth as a cosmic body. The three essential elements of an Earth notion are presented as variables appearing in various forms between the two extreme alternatives.

Evolution of children's conceptions with age and conventional instruction

Frequency of each of the five notions in the different school grades—cross-age studies

In two studies[3,6] I attempted to trace the development of the Earth concept in children of various ages in Israel, where it is first introduced at the fifth grade (11 years old). This was done by interviewing samples from grades two, four, six and eight (8, 10, 12 and 14 years old), in two Israeli schools. Each sample included about 50 pupils. Frequencies expressed in percentages were calculated for each of the five notions described above. The findings are presented in Figure 9.16. The frequency values in the figure are joined by lines to show clearly the notion distribution profile found for each age level.

The profile of the eighth grade shows that about 70 per cent of pupils held notions 4 and 5, while of the second graders, 80 per cent held notions 1 and 2. The remainder of each group was distributed between the remaining three notions, while the profile declined at notions 1 and 5 respectively. The profiles for the fourth and sixth grades show two intermediate states between those of the second and eighth grades.

Two other cross-age studies by other researchers investigated the

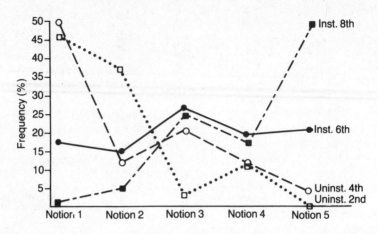

Figure 9.16: Frequency profiles of the various notions at various age levels.

development of the concept with age in other ethnic groups. The first[4] investigated pupils' Earth notions in Nepal among groups of eight, ten and twelve-year-olds. They used their own version of the original interview procedure. Their findings confirmed the existence of these notions about the Earth among pupils, and that there is a change in the notion frequency profiles with change of age. They reported that the concept development in Nepal, as seen in the frequency profile for the different age groups, lagged behind the norm of a sample of American second graders[2] by a few years.

The second cross-age study was conducted in California[5] using a modification of the original interview procedure. The findings supported all the basic findings of the previous studies.

The cross-age studies: interpretations and implications

A comparison between the four profiles in Figure 9.16 suggests that they represent a group conceptual progress that takes place with age (or with schooling). One may reasonably argue that if the present eighth grade was interviewed two years earlier, it would have shown a profile very similar to the one of the present sixth grade. Similarly, one may argue that if the same interview had been conducted with the present eighth grade class, four and six years earlier, the frequency profiles would have resembled the profiles obtained for the present fourth and second grades. This interpretation suggests that the conceptual change within the individual pupils does not occur as a fast revolution following some formal relevant instruction. It should be remembered here that in Israel the Earth concept is formally introduced into the curriculum at the fifth grade (11 year olds). If this conventional instruction was fully effective one would expect to find the vast majority of sixth grade pupils holding notions 4 or 5. The findings presented in Figure 9.16 do not support this expectation but rather suggest that the conceptual change takes place as a long-term gradual evolution. In each stage of this evolution a partial accommodation occurs in some of the conceptual elements but not necessarily in all of them. It is interesting to note that this suggestion is compatible with current trends, in the history of science which describes the development of scientific notions as a multi-step evolution rather than as a few-step revolution.[1]

The impact of a specially designed instruction on young children's notions about the Earth

In this section I report on my attempt to use the potential of the findings of the various studies described above in a teaching experiment.[6] I chose to conduct this experiment with rather young children (second grade pupils, i.e. 8-year-olds), since any significant success in teaching the concept to them would imply a hope for even higher success with older children.

A special unit of individualized instruction was prepared for teaching the Earth concept. The individualization was achieved by applying the audio-tutorial (AT) technique. Headphones were used to receive the audio-taped instruction provided in a tutorial style. The instruction involved the pupils in a rich variety of observations of visual and hands-on activities which kept the children busy throughout a 20-minute lesson period. The taped script included explanations, stories, questions for stimulating thinking, guidance for analytical observation of the visuals, and instructions for manipulating the concrete props. Six AT lessons constituted the teaching unit. The various activities focused on the three essentials of the concept: (1) the Earth's shape, (2) the Earth being surrounded by space, and (3) the Earth's centre as the reference point for the 'down' direction (i.e. the direction of gravity).

In order to evaluate the impact of the instruction on the pupils' Earth notions an interview test was administered pre- and post-instruction. The pre-test was administered to each child about two weeks before starting the Earth-related lessons. The post-test was administered to each child about five weeks after the last AT lesson (see Figure 9.17). This long interval was designed intentionally to increase the probability that we would be truly testing for long-term retention of meaningfully learned concepts.

A comparison between the notion frequency profiles before and after the instruction is given in Figure 9.18. It is clear from this comparison

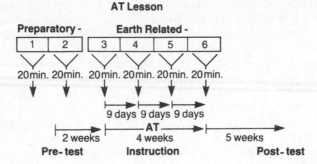

Figure 9.17: Timetable for the various experimental components.

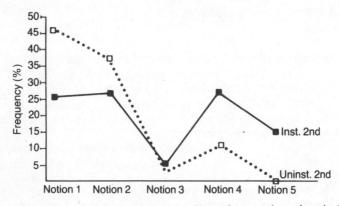

Figure 9.18: The notion frequency profiles of second graders before and after instruction.

that while only 12 per cent of the pupils held notions 4 and 5 before the instruction, after its completion 42 per cent of them held these two notions. These results should not be overlooked.

Figure 9.19 compares the profile of the instructed second grade with the profiles of the fourth and sixth grade groups. The notion frequency profile of the instructed second grade group is clearly *more* advanced that that of the fourth grade group which did not have any relevant formal instruction. The achievements of the second grade were not much lower than those of the conventionally instructed sixth grade. Note that the combined frequency of notions 4 and 5 of the second grade is the same as that of the sixth grade. Piaget's theory would have predicted that second graders are too young to understand the Earth concept, since they cannot overcome the egocentric point of view. This experiment shows that teaching centred upon the essential ideas of the Earth concept can be effective even with such young children.

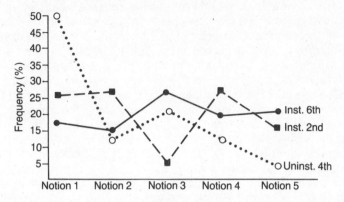

Figure 9.19:   A comparison between Notion frequency and profiles of the instructed second grade and those of the fourth and sixth grades.

Conclusion

This chapter has described five different notions about the Earth as a cosmic body which were found as prevailing among children. These notions were repeatedly found by different studies conducted in different countries on childen of various ages. These notions range from a very primitive belief in a flat Earth through 'more advanced' alternatives to a notion whose essential elements resemble the essentials of the scientific notion. The findings of the various studies suggest that, generally, the Earth concept undergoes evolution in children as they grow older or as they encounter more formal or informal instruction. The important point is that the scientific concept is not internalized as intended immediately with its formal teaching in school. Rather, it was shown that primitive elements tend to persist for some time in children's notions despite formal instruction.

It was argued at the beginning of this chapter that conventional instruction on science topics is generally designed with reference to the subject-matter only and does not include an analysis of the cognitive demands presented by the particular topic. This fact might be the reason why conventional instruction is inefficient. With regard to teaching the Earth concept, educators have the illusion that providing some proofs of the spherical shape of the Earth will convince the pupils about the Earth's shape and, as a by-product, will change their understanding of the 'nature' of cosmic space. Such proofs when given without considering pupils' preconceptions and without confronting them explicitly, often do not serve this purpose. They do not have the intended effect of causing pupils to modify their belief about the Earth's shape and, needless to say, they do not influence pupil's notions of cosmic space. The notion of cosmic space requires direct and explicit didactic treatment. The idea of 'down' directions on the Earth is also mistreated in conventional instruction. It is not enough to state that an object falls because of the Earth's gravity. It is important to relate gravity explicitly to the Earth's centre. From our experience the very idea of where the centre of a sphere is, is not clear to young pupils and requires an explicit and direct treatment.

Towards the end of this chapter I reported on a study in which a relatively short instructional unit was specially designed to deal explicitly with the three elements of the concept. This unit integrated explanations with viewing aids and concrete props, and was taught to second grade pupils. This short instruction advanced pupils understanding of the concept quite significantly. This finding gives the hope that by further improvement of the teaching, paying more attention to the cognitive difficulties of pupils, we should be able to encourage the vast majority of pupils to internalize the concept much earlier and more meaningfully than usually happens.

References

[1]Toulmin, S. E. and Goodfield, J. (1967). *The Fabrics of Heavens*. Hutchinson: London.
[2]Nussbaum, J. and Novak, J. D. (1976). An Assessment of children's concepts of the Earth utilizing structured interviews. *Science Education* 60 (4) 535-50.
[3]Nussbaum, J. (1979) Children's conception of the Earth as a cosmic body: a cross-age study. *Science Education* 63 (1) 83-93.
[4]Mali, G. B. and Howe, A. (1979). Development of Earth and Gravity concepts among Nepali children. *Science Education* 63 (5), 685-91.
[5]Snieder, C., and Pulos, S. (1983). Children's cosmographics: understanding the Earth's shape and gravity. *Science Education* 67 (2), 205-22.
[6]Nussbaum, J. and Sharoni-Dagan, N. (1983) Changes in second grade children's preconceptions about the Earth as a cosmic body resulting from a short series of audio-tutorial lessons. *Science Education* 67 (1), 99-114.

CHAPTER 10

Some Features of Children's Ideas and their Implications for Teaching

Rosalind Driver, Edith Guesne and Andrée Tiberghien

General features of children's conceptions

A number of features of children's ideas were evident in the studies reported in the previous chapters. Here we will draw out what appear to be some of the general issues.

Perceptually dominated thinking

A theme which runs through a number of chapters is the tendency for pupils initially to base their reasoning on observable features in a problem situation. For example, light is only considered to exist when it is intense enough to produce perceptible effects, such as a patch of light on a surface, rather than being thought of as an entity which travels through space. In the same way sugar 'disappears' when it dissolves rather than continuing to exist but in the form of particles too small to see, the Earth is a flat plane with the sky above it.

In teaching science we are leading pupils to 'see' phenomena and experimental situations in particular ways; to learn to wear scientist's 'conceptual spectacles'.[1] This involves pupils in constructing mental models for entities which are not perceived directly, such as light, electric current, particles of matter. The modelling process which is involved is complex; it requires pupils to construct and use certain *entities*, which may be sets of objects or systems, to describe these in exact ways using certain *parameters* (e.g. mass, volume temperature, charge) and to account for the processes of *interaction* between the parameters by describing relationships between them (using ideas such as forces, heat, electric current). The construction of such complex models involves considerable effort on the part of a learner and it is likely to take time before such ways of seeing the world become a stable and useful part of a young person's conceptual 'armoury'.

Limited focus

In many cases we have seen evidence for children considering only limited aspects of particular physical situations, with the focus of their attention appearing to depend on the saliency of particular perpetual features. In Chapter 8 for example, the question concerning burning phosphorus in a closed container drew pupils' attention to a number of features which changed during combustion: the phosphorus itself burning, the 'smoke' being emitted, the 'smoke' then dissolving. In making their prediction about the mass of the system pupils tended to focus on one of these obviously changing features rather than considering the interaction of the contents of the container as a closed system.

Associated with this tendency to focus on limited aspects of a given situations, is the propensity of children to interpret phenomena in terms of absolute properties or qualities ascribed to objects rather than in terms of interaction between elements of a system. For example, some children chose an iron container to keep ice cold for as long as possible because of specific properties of iron (e.g it is a solid, or it is naturally cold): they tended not to think about the problem in terms of the interaction between the ice and the container and the ambient air. Similarly in explaining the action of a straw or syringe, we saw how many pupils considered only what was happening in the inside, attributing the motion of the liquid to the power of 'suction', rather than considering the flow of the liquid being a consequence of pressure differences inside and outside the straw or syringe. From a scientist's perspective the process of burning involves the interaction of the burning substance and oxygen; children however tend to consider whether a substance burns or not as being solely a property of the substance itself.

Focus on change rather than steady-state
situations

This tendency for children to focus on change rather than on steady-state situations may be considered as a type of limited focus. However, we think it is such a significant feature in children's thinking that we are commenting on it separately.

In many of the chapters we have seen examples of the children's tendency to focus on sequences of events or modifications of situations with time. This means they tend to focus on transient states of a system rather than on equilibrium states. In reasoning about fluids, for example, children tended to consider that pressure is acting only in a disequilibrium situation ignoring the pressures acting in equilibrium. A parallel situation seems to occur in mechanics where children acknowledge that a force is acting when motion is observed; forces are less likely to be considered to be acting in systems in static equilibrium. In simple electrical circuits we suspect there is also a conceptual problem due to pupils' confusion of steady-state situations and transient states (for example, when a switch is closed or opened in a circuit). Although the analytical treatment of transient currents requires quite sophisticated mathematics we suggest that making the distinction descriptively between transient and steady state situations in teaching may be helptul to pupils' learning.

This tendency to consider changing rather than equilibrium states is perhaps understandable in terms of what children think it is necessary to explain. It reflects an important aspect of children's causal reasoning, namely that change requires an explanation, it requires them to postulate a mechanism however simple to link different states of a system in time; equilibrium situations on the other hand, because there is no change with time, do not require explanation–they are 'how things are'.

Linear causal reasoning

When children explain changes, their reasoning tends to follow a linear causal sequence. They postulate a *cause* which produces a chain of *effects* as a time-dependent sequence. This tendency to think of explanations in terms of preferred directions in chains of events means that pupils can have problems appreciating the symmetry in interactions between systems. For example, in considering a container being heated, they think of the process in directional terms with a source supplying heat to a receptor; whereas, from a scientific point of view, the situation is symmetrical with two systems interacting, one gaining energy the other losing it. In mechanics, as we have seen, pupils tend to think of a force, or action, producing an effect such as motion; the reciprocal nature of the forces acting (i.e. Newton's third law) is not easy to appreciate from this perspective since it requires pupils to abandon this sequential way of thinking with its 'preferred' direction.

Another consequence of this tendency to think sequentially and to have a preferred direction when reasoning about events, is that processes which a scientist sees as reversible are not necessarily seen this way by pupils. We have seen, for example, that pupils appreciate the effect of an increase in pressure on an enclosed body of gas, yet they have difficulty anticipating the effect of a reduction in pressure. Similarly, pupils can understand that an input of energy may change a solid to a liquid; what happens, however, when a liquid turns to a solid is much more difficult to appreciate.

Undifferentiated concepts

Some of the ideas children use have a range of connotations which can be different and considerably more extensive than those used by scientists. For example, in order to describe or interpret a simple electric circuit, children use one notion (which they call electricity, current, power). This notion has some of the properties of several scientific concepts including current, charge and potential difference. Similarly, children's notions of weight often carry connotations of volume, pressure and density. 'Air' tends to have considerably more extensive meanings for children than it does for scientists, including the notion of a general mediator in situations where there is action at a distance such as forces due to gravitational or magnetic fields, or as a necessary medium for the transmission of 'heat'.

The fact that children's notions tend to be more inclusive and global than those of scientists means that in some circumstances children tend to slip from one meaning to another without necessarily being aware of it. For example, the word conductor or insulator may be used to mean both 'to heat quickly or slowly' and 'to hold warmth or coldness'. These are notions which are clearly differentiated from a scientist's perspective, however, at their level of interpretation of events pupils have not seen the need to make such distinctions.

Context dependency

The previous section showed how different scientific concepts may be undifferentiated in children's thinking. Conversely, children often call upon different ideas to interpret situations which a scientist would explain in the same way. Thus, in the chapter on heat, we saw a child choosing an aluminium pan to keep soup hot, because 'coffee pots keep the heat in well, aluminium keeps the heat in well'; yet, when asked to choose a container in which hot water would stay hot for a short time, she took a metal one because 'it's a conductor... the hot water's heat will go up the sides... then through'. In the same way, we saw that 13 to 14-year-olds tended to make opposite statements about the reflection of light depending on whether or not they could see a patch of light on the surface.

As these examples demonstrate, different concurrent ideas can be drawn on in situations which differ in some perceptual features. Indeed, one of the problems involved in investigating children's ideas is devising ways of probing thinking which enables us to sort out the status of the responses we obtain; to distinguish between those ideas which play a significant part in the thinking of an individual or a group and those which are generated in an ad hoc way in response to the social pressure to produce an answer in an interview or test situation.

Some predominant conceptions

So far we have identified a number of general features which characterize children's thinking about physical phenomena. Although such general points are useful for teachers and curriculum developers to bear in mind, specific information about children's thinking about particular types of phenomena is important when it comes to planning and teaching specific topics.

The reader may have noticed that a number of alternative conceptions tended to reappear in studies of various topic areas; apparently there are a number of ideas which are quite prevalent and influence children's thinking about a range of situations. One of these more dominant notions is the association made between the action of a force and resultant motion. Not only does this idea appear in pupils' interpretations of the motion of objects in their everyday world, but we have also seen evidence that the idea influences their thinking in other areas. In the case of fluids, for example, we have seen how pupils tend to consider pressure in one direction only—the direction in which some 'action' is applied. Problems pupils have in appreciating the intrinsic motion of particles may also stem from their belief that motion requires a force to maintain it. Other ideas which appear to be used in a variety of different situations include the notion of vacuums 'sucking'. This perceptually based idea was invoked not only to describe the motion of liquids but even to provide the necessary motive force for gas particles. Ideas such as the lightness of air was seen to enter children's understanding of the behaviour of atmospheric air and it also influenced their interpretations of phenomena associated with burning.

These recurring ideas, which permeate pupils' understanding of a range of natural phenomena, reflect many of the general features we have just described; they tend to derive from perceptions and reflect linear causal reasoning with a single action producing an effect. Although these ideas may not constitute coherent and well articulated models on the part of individuals, we do note the prevalence of such ideas in the population as a whole. There is also evidence that such ideas are deepseated and recur despite teaching. They may need therefore to be given particular consideration in planning for long term learning by pupils during the secondary school years.

The development of conceptions

Children's ideas and the history of science

In some areas it is tempting to draw parallels between children's ideas and the progression of ideas in science itself. In several chapters indeed, some ideas held by children may have struck reminiscent of scientific theories which were in favour in the past. We saw heat decribed as a substance as in the caloric theory. We heard children describing vision as proceeding from the eyes to the object, reminding us of the 'visual fire' of the pythagorean school. We noticed motion explained by a force inherent in the object, as in the impetus theory, which stated that motion implies a cause and that this cause can be found inside the moving body.

It would be unwise, however, to press the parallel betwen the history of science and children's ideas too far. Firstly, there are often only a few features in common between a given idea used by children and its historical counterpart. When children describe vision as a movement starting from the eyes, this does not have the substantive connotations of the 'visual fire' of the ancient theories. Secondly, the ideas when used by scientists in the past were part of coherent conceptual systems, whereas the ideas used by children tend to be far less coherent. Children's ideas about force and motion, for example, do not have the breadth and internal consistency of the pre-Galilean impetus theory, (which, unlike the thinking of most pupils, included a clear understanding of relativistic ideas[2]).

Conceptual change as a long term process

Where conceptual change does occur, it appears that it is a long-term and slow process. Like all human beings, children have a tendency to interpret new situations in terms of what they already know, thus reinforcing their prior conceptions. An exception to this is where a learner is unable to interpret a situation in a coherent way. There may be alternative, possibly conflicting, interpretations which the learner can give, or the situation may be such that the learner is unable to construct any meaningful interpretation for it at all. It is such situations, where the learner sees the need to construct a coherent meaning, that may provide the necessary conditions for conceptual learning.

In the previous chapters we have seen examples of learning without conceptual change. In some cases the result of teaching appears to be the 'grafting on' of scientific vocabulary to pupils' prior conceptions. In the chapter on the gaseous state, for example, we noted pupils using the taught word 'pressure' but implying by it the notion of 'suction'. Similarly, pupils added the words 'conductor' and 'insulator' to their vocabulary without substantially changing their ideas about heat transfer.

We also noted cases where new ideas were modified by pupils to fit in with their present ways of thinking. In the chapter on the Earth concept, there were cases of pupils initially acknowledging that the Earth is round, yet when probed, their conceptions of what this meant were adaptations of the flat Earth model. In studying the role of oxygen in burning pupils readily accepted that oxygen was necessary but rather than develop the ideas of chemical combination they tended to see the oxygen as being 'burnt away'.

In other cases children start to use a given concept in a limited number of situations. However, the integration and consistent use of new concepts is a much longer term process. When new ideas conflict with children's points of view, they can be obstacles to learning. To integrate such new concepts, children may have to modify the organization of their ideas in a radical way, which amounts to undertaking a kind of 'revolution' in their thinking.[3] Even when this happens, new and old ideas may co-exist. This kind of learning, which does not occur frequently, requires children to accumulate new information and ideas as a basis for reorganizing their conceptions.

It is often difficult to assess the effectiveness of teaching in promoting conceptual change in the short term. Indeed we may need to rethink our view of teaching by being prepared to adopt longer-term goals for pupils' conceptual learning. Children do not adopt new ideas or change their existing ideas radically in the period of time usually allocated to a lesson or even to a sequence of lessons. They may, however, be encouraged to use accepted scientific ideas in a progressively wider range of situations over an extended period of time.

Some issues for curriculum planning

Taking account of the learner's prior knowledge

Conventionally curriculum planning in the sciences has started with a conceptual analysis of the subject matter itself. Possible teaching sequences are prepared by analysing which are the most basic ideas, from a scientific perspective, and building the curriculum from there. We would argue that the evidence in this book suggests that our science schemes may make assumptions that children have already constructed certain basic ideas and this may well not be the case. Ideas such as light travelling through space, matter being conserved or the Earth as a sphere in space may be assumed to be a starting point in our teaching schemes yet they may not have been constructed in a meaningful way by pupils taking the science courses.

This suggests that in curriculum planning it is necessary not only to consider the structure of the subject but also to take into account the learner's ideas. This may mean revising what we consider to be the starting points in our teaching—the ideas that we can assume pupils have available to them.

Knowledge of pupils' ideas is also important in planning specific learning tasks. When we know the types of ideas that are prevalent we can suggest activities which may challenge or extend the range of application of these ideas. Here we outline some strategies suggested by a number of research studies, some of which have been mentioned in earlier chapters, which together could be helpful in promoting conceptual learning.

(1) *Providing opportunities for pupils to make their own ideas explicit.*   Opportunities for this to happen can be provided in small group situations, in whole class discussions or by asking pupils to write down, to draw or in some other way to represent how they are thinking about a situation.

(2) *Introduce discrepant events.*   Observing an event which is unexpected may stimulate pupils to think about the situation. The conceptual conflict thus produced may make a pupil dissatisfied with his or her current ideas and hence to see the need for change. However, discrepant events by themselves have a limited effect. As Nussbaum pointed out in Chapter 7, unless pupils are already aware of the elements of their existing conceptions from which their particular expectations about situations derive, they may not even see the event as discrepant. Also even if conceptual conflict is produced in a pupil, this does not itself produce an alternative conceptual scheme.

(3) *Socratic questioning.*   Where pupils ideas are inconsistent and unrelated to one another, Socratic questioning can help pupils to appreciate the possible lack of consistency in their own thinking and to reconstruct their ideas in a more coherent way. Giving pupils opportunities to explore their ideas in discussion with their peers in small groups can serve a similar purpose.

(4) *Encouraging the generation of a range of conceptual schemes.* If pupils are to construct meanings for themselves this requires them to be actively involved in reflecting on their own thinking. One of the factors which undermines this process is the 'right answer' syndrome.

Pupils and teachers conspire together in many classrooms to undermine pupils' scientific understanding often without realizing it; both parties adopt the view that getting the 'right answer' is what matters and pupils will use irrelevant cues in teacher questioning routines, the wording of worksheets or questions in textbooks to obtain this goal. We suggest, therefore, that children be encouraged to consider a range of possible interpretations for events and to attempt to evaluate these for themselves.

The generation of alternative conceptual schemes can be promoted in classrooms by pupils themselves, through discussion in small groups, 'brainstorming' in the class as a whole, and by the introduction of new ideas by the teacher or through instructional materials. In whatever way the new ideas are introduced individual pupils have still to make them meaningful to themselves: just because someone is told something does not mean they understand it in the way intended.

(5) *Practice in using ideas in a range of situations.*   The problem of generalization is an important one and opportunities may need to be explicitly provided to encourage it to happen. In particular, the role of the experiment in science teaching needs careful consideration. To a scientist the results of an experiment give general information about

a class of phenomena; the particular objects and apparatus used are seen to 'stand for' a range of situations. Children, on the other hand, may not see the particular features of a given experimental arrangement in such general terms and as a consequence what they learn from an experiment may be restricted to the particular context in which it was performed. Opportunities for pupils to check out the range and limits of applicability of experimental results are therefore important. In this way pupils may gain confidence in new ideas and see them as useful.

These suggestions for ways of promoting conceptual change in classrooms are only tentative at this stage as they are based on a small number of exploratory studies.[4] We hope that in the next few years further collaborative work between teachers and researchers will enable us to build on what we already know about children's ideas; to work out ways in which classrooms can become places where learning science can become more meaningful and interesting and where the ideas of pupils are valued and encouraged to develop.

References

[1]Modern philosophers of science have argued that observations are theory laden. Karl Popper in *Conjectures and Refutations* (p. 47) states that 'observation statements and statements of experimental results are always *interpretations* of the facts observed... they are interpretations in the light of theories'.
[2]E. Saltiel and L. Viennot. (1985). What do we learn from similarities between historical ideas and the spontaneous reasoning of students. In *The many facets of teaching and learning mechanics*, 199-214, Ed. P. L. Linjse, WCC-Utrecht.
[3]Posner, G. J., Strike, K. A., Hewson, P. W. and Gertzog, W. A. Accommodation of a scientific conception: towards a theory of conceptual change. *Science Education*, 66 (2), 211-227.
[4]Readers interested in further information on conceptual change in classrooms may find the following references useful:
Bell B., Watts, D. M. and Ellington, K. (Eds) (1985) *Learning, doing and understanding in science*. SSCR: London.
Driver, R. (1985) Changing perspectives on science lessons. In *Recent advances in classroom research*. Eds N. Bennett and C. Desforges, British Journal of Psychology Monograph.
Driver, R. and Erickson G. (1983) Theories-in-action, some theoretical and empirical issues in the study of students' conceptual frameworks in science. *Studies in Science Education*, 10, 37-60.
Gilbert, J. K. and Watts, D. M. (1983) Concepts, Misconceptions and Alternative Conceptions: Changing Perspectives in Science Education. *Studies in Science Education*, 10, 61-98.
Osborne, R. J. and Freyberg P. (Eds) (1985) *Learning in science: the implications of children's science*. Heinemann Educational Books.
Osborne, R. J. and Whittrock, M. C. (1983) Learning Science: A Generative Process. *Science Education*, 67 (4), 489-508.
Research on physics education: proceedings of the first international workshop (1984), La Londe les Maures, Editions du CNRS, Paris.
West, L. H. T. and Pines, A. L. (1985) *Cognitive Structure and Conceptual Change*. New York: Academic Press.

Index

3642